2nd edition

C000297619

Got it!

1

Student Book
& Workbook

Philippa Bowen

Denis Delaney

Christina de la Mare

OXFORD
UNIVERSITY PRESS

Contents

be: Simple present	Simple present	Imperatives
There is / isn't, There are / aren't	Adverbs of frequency	*can* (ability)
Demonstratives: *this, that, these, those*	*How often …?*	Present progressive

Communication	Skills
Making requests	**Reading:** A website article about a music festival **Listening:** A phone conversation about a festival **Speaking:** A conversation about festival **Writing:** A blog post about a festival
Describing people	**Reading:** An article about America's favorite people **Listening:** A conversation about John Lennon and his band **Speaking:** Factfiles of Great Garbo, Geoffrey Chaucer, and Diego Rivera **Writing:** A profile of Geoffrey Chaucer and Diego Rivera

Talking about vacations	**Reading:** An article about the discovery of Antarctica **Listening:** A biography of Sir Edmund Hillary **Speaking:** A presentation of the important events in someone's life **Writing:** A description of the important events in your life
Going to the movies	**Reading:** A web page about movies **Listening:** A conversation about a movie **Speaking:** Discussing a movie **Writing:** A review of a movie

Ordering food and drink	**Reading:** An article about the history of school lunches in the U.S. **Listening:** A radio interview about the Okinawa diet **Speaking:** Discussing favorite types of food **Writing:** A food article about the American hot dog
Inviting and making arrangements	**Reading:** An article about a very long bus ride **Listening:** Two teenagers talking about a vacation **Speaking:** Making arrangements for a vacation **Writing:** An itinerary for a vacation

Asking for tourist information	**Reading:** A magazine article about our changing planet **Listening:** A radio interview about a volcano **Speaking:** Talking about a scary incident **Writing:** A story about a scary experience
Making a phone call	**Reading:** An article about the '-est' moment of your life **Listening:** A radio interview about the results of a survey **Speaking:** Comparing your country with other countries **Writing:** A report about your country

Vocabulary

Countries and nationalities

1 Match the countries with the flags. Then write the nationalities.

> Brazil   Canada   Japan   ~~South Korea~~   the United Kingdom   the United States

1 _South Korea_
  Korean

2 _____

3 _____

4 _____

5 _____

6 _____

The family

2 Look at Alicia's family tree. Complete the sentences.

> Bruno is the children's _grandpa_.

1 Bruno is David's _____.
2 Gabriel is Alicia's _____.
3 Sophia is Hugo's _____.
4 Hugo is Alicia's _____.
5 Julia is Sophia's _____.
6 David is Hugo's _____.
7 Esther is Alicia's _____.
8 Bruno and Esther are Sophia's _____.
9 Julia is Gabriel's _____.
10 Laura and Samuel are Hugo's _____.

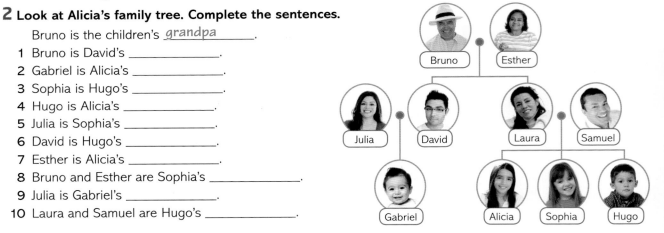

Daily routines and sports

3 Look at the pictures. Complete the daily routine for Jackson Williams, high school sports star!

I _have breakfast_ at six thirty, then I ¹ _____

before school. At school, I ² _____ – I'm on the team! After school,

I ³ _____ and ⁴ _____. Then,

I ⁵ _____. I always ⁶ _____ late. It's a long day!

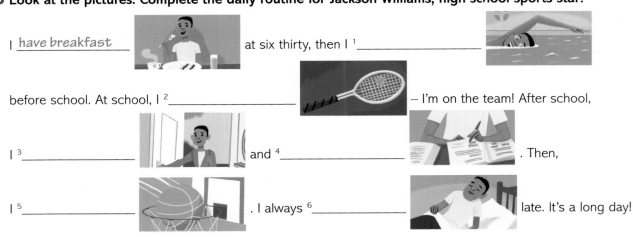

House and furniture

4 Complete the rooms and the furniture with the missing letters.

Room	b e d r o o m	¹b _ _ t _ r _ _ _ m	²k _ _ _ c _ _ _ n	³l _ _ _ i _ g r _ _ _ m	⁴di _ _ _ _ _ g r _ _ _ _
Furniture	⁵b _ _ _ ⁶c _ _ _ _ _ _	⁷t _ _ _ _ _ _ ⁸s _ _ _ _ _ _ _	⁹s _ _ _ _ _ _ ¹⁰s _ _ _ _	¹¹s _ _ _ _ ¹²a _ _ _ _ _ _ _ _	¹³t _ _ _ _ _ ¹⁴c _ _ _ _ _

Possessions

5 Look at the pictures. Complete the word puzzle.
What is the mystery possession?

1
2
3
4
5
6
7

1	s	k	a	t	e	b	o	a	r	d
2										
3										
4										
5										
6										
7										

Mystery possession: _____

School subjects

6 Complete the sentences with the correct school subjects.

Isabel likes _art_ 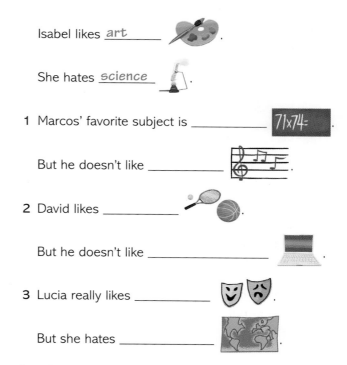.

She hates _science_.

1 Marcos' favorite subject is _____

But he doesn't like _____

2 David likes _____

But he doesn't like _____

3 Lucia really likes _____

But she hates _____

Clothes and prices

7 Complete the sentences with the correct clothes.

Jen's _jacket_ is $30.
1 Her _____ is $18.
2 Her _____ is $22.
3 Her _____ are $50.
4 Juan's _____ is $20.
5 His _____ is $35.
6 His _____ are $45.
7 His _____ are $60.

Grammar

be: Simple present

1 Read the factfile. Then complete the sentences about Eduardo. Use the affirmative or negative form of the verb *be*.

Factfile

Name:	Eduardo Ruiz
Age:	14
Country:	Brazil
School:	The American College of Sao Paulo
Favorite subject:	history
Friends:	Taylor (American), Markus (German)
Favorite bands:	Paramore, Maroon 5

Eduardo's surname _isn't_ Ramos.

1 Eduardo _____ 14.

2 Eduardo _____ from the U.S.

3 Taylor and Markus _____ Eduardo's teachers.

4 History _____ his favorite school subject.

5 His friends _____ from the U.S. and Germany.

6 His favorite bands _____ Linkin Park and Green Day.

2 Write questions. Then answer the questions with information about you.

What / your name?
What's your name? _____

1 How old / you?
_____

2 Where / you from?
_____

3 art / your favorite subject?
_____

4 Who / your friends?
_____

5 Paramore / your favorite band?
_____

There is / isn't, There are / aren't

3 Look at Sara and Frank's perfect rooms. Complete the sentences with *there is*, *there are*, *there isn't*, or *there aren't*.

In Sara's perfect bedroom _there is_ a big bed. [1]_____ a lot of posters on the walls, too. [2]_____ a closet and a mirror, but [3]_____ a chair. And [4]_____ any shelves.

In Frank's perfect living room [5]_____ a big TV. [6]_____ sofas, too, but [7]_____ any armchairs. [8]_____ shelves for games and DVDs, but [9]_____ a table.

Demonstratives: *this, that, these, those*

4 Complete the sentences with *this, that, these,* or *those*.

These are my parents, Sally and Michael.

1 _____ is my dog, Pugsy.

2 _____ is my house.

3 _____ boys are my brothers.

Simple present

5 Look at the information in the chart. Write questions. Then answer the questions.

	Amy	Tom	Mia	Leo
have / lunch at 1:15		✓		
play / basketball		✓		✓
get up / at 7:30	✓			
like / track and field	✓		✓	
go / to bed late				✓

(Amy / get up / 6:30)

Does Amy get up at 6:30?

No, she doesn't. She gets up at 7:30.

1 (you / have lunch / 1:30, Tom)
2 (Amy and Mia / like / basketball)
3 (you and Tom / play baseball, Leo)
4 (Leo / go to bed / early)

6 Complete the blog post with the correct form of the verbs in parentheses.

Hi! My name's Alanna.
I _live_ (live) in Detroit,
Michigan. I ¹_____ (go)
to Roosevelt Junior High
School. I ²_____ (get
up) at 7 a.m. I ³_____
(have) breakfast with my
family. My sister ⁴_____
(go) to my school, too. She
⁵_____ (play) the violin.
I ⁶_____ (not like) music lessons, but P.E. is
great. School ⁷_____ (start) at 8:45 a.m. and
it ⁸_____ (finish) at 3 p.m. I ⁹_____ (get)
home at around 3:30 p.m. I usually
¹⁰_____ (watch) TV for an hour, and then
I ¹¹_____ (do) my homework. Dad ¹²_____
(get) home from work at 6:30 p.m., and then we
¹³_____ (have) dinner. My sister and I
¹⁴_____ (not go) out on school nights. After
dinner, I ¹⁵_____ (listen) to music, or I
¹⁶_____ (chat) with my friends on the Internet.
I ¹⁷_____ (go) to bed at 10:30 p.m.

7 Write questions about Alanna. Then answer the questions.

Where / she / live?

Where does she live?

She lives in Detroit, Michigan.

1 Where / she / go to school?
2 Who / she / have breakfast with?
3 What / her sister / play?
4 What time / school / start?
5 What / she / do / before dinner?
6 What / Alanna and her friends / do after dinner?

Adverbs of frequency

8 Write the adverbs of frequency in the correct order.

always   never   often   rarely
sometimes   usually

always	●●●●●
1 _____	●●●●○
2 _____	●●●○○
3 _____	●●○○○
4 _____	●○○○○
never	○○○○○

9 Rewrite the sentences with the correct adverbs of frequency in the correct place.

I play tennis on the weekend. (●●●●○)

I usually play tennis on the weekend.

1 Cecilia takes a bath in the evening. (●●●●●)
2 Our teacher is late for class. (○○○○○)
3 They go out on school nights. (●○○○○)
4 Ken gets up at eight o'clock. (●●●○○)
5 Luke goes to a café after school. (●●○○○)
6 We go shopping on Fridays. (●●●○○)

How often ...?

10 Look at Kelly's school schedule. How often does she do things? Write questions and answers.

Washington Junior High School Schedule				
Monday	Tuesday	Wednesday	Thursday	Friday
P.E.	science	P.E.	history	art
math	computer science	Spanish	geography	Spanish
B	R	E	A	K
science	math	history	music	music
L	U	N	C	H
math	P.E.	art	Spanish	history
computer science	computer science	no lessons	music	geography

How often / have P.E.?
How often does she have P.E.?
She has P.E. three times a week.

1 How often / eat lunch at school?
_____
_____
_____

2 How often / study geography in the morning?
_____
_____
_____
_____

3 How often / have computer science in the afternoon?
_____
_____
_____
_____

4 How often / go to art class?
_____
_____
_____

Imperatives

11 Complete the school rules with the affirmative or negative imperative form of the verbs in the box.

| be   eat   finish   leave   use   walk   wear |

Don't wear jeans. (✗)
Be _____ on time for class. (✓)

1 _____ cell phones. (✗)
2 _____! Don't run! (✗)
3 _____ or drink during class. (✗)
4 _____ the school at lunchtime. (✗)
5 _____ your homework on time. (✓)

can (ability)

12 Look at the pictures. Write sentences about what the people can and can't do.

Bella
Can Bella sing?
Yes, she can, but she can't dance.

(✗)

(✗) 1 Grandpa
_____
_____

(✓)

2 The children
_____
_____
_____

(✗)

3 Alícia
_____
_____
_____

(✗)

(✓)

4 Miguel
_____
_____
_____

(✗)

(✗) 5 Your little brother
_____
_____

(✓)

Present progressive

13 **Look at the picture of the picnic. What are teenagers 1–5 doing? Write present progressive sentences.**

1 She *'s talking* on her cell phone.
2 They_____ about something.
3 They_____ soccer.
4 She_____ to her MP3 player.
5 He_____ a cola.

14 **The sentences about teenagers 6–10 are incorrect. Correct the mistakes.**

6 He's exercising.
  He isn't exercising. He's eating.

7 He's sending a message.
  _____
  _____

8 They're talking.
  _____

9 She's playing tennis.
  _____

10 He's dancing.
  _____

15 **Write questions in the present progressive. Then answer the questions.**

What / the girl with the cell phone / wear?
What is the girl with the cell phone wearing?
She's wearing a red dress.

1 What / the boy / eat?
  _____
  _____

2 How many people / sit down?
  _____
  _____

3 How many people / stand up?
  _____
  _____

4 What / the girl / read?
  _____
  _____

16 **Complete the dialogue with the present progressive form of the verbs in parentheses.**

Sophie Hi, Gabriel! Where are you? Are you at home?

Gabriel Yes, *I'm watching* (I / watch) TV. What about you?

Sophie [1]_____ (I / sit) in the park. A lot of people from school are here.

Gabriel That sounds good. I can hear music.

Sophie That's Sam. [2]_____ (he / play) the guitar.

Gabriel [3]_____ (what / Lucy and Harry / do)?

Sophie Well, [4]_____ (Lucy / listen) to her MP3 player. Very boring! [5]_____ (she / not talk) to us. [6]_____ (Harry / eat). Like always!

Gabriel Is Diego there?

Sophie Yes, he is. [7]_____ (he / ride) his bike.

Gabriel And what about Maria and Paul?

Sophie They're here. [8]_____ (they dance). Jack and Luis are here, too.

Gabriel [9]_____ (they / play) baseball?

Sophie [10]_____ (no / they). [11]_____ (they / play) soccer.

Gabriel Great! [12]_____ (I / leave) the house now!

1 What's Zac doing?

1 🔊 1.02 **Read and listen** Which competition is the band practicing for?

Dylan Stop! Stop! Where's Zac? What's he doing?

Lewis He's on the phone. He's talking to his girlfriend again.

Rosie He calls her twenty times a day …

Dylan … and he's always late for practice!

Ten minutes later …

Zac OK, guys. I'm here. Let's rock!

Dylan Zac! Are you serious about this band?

Zac Yes, I am. This is *my* band.

Dylan *Yours*?

Zac Yes! You play the bass, Rosie plays the guitar, and Lewis plays the drums, but I'm the singer and the star.

Rosie Oh, stop it! Let's practice! We're in the Battle of the Bands next month.

Lewis And we're playing terribly!

Dylan Yes, we are.

Rosie I know. Let's practice now. It's getting late.

Zac Wait, my phone is ringing again.

Rosie What are you doing now?

Zac I'm listening to a message from my girlfriend.

Dylan I give up! You're impossible, Zac!

2 Comprehension Answer the questions.

Who is Zac talking to on the phone?
He's talking to his girlfriend.

1 How often is he late for band practice?
2 What musical instruments do Dylan, Rosie, and Lewis play?
3 Who is the singer of the band?
4 When is the Battle of the Bands?

Language focus

3 Dialogue focus There are six more mistakes in the dialogues. Find and correct the mistakes.

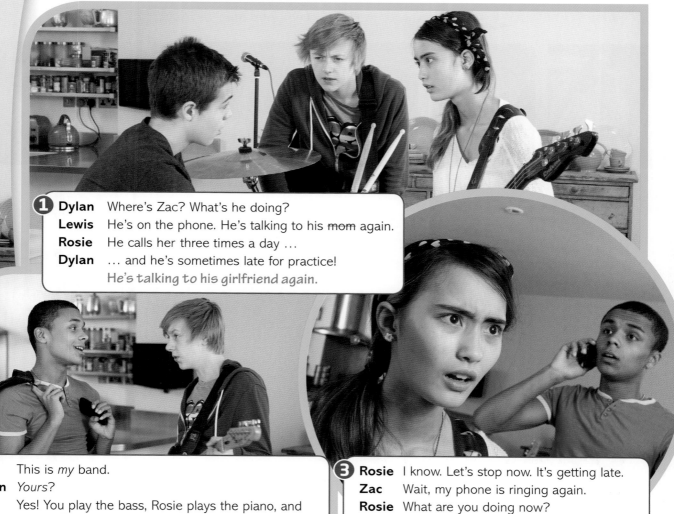

1 Dylan Where's Zac? What's he doing?

Lewis He's on the phone. He's talking to his ~~mom~~ again.

Rosie He calls her three times a day …

Dylan … and he's sometimes late for practice!

He's talking to his girlfriend again.

2 Zac This is *my* band.

Dylan *Yours?*

Zac Yes! You play the bass, Rosie plays the piano, and Lewis plays the drums, but I'm the actor and the star.

3 Rosie I know. Let's stop now. It's getting late.

Zac Wait, my phone is ringing again.

Rosie What are you doing now?

Zac I'm listening to a message from my sister.

4 🔊 1.03 **Listen and check. Listen again and repeat.**

5 Focus on you Read dialogue 3 in exercise 3 again. Then write three similar dialogues. Use the activities in the box.

> do my homework   go to the gym   have breakfast / lunch / dinner
> listen to music   play computer games   play soccer
> practice the guitar   read a magazine   watch TV   write an e-mail

A What are you doing now?
B I'm reading a magazine.

6 Pairwork Imagine it is Saturday morning. Ask and answer questions about what you and your family are doing. Use the present progressive. 😊

A What are you doing now?
B I'm …
A What's your sister doing now?
B She's …

1 Vocabulary

Musical genres and instruments

1 🔊 1.04 **Match the pictures of the singers and bands with the music genres in the box. Then listen and check.**

classical   heavy metal   hip-hop   ~~pop~~   reggae   rock

pop   1 _____   2 _____   3 _____   4 _____   5 _____

2 🔊 1.05 **Listen. Can you identify the musical genres?**

pop   1 _____   2 _____   3 _____   4 _____   5 _____

3 🔊 1.06 **Label the pictures with the words in the box. Then listen and check.**

~~drums~~   flute   guitar   piano   recorder   saxophone   trumpet   violin

drums   1 _____   2 _____   3 _____

4 _____   5 _____   6 _____   7 _____

Look!

Instrument	Musician
piano	a pianist
guitar	a guitarist
drum	a drummer
trumpet	a trumpeter

4 Pairwork Ask and answer questions about ... 🙂

- your favorite type of music and your favorite singer / band.
- the musical instruments that you can play.

A What's your favorite type of music?
B I like heavy metal.
A What's your favorite heavy metal band?
B It's Metallica. It's fantastic!

B Can you play a musical instrument?
A Yes, I can. I can play the piano and the guitar. What about you?
B I can't play an instrument.

Workbook p.4   Extra practice online

Simple present / Present progressive

What's Zac **doing**?
He'**s talking** to his girlfriend.
He **calls** her twenty times a day.
He's **always** late for practice.

Think!

Answer the questions. Use *simple present* **or** *present progressive*.

Which tense do we use

- to talk about actions in progress now?

  ¹_____

- to talk about habits? ²_____

Rules p.W2

1 Circle the verb in each sentence. Is it an action in progress now (N), or a habit (H)?

Sam often (watches) movies   H
Sam'(s watching) a DVD at the moment.   N

1 I always listen to my MP3 player on the bus. ___
2 Kate practices her flute three times a week. ___
3 Are you using your computer at the moment? ___
4 Mom and Dad go shopping on the weekend. ___
5 Quick! *Glee* is starting right now! ___
6 Do you study math every day? ___

2 Underline the adverbs of frequency and other time expressions in exercise 1. Use them to complete the chart.

Simple present	Present progressive
often	at the moment

3 Choose the correct answers.

Tom often (meets) / is meeting his friends after school.

1 Our orchestra **does** / **is doing** a concert twice a year.
2 I **don't play** / **'m not playing** sports every day.
3 **Do you study** / **Are you studying** at the moment?
4 Shh! We **listen** / **'re listening** to this CD.
5 Kevin **doesn't watch** / **isn't watching** TV very often.
6 Listen! Luisa **plays** / **is playing** her violin.
7 Dad always **cooks** / **is cooking** on Saturdays.
8 I **don't have** / **'m not having** lunch now. It's only eleven o'clock!

4 Write the sentences and questions in the simple present or present progressive.

He / not get up early / on Sundays.
He doesn't get up early on Sundays.
Ellen / do her math test / now?
Is Ellen doing her math test now?

1 Luke / play the guitar / at the moment.
2 My teacher / go to the U.S. / every summer.
3 You / study English / every evening?
4 Dan / not do his homework / now.
5 I / not see my grandparents / very often.
6 What / Harry do / at the moment?

5 Complete the dialogues with the correct form of the verbs in parentheses. Add a short answer if necessary.

1
Dad   <u>Are</u> you <u>going out</u>
     (go out), Jake?
Jake Yes, ¹_____.
Dad Where ²_____ (you / go)?
Jake I ³_____ (go) to band practice.
Dad Oh yes, of course! ⁴_____
     (Gemma / play) in the band, too?
Jake Yes, she ⁵_____. We usually
     ⁶_____ (practice) at her house.
     Oh, no! I'm late. See you later!

2
Toby Mom, ⁷_____ (Amy / play) her
     recorder in the living room!
Mom Good! She ⁸_____ (not
     practice) very often.
Toby But I ⁹_____ (watch) TV!
Mom What about your homework, Toby?
Toby It's Monday. I ¹⁰_____ (not have)
     homework on Mondays!

6 Answer the questions. Use information about you.

1 What are you doing now?
2 What do you usually do in your free time?
3 How often do you play sports?

Finished?

Think about a friend or family member. What are they doing now? What do they do every day? Write sentences.

My dad is sitting in his office. He's ...

Puzzle p.104

1 Communication

Making requests

1 🔊 1.07 **Read and listen to the dialogues. Match them with the pictures. Listen again and check. Then listen and repeat.**

1 __c__
A Can I open the window, please?
B Yes, you can. It's hot in here.
A Thank you.

a

2 ____
A Can I borrow your pen, Susana?
B Not now. I'm doing my homework. You can borrow it later.

b

3 ____
A Can I use an English dictionary?
B No, you can't! You can do the exercise without it.

c

Learn it, use it!

You ask	You answer
Can I open the window, please?	Yes, you can. / Yes, OK.
Can I borrow (your pen), please?	Not now. / You can borrow (it) later.
Can I use an English dictionary?	No, you can't.

2 🔊 1.08 **Pronunciation** Listen and repeat.

Can I open the window, please? → Yes, you can.
Can I use your eraser, please? → Not now. I'm using it.
Can I borrow your dictionary? → No, you can't.

3 🔊 1.09 **Listen and complete the requests. Check (✓) the positive replies and cross (✗) the negative replies. Listen and check.**

Can I _sit next to you_ ? [✗]
1 Can I _____? I don't have mine. [ ]
2 Can I _____? [ ]

4 Pairwork Make requests with the expressions in the box. Use the dialogues in exercise 1 as a model. Accept or reject your partner's requests. 😊

borrow your book   close the window   copy your homework
have some water   sit next to you   use a dictionary   use your pen

Workbook p.6   **Extra practice** online

Possessive pronouns

"This is **my** band." "**Yours**?"

Possessive adjectives	Possessive pronouns
my	mine
your	yours
his	his
her	hers
its	–
our	ours
your	yours
their	theirs

Think!

Read the sentences. Are the rules true (T) or false (F)?

It's **your guitar**. It's **yours**.

- [1]We use possessive adjectives before a noun. ___
- [2]We use possessive pronouns before a noun. ___
- [3]We use possessive pronouns to replace a possessive adjective and a noun. ___

Rules p.W3

1 Complete the sentences with the correct possessive pronouns.

This isn't my guitar. Where's _mine_ ? (my guitar)

1 These are my pens, and those are _____. (your pens)
2 Whose books are these? Are they Paula's? Yes, they're _____. (her books)
3 That isn't their pizza. _____ is on the kitchen table. (Their pizza)
4 Your house is big. _____ is smaller. (Our house)
5 David's saxophone is new. This isn't _____. (his saxophone)

2 Choose the correct answers.

Here's (your)/ yours jacket.

1 "Whose are these books?" "They're **my / mine** ".
2 Those bags are Jason's. They aren't **our / ours** .
3 "Are these Elizabeth's keys?" "No, these are **her / hers** ".
4 Is this **their / theirs** address?
5 **My / Mine** dad is taller than **your / yours** .

Adverbs of manner

… and he's always **late** for practice! And we're playing **terribly**.

Regular adverbs

Adjective	Adverb
bad	badly
terrible	terribly
happy	happily
impossible	impossibly

Rules p.W3

Irregular adverbs

Adjective	Adverb
good	well
early	early
late	late
fast	fast

Rules p.W3

Think!

Read the sentence. Choose the correct word.

He's a bad singer. He sings **badly**.

- Adverbs of manner come **before** / after the verb.

Rules p.W3

3 Rewrite the sentences with adverbs.

You have neat handwriting. You write _neatly_ .

1 Jay goes to bed at midnight. He goes to bed _____.
2 Lydia's a fast runner. She runs _____.
3 My mom's a good artist. She paints _____.
4 You're a terrible dancer! You dance _____.
5 My brother's a happy baby. He always plays _____.

Finished?

Write true sentences about you or your family. Use the adverbs in the box.

badly   beautifully   early   fast   happily

My brother sings badly.

Puzzle p.104

TEEN NEWS

ACL Rocks!

Abbie Draper (17) is at the Austin City Limits Music Festival in Texas. Her parents work there every year, and this year she's working, too. She's telling us about the festival.

"It's a beautiful warm evening in October, and I'm having a fantastic time with 75,000 other people. I'm watching Florence and the Machine on one of eight stages, and they are fantastic. Everyone is singing and dancing, and enjoying the atmosphere. But where are we? The Austin City Limits Music Festival of course!

The festival is now very popular in the U.S. It happens for three days in September or October every year in the Zilker Park near Austin, Texas. People travel from a lot of different places to come here. A lot of famous singers and bands play at the festival. But they aren't the only attraction. There are a lot of other activities including a place to watch NFL football games!

You can play beach volleyball, too!

My parents help organize the festival. I don't see them very much because they are always busy. But that's OK. I'm very lucky because I come here every year. And this year is different because I'm working here for the first time. My job is to help in the children's zone, *Austin Kiddie Limits*. There are art and music activities, and a lot of games. So while the adults are enjoying the music, the children are having a fantastic time, too!

I'm watching the fans and I can see a lot of happy people. There is always fantastic music at the ACL. Tomorrow, one of my favorite musicians is on stage: Jack White. I'm so excited! And I can meet him afterwards with my dad! ACL rocks!"

Culture focus

The U.S. has some big music festivals and they are very popular. These festivals have a lot of stages and visitors can see many different musicians. Some of these festivals also have art, movies, theater, dance, and literature. There is a lot of culture, and a lot of fun for visitors to the festivals.

Check it out!

Find these words and check their meaning.

stage   busy
a lot of   zone

Reading

1 🔊 1.10 **Read and listen** to the article. Then answer the questions.

How many stages are there?
There are eight stages.

1 How many days does the festival last?
2 When and where is the Austin City Limits Festival?
3 What attractions are there for visitors?
4 Why does Abbie go to the festival every year?
5 What is she doing there this year?
6 Who is Abbie excited about meeting?
7 What do you think of the Austin City Limits Festival? Are there similar festivals in your country?

Listening

My listening skills

Predicting the content of a listening text

Before you listen to a recording, it is a good idea to predict the content. This can help you to understand the language better.

Read the instructions for the exercise. Find out who is speaking and where they are. Then, look at the questions. Some words in the questions give you more information about the text.

2 (◄)) 1.11 **Listen to Bella's phone conversation with her friend Harry about a festival. Choose the correct answers.**

Harry wants to **stay at home** / **go out** tonight.

1 Bella **is** / **isn't** free now.
2 Bella is at **the movie theater** / **a music festival**.

3 She's there with her **parents** / **friend**.
4 She's staying **with her aunt** / **in a hotel**.
5 Bella **likes** / **doesn't like** Guns N' Roses.
6 Harry wants to go to the movie theater next **Thursday** / **Friday**.

Speaking

3 Imagine that you are at one of these festivals and make notes. Decide …

- which festival you are at.
- which bands you are watching.
- which other activities you can do.
- who is with you at the festival.
- how long you are staying.

4 Pairwork Ask and answer questions about one of the festivals in exercise 3. Use the simple present and the present progressive. 😊

- Which festival / you at?
- Where / happen?
- Who / you with?

A Which festival are you at?
B I'm at …

- How long / you stay?
- What bands / play at the festival?
- What / other activities can you do?

Writing

5 Look at the posters in exercise 3. Complete the e-mail.

6 Imagine you are at the Lollapalooza festival. Write a blog post with the information in the poster. Use the e-mail in exercise 5 as a model.

Hello, friends,
I'm at the …

Sent: Friday July 27th, 15:33

Hello, friends,

I'm at the Bonnaroo Festival in Tennessee! It's my second time here. This year it starts on June __13th__ and ¹_____ on the 16th. I ²_____ here with my friends, and ³_____ having a great time.

Right now, I'm having an electric guitar lesson. Tonight, my favorite ⁴_____ The XX are on stage. It's fantastic here!

More news soon,

Zac

2 Where were you?

1 🔊 1.12 **Read and listen** Where was Zac last night?

Dylan Where were you last night, Zac?

Zac I was at home. Why? Was it band practice?

Dylan Yes, it was, and you weren't there again!

Zac Calm down, Dylan. *The Amazing Spider-Man* was on TV.

Lewis Cool! I love *Spider-Man* movies!

Dylan Who cares about *Spider-Man* movies? We were there for band practice, Zac, and you weren't!

Zac Practice is for you guys, Dylan. I'm already a star.

Dylan We're a band, Zac. There aren't any stars.

Rosie Look, guys! The Misfitz are over there. They're entering the Battle of the Bands, too.

Zac Who's the girl with the brown hair?

Rosie Her name's Kelly. She's the keyboard player in The Misfitz.

Lewis She's a brilliant player, but their singer's terrible.

Zac Their singer's terrible … hmm … interesting.

Check it out!

Find these words and check their meaning.

Calm down.   Who cares about …?

2 Comprehension Complete the sentences with *Dylan*, *Zac*, *Rosie*, *Lewis*, or *Kelly*.

<u>Dylan</u> isn't happy with Zac.

1 _____ sometimes doesn't go to band practice.

2 _____ thinks he's a star.

3 _____ sees The Misfitz.

4 _____ is the keyboard player in The Misfitz.

5 _____ says Kelly is a brilliant player.

Language focus

3 Dialogue focus Reorder the sentences to form dialogues. Then write them again.

① ___ I was at home. Why? Was it band practice?

___ Yes, it was, and you weren't there again!

_1_ Where were you last night, Zac?

Dylan ¹ *Where were you last night, Zac?*

Zac ² _____

Dylan ³ _____

② ___ Who cares about *Spider-Man* movies? We were there for band practice, Zac, and you weren't!

___ Cool! I love *Spider-Man* movies!

___ *The Amazing Spider-Man* was on TV.

Zac ⁴ _____

Lewis ⁵ _____

Dylan ⁶ _____

_____

③ ___ Her name's Kelly. She's the keyboard player in The Misfitz.

___ She's a brilliant player, but their singer's terrible.

___ Who's the girl with the brown hair?

Zac ⁷ _____

Rosie ⁸ _____

Lewis ⁹ _____

4 🔊 1.13 **Listen and check. Listen again and repeat.**

5 Focus on you Read the example dialogue. Then write four similar dialogues. Use the activities in the boxes.

> at Bella's party   at Giovanni's pizza restaurant
> at a rock concert   at the movies   at the swimming pool

> basketball practice   drama club   music practice
> soccer practice   track and field club

A Where were you yesterday evening?

B I was at Bella's party. Why? Was it basketball practice?

A Yes, it was. And you weren't there.

B I'm sorry. But I love Bella's parties.

6 Pairwork Practice the dialogues in exercise 5.

Physical descriptions

1 🔊 1.14 **Match the descriptions with four of the people in the picture. Write the correct names under the people. Then listen and check.**

1 _____

2 David _____

3 _____

4 _____

a Olivia is short and very slim. She has long, blond, wavy hair and blue eyes. She has braces. She's young. She's about 15.

b Ron is tall and overweight. He's bald, but he has a gray beard. His eyes are brown and he wears glasses. He's pretty old. He's about 70.

c Julia is average height and pretty slim. She has shoulder-length, red, straight hair and freckles. Her eyes are green. She's middle-aged. She's about 45.

d David is tall and average weight. He has short, black, curly hair, and a mustache. He has brown eyes and he's about 45, too.

2 **Underline the adjectives and other description words in exercise 1. Then complete the chart.**

Age	Height	Weight	Hair	Eyes	Other
young	short	very slim	bald	blue	braces
			length: long …		
			color: blond …		
			style: wavy …		

3 🔊 1.15 **Complete the descriptions of Sarah and Jack, two members of the family in exercise 1. Then listen and check.**

A Sarah is __short__ and pretty [1]_____. She has short, [2]_____, [3]_____ hair and blue [4]_____. She's pretty [5]_____. She's about 70.

B Jack is pretty [6]_____ and [7]_____. He has [8]_____, brown, [9]_____ hair and green eyes. He wears [10]_____. He's young. He's [11]_____ 18.

4 **Pairwork** **Describe two members of your family to your partner. Use the information in the box. Can your partner guess who you are describing?**

age eyes hair height name other weight

He's 16. He's average height and slim. He has short, black, straight hair, and brown eyes. He wears glasses.

Workbook p.10   **Extra practice** online

be: Simple past

Affirmative

I **was** at home.　We **were** at band practice.

I	was
you	were
he / she / it	was
we	were
you	were
they	were

Think!

Complete the chart with *was* and *were*.

I / he / she / it	1 _____
you / we / they	2 _____

Rules p.W8

1 Complete the sentences with *was* or *were*.

Ana <u>was</u> in my class in elementary school.

1 Your glasses _____ on the desk.
2 Tom _____ 12 in this picture.
3 I _____ very happy on my birthday.
4 Mr. and Mrs. Hernandez _____ at home.
5 The man _____ very tall.
6 The students _____ in class.

Negative

I **wasn't** at home.　You **weren't** at band practice!

Full forms	Short forms
I **was not**	I **wasn't**
you **were not**	you **weren't**
he / she / it **was not**	he / she / it **wasn't**
we **were not**	we **weren't**
you **were not**	you **weren't**
they **were not**	they **weren't**

Rules p.W8

2 Rewrite the sentences in exercise 1 in the negative form.

Ana wasn't in my class in elementary school.

3 Correct the sentences with the words in parentheses.

Elvis Presley was British. (American)
Elvis Presley wasn't British. He was American.

1 Marilyn Monroe was a writer. (actress)
2 Bob Marley was a jazz singer. (reggae singer)

3 Charlie Chaplin and Cory Monteith were musicians. (actors)
4 Selena was an actress. (singer)
5 The Jackson Five pop group were friends. (brothers)
6 Mário de Andrade was a singer. (writer)

Past time expressions

Where **were** you **last night**?

yesterday (yesterday morning / afternoon / evening)

last night (last Monday / week / summer / Christmas / year)

a year **ago** (ten minutes / two days / a week / a month **ago**)

in 2013 (**in** June / the 1990s / the twentieth century)

Think!

Read the sentences. Choose the correct words.

I was at school **last Monday**.
Last Monday I was at school.
• English time phrases [1] **can / can't** go at the beginning of a sentence. They [2] **can / can't** go at the end of a sentence.

Rules p.W8

4 Write the past time expressions in the correct order. Start with *ten minutes ago*.

a month ago　an hour ago　last night
last week　last year　~~ten minutes ago~~
two weeks ago　yesterday morning

<u>ten minutes ago</u>

1 _____　　4 _____
2 _____　　5 _____
3 _____　　6 _____
　　　　　　　　　　7 _____

5 Write five true sentences with the past time expressions in exercise 3 and the affirmative and negative forms of *be*.

I wasn't at home last night.

Finished?

Think of a famous person from the past and write five sentences about them. Describe their profession and their physical appearance with the simple past form of *be*.

Elvis Presley was a singer. His hair was short and black, and his eyes were …

Puzzle p.104

2 Communication

Describing people

1 🔊 1.16 **Listen and complete the dialogues with the words in the box. Listen again and check. Then listen and repeat.**

| about   boy   brown   glasses   ~~math~~   Spain   very   young |

1

Mom Who's Miss Riley?
Kate She's our new __math__ teacher.
Mom Oh, what's she like?
Kate She's OK, but she's pretty strict.
Mom Is she ¹_____?
Kate Yes, she is. She's ²_____ 30.
Mom What does she look like?
Kate She's short and she has blond hair. She wears ³_____.

2

Ellen Who's Carlos?
Tom He's a new ⁴_____ in my class.
Ellen Oh. Where does he come from?
Tom He comes from ⁵_____.
Ellen Really? What does he look like?
Tom Um … he's tall and he has ⁶_____ hair.
Ellen What's he like?
Tom He's nice. He's ⁷_____ friendly.

Learn it, use it!

You ask	You answer
What's (she) like?	(She)'s nice. / (She)'s friendly. / (She)'s OK. / (She's) strict.
What does (he) look like?	(He)'s tall and (he) has …

2 🔊 1.17 **Listen to the three conversations about Gemma, Tina, and Marie. Write the correct names under the photos.**

1 _____   2 _Gemma___   3 _____

3 🔊 1.17 **Listen again. Write _Gemma_, _Tina_, or _Marie_. Listen and check.**

She's about 15. _Gemma___
1 She's a new girl at school. _____
2 She comes from Canada. _____
3 She's very nice. _____
4 She's my brother's new girlfriend. _____
5 She's very friendly. _____

4 Pairwork **Write the names of five people you know. Then ask and answer with the words in the box. Use the dialogues in exercise 1 as a model.**

| (not) cool   (not) friendly   (not) nice   (not) strict |

A Who's João?
B He's my piano teacher.

Workbook p.12   **Extra practice** online

be: Simple past

Questions and short answers

> Was it band practice?
> Were you at home yesterday?

Questions	Short answer	
	Affirmative	**Negative**
Was I?	Yes, you **were**.	No, you **weren't**.
Were you?	Yes, I **was**.	No, I **wasn't**.
Was he / she / it?	Yes, he / she / it **was**.	No, he / she / it **wasn't**.
Were we?	Yes, you **were**.	No, you **weren't**.
Were you?	Yes, we **were**.	No, we **weren't**.
Were they?	Yes, they **were**.	No, they **weren't**.

Rules p.W9

1 Write the questions in the correct order. Then give short affirmative (✓) or negative (✗) answers.

in the park / was / yesterday / Tom ? (✗)
Was Tom in the park yesterday?
No, he wasn't.

1 last night / *Scrubs* / on TV / was ? (✓)
2 you and Miguel / at the soccer game / were / on Saturday ? (✓)
3 good / the concert / was ? (✗)
4 Mrs. Jones / yesterday / at school / was ? (✓)
5 Matt and Clare / were / at the sports center ? (✓)
6 in London / last week / the students / were ? (✗)

2 Complete the dialogue with the correct simple past form of *be*.

LAUREL AND HARDY, MASTERS OF COMEDY

A <u>Were</u> Stan Laurel and Oliver Hardy actors?
B Yes, they ¹_____. They ²_____ famous for their comedy movies in the 1920s and 1930s.
A ³_____ they American?
B Oliver Hardy ⁴_____ American, but Stan Laurel ⁵_____ British. He ⁶_____ from the north of the U.K.

Question words + *was* / *were*

> Where were you last night?
> What was on TV?

When	**were** you	born?
Why	**was** he	at home?
Where	**were** you	yesterday?
Who	**was** she?	
How old	**were** you	last year?

Think!

Read the sentences. Choose the correct alternative.

> When **were** you **born**?
> I **was born** in 2001.

• When we talk about our date of birth, we use the simple present / **simple past** of *be* + *born*.

Rules p.W9

3 Look at the underlined words in the answers. Then complete the questions with the words in the box.

How old   When   ~~Where~~   Where   Who   Why

<u>Where were you</u> at eight o'clock?
I was <u>at home</u> at eight o'clock.

1 _____ last weekend?
I was <u>in Chicago</u> last weekend.
2 _____ English teacher last year?
My English teacher last year was <u>Mrs. Smith</u>.
3 _____ born?
I was born <u>in 2010</u>.
4 _____ at Kelly's house?
I was at Kelly's house <u>because it was her birthday</u>.
5 _____ in 2012?
Tom was <u>8 years old</u> in 2012.

Finished?

Write five questions for a partner with the simple past form of *be* and question words. Use the questions in exercise 3 as a model. Then ask and answer the questions.

Puzzle p.104

America's FAVORITES

**Who are America's favorite people?
Some are real, but others are
characters in books and cartoons!
Read and find out more.**

John F Kennedy

John F Kennedy (JFK) (1917–1963) was born in Massachusetts, U.S. He was president of the U.S. from 1961 to 1963, and he was very popular with American people. He was only 43, but he was a strong leader and, with his short, brown hair and blue eyes, he looked like a movie star, too. But JFK's time as president was short. Lee Harvey Oswald assassinated him in 1963.

Diana Ross and the Supremes

Diana Ross and the Supremes were a famous singing group in the 1960s. The three women were from Detroit in the U.S. Their music was popular all over the world, and twelve of their songs were number one in the U.S. Some of their famous songs are *Where Did Our Love Go*, *Baby Love*, and *Stop! In the Name of Love*. The group was also popular for its look: the women were very slim with short, black hair.

Bart Simpson

With his short, yellow arms and legs, and yellow hair, Bart Simpson doesn't look like a typical 10-year-old boy. But Bart isn't real; he's a cartoon character in the TV show *The Simpsons*. Bart loves doing crazy things, and he doesn't like rules. Some parents weren't happy about this! But Bart is a very popular character in the U.S.!

Katniss Everdeen

Katniss Everdeen is a character in the book and movie series *The Hunger Games* by Suzanne Collins. Katniss lives in the imaginary country Panem, in an area with little money. Life can be very tough, but Katniss is a strong girl. In the movies, the beautiful actress Jennifer Lawrence plays the part of Katniss. She is slim with long, brown, wavy hair and gray eyes.

Check it out!

Find these words and check their meaning.

leader
little
tough

Reading

1 🔊 1.18 **Read and listen** to the article. Then answer the questions.

When was JFK born?
He was born in 1917.

1 When was he president of the U.S.?
2 Where were Diana Ross and the other women in her group from?
3 What did they look like?
4 What is Katniss Everdeen like?
5 In the movies, what does Katniss look like?
6 What does Bart Simpson look like?
7 Who weren't happy about the Bart Simpson character?
8 Who is your favorite person in the article? Why?
9 Who is your favorite person in your country? Why?

Listening

2 🔊 1.19 **Listen to the conversation about a famous singer and his band. Check (✓) the correct answers.**

John Lennon was a ... .
- **A** writer ☐
- **B** singer and songwriter ✓
- **C** actor ☐

1 He was a member of ... .
- **A** Metallica ☐
- **B** U2 ☐
- **C** The Beatles ☐

2 Their first song was ... .
- **A** *Yellow Submarine* ☐
- **B** *Yesterday* ☐
- **C** *Love Me Do* ☐

3 The song was from ... .
- **A** 1960 ☐
- **B** 1962 ☐
- **C** 1965 ☐

4 The band's nickname was ... .
- **A** The Fab Four ☐
- **B** The Beat Fans ☐
- **C** The Fab Fans ☐

5 They were famous ...
- **A** in the U.K. ☐
- **B** in the U.S. ☐
- **C** all over the world. ☐

Speaking

3 Pairwork **Use the words and the factfiles to ask and answer questions about the famous people.** 🙂

- What / name?
- Where / born?
- Why / famous?
- What / famous (movie / painting / poem …)?

A *What's her name?*
B *Her name is Greta Garbo.*

Writing

4 **Complete the profile of Greta Garbo. Use the factfile in exercise 3 as a model.**

Greta Garbo was born on <u>September 18th, 1905</u> in ¹_____, in Sweden. She was an ²_____, and she was famous all over the world. One of her famous movies was ³_____. Greta Garbo was a slim, beautiful woman. Her eyes were blue and her ⁴_____ was blond. She died on April 15th, ⁵_____.

5 **Write profiles of Geoffrey Chaucer and Diego Rivera.**

My speaking skills

Preparing for a role play
Prepare for your role play before you start speaking.
Look at the prompts and use them to form questions. Which tense do you need?
Look carefully at the information. What are the questions asking exactly? How can you form your answers with the correct grammar and the correct information?

Greta Garbo
(September 18th, 1905 – April 15th, 1990)
Place of birth: Stockholm, Sweden
Profession: actress
Famous movie: *Anna Karenina*

Geoffrey Chaucer
(c. 1343 – October 25th, 1400)
Place of birth: London, England
Profession: writer and poet
Famous poem: *The Canterbury Tales*

Diego Rivera
(December 8th, 1886 – November 24th, 1957)
Place of birth: Guanajuato, Mexico
Profession: artist
Famous painting: *The Flower Carrier*

 **Review**

Vocabulary

1 Complete the musical genres and instruments with *a*, *e*, *i*, *o*, and *u*.

r_e_c_o_rd_e_r   5 s__x__ph__n__
p_o_p   6 cl__ss__c__l
1 fl__t__   7 tr__mp__t
2 g__ __t__r   8 h__p-h__p
3 r__gg__ __   9 h__ __vy m__t__l
4 v__ __l__n   10 p__ __n__

2 Reorder the letters to complete the physical descriptions of Estela and Max.

A Estela is average t g h h i e _height_ and is pretty ¹m i l s _____. She has shoulder-²l n h e t g _____ brown, ³u c r y l _____ hair. She wears ⁴s a g s e s l _____.

B Max is pretty ⁵l a l t _____ and ⁶r t o e w g e v i h _____. He has ⁷r h t s o _____, ⁸d o b n l _____, ⁹t t i r a g s h _____ hair. He has a ¹⁰d r a b e _____ and a ¹¹c h u s a t e m _____.

3 Choose the correct answers.

1 Calm down. / Who cares? Everything is OK.
2 Let's rock! / I give up! The music is great!
3 I give up / Who cares about math homework? It's Friday!
4 I give up! / Calm down! You never arrive at soccer practice on time!

Grammar

4 Complete the sentences with the simple present or present progressive form of the verbs in parentheses.

Lara _practices_ the piano every day. (practice)
Emilio _isn't using_ the computer now. (not use)
1 Koji usually _____ sports after school. (play)
2 What book _____ at the moment? (you / read)
3 We _____ P.E. on Wednesdays. (not have)
4 Eva _____ this week. She's on vacation. (not work)
5 _____ his bike very often? (your brother / ride)
6 Listen! Tom _____ the piano. (play)

5 Complete the sentences. Use one possessive pronoun and one adverb in each sentence. Use the adverb form of the adjectives in parentheses.

The children play their recorders in a music group. Tim plays _his_ _beautifully_. (beautiful)
1 I can't read my homework! You always do _____ _____. (neat)
2 My sister needs a new laptop. _____ is working very _____. (bad)
3 My parents want a fast new car. _____ goes very _____. (slow)
4 My brother is eating his ice cream _____. But my sister and I aren't enjoying _____. (happy)
5 My friends and I have school tests tomorrow. I hope I do _____ on _____. (good)

6 Rewrite the sentences in the simple past. Use the time expressions in parentheses.

I'm 13. (last week)
I was 13 last week.
1 Is Jamie in Paris? (yesterday)
2 Katie isn't at home. (an hour ago)
3 We're at the movies. (last night)
4 Tina's hair is long. (two years ago)
5 Are cell phones common? (30 years ago)
6 You aren't in the band. (last year)
7 I'm not in New York. (last month)

7 Complete the dialogue with the simple past form of *be*.

Megan Who _was_ Bob Marley, Mom?
Mom He ¹___ a singer.
Megan ²___ he a pop star?
Mom No, he ³___. He ⁴___ in a famous reggae band called Bob Marley and the Wailers.
Megan Who ⁵___ the other members?
Mom Well, the first members ⁶___ Peter Tosh and Bunny Wailer.
Megan ⁷___ they American?
Mom No, they ⁸___. They ⁹___ Jamaican.
Megan You know a lot about the band, Mom.
Mom Well, it ¹⁰___ a great band. And Bob Marley ¹¹___ a great singer. He ¹²___ good-looking, too. His hair ¹³___ long, and his eyes ¹⁴___ brown. He's still my favorite singer!

26 twenty-six

Communication

8 🔊 1.20 **Complete the dialogue. Then listen and check.**

Isabel I have a ticket to see the band Shouter tonight. You know the singer with the big, blue _eyes_____?

Selma Yes! She's fantastic! ¹_____ I come?

Isabel Yes, but I don't have a ticket for you.

Selma Well, ²_____ I buy a ticket?

Isabel ³_____, you can. Ask Carlos. He's in my brother's class.

Selma What does he ⁴_____ like?

Isabel He's very tall, with ⁵_____-length, blond, wavy ⁶_____.

Selma Oh, *that* Carlos! Wow! What's he ⁷_____?

Isabel He's very cool!

Pronunciation

The sound schwa /ə/

9 🔊 1.21 **In English words with more than one syllable, we usually put the stress on one syllable only. Listen to the stressed syllables in the words below.**

● •   ● • ••   • ●• •   • ●   •• ●
brother   classical   computer   tonight   relax

The other syllables in the words are unstressed. Often we pronounce them with a sound called schwa /ə/. Listen to the words again and listen for the schwa sounds. Then listen and repeat.

10 🔊 1.22 **Listen to the different pronunciation of the syllables. Then listen and repeat.**

stressed	unstressed
man	human
fast	breakfast
board	cupboard

11 🔊 1.23 **Listen to the words. Underline the syllables with the stress and circle the syllables with the sound schwa /ə/. Then listen again and repeat.**

ⓐbout   2 awesome   4 pizza   6 again

1 priceless   3 president   5 August   7 parents

Listening

12 🔊 1.24 **Listen to four short conversations. Check (✓) the correct answers.**

What is Brad doing?
A He's doing his homework.   ☐
B He's reading a magazine.   ✓
C He's taking a math test.   ☐

1 Why does Rosa look different?
A Her hair was curly last year.   ☐
B Her hair was straight last year.   ☐
C Her hair was long last year.   ☐

2 What does Andres look like?
A He has short, brown hair and glasses.   ☐
B He has short, brown hair and a beard.   ☐
C He has curly, black hair and a beard.   ☐

3 Where was Pablo yesterday afternoon?
A He was at his grandma's birthday party.   ☐
B He was at a friend's 18th birthday party.   ☐
C He was at band practice.   ☐

13 🔊 1.25 **Listen to the conversation. Claudia is describing a picture of her family. What are the people in the picture doing? Complete the sentences with the present progressive form of the verbs in the box.**

eat   not have a good time   not sit down
play soccer   read   ~~swim~~   talk

Lia _is swimming_____.
1 Jose _____.
2 Pedro _____.
3 Nuria _____.
4 Miguel and Eduardo _____.
5 Antonio _____.
6 Josefina _____.

Rosa Parks

To most people around her, Rosa Parks was an ordinary woman with an ordinary life in Montgomery, Alabama in the U.S. With her slim figure, black hair and brown eyes, she looked like a typical African American woman in the 1950s. But Rosa Parks was not ordinary. Life for African American people was very difficult in those years, and Rosa was one solution to their problems.

In 1950s America, black people's lives were very different from those of white people. Their jobs were bad, and their schools were terrible. Everything for white people was better. But Rosa's actions on one evening in 1955 were very important for change.

Imagine you are a black person sitting on a bus. The bus is full, and a white person climbs on. The bus driver says to you, "Stand up and give this person your seat." What do you do?

Rosa's decision was to stay in her seat. The bus driver was very angry, and Rosa was in trouble with the police. But the incident was soon very famous all over America. And with support from other black people in her community, there was a boycott of the bus company, too – for over a year! Now it was clear to all Americans that black people were not happy with their lives. After a change in the law in 1956, there were more equal rights for black people in the U.S. Rosa Parks' story shows that one person's simple action can make a great difference for millions of people.

Check it out!

Find these words and check their meaning.

in trouble
boycott
law
equal rights

1 Scan the article and choose the correct answers.

Rosa Parks was English / (American).

1 She was **in trouble** / **happy** with the police.
2 Rosa's decision was **bad** / **good** for black people in the U.S.

2 🔊 1.26 **Read and listen** to the article. Then answer the questions.

Where was Rosa Parks from?
She was from Montgomery, Alabama.

1 What did she look like?
2 Why was life difficult for Rosa and many others like her?
3 How long was the Montgomery bus boycott?
4 Imagine you are another black person on the bus. You hear the conversation between Rosa and the bus driver. What do you think about Rosa? What do you think about the driver?

3 **Presentation** Look at the pictures of two American classrooms in the 1940s and 1950s. Make questions with the prompts below. Then write answers to the questions. Use your answers to prepare a short presentation.

Who / in the pictures?
Who are in the pictures?

1 What / the classroom in picture 1 like?
2 What / the classroom in picture 2 like?
3 What / the classrooms (not) have?
4 What / life like / children in the pictures?
5 How / life / different for American children now?

Vocabulary and speaking

I can identify musical genres and instruments. (p.12)   A2

1 Reorder the letters to form musical genres and instruments.

1 Dad's favorite music is e g a r g e _____.
2 My sister plays the t r m u p t e _____.
3 I want a u g r t a i _____ for Christmas.
4 Do you play the n a p i o _____?
5 I like listening to r c o k _____ music.   __ / 5

I can make requests. (p.14)   A2

2 Complete the dialogue.

Felipe Can I [1]_____ the window, please?
Olivia Yes, of course you [2]_____.
Felipe And can I have a [3]_____?
Olivia Yes. What do you want? Cola, or water?
Felipe [4]_____ I [5]_____ a cola, please?
Olivia Yes. Here you go.   __ / 5

I can ask and answer questions about a music festival. (p.17)   A2

3 Choose the correct answers.

Fabio Hi, Zoe, what are you [1]doing / making at the moment?
Zoe Hi, Fabio! I'm at a festival. A lot of [2]famous / favorite musicians are here.
Fabio Really? Who's [3]listening / playing?
Zoe Tinie Tempah – he's awesome!
Fabio And [4]what / where is it?
Zoe It's in New York.
Fabio Well, I hope you're [5]liking / having a great time! Talk soon!
Zoe Bye!   __ / 5

I can identify words for physical description. (p.20)   A2

4 Complete the sentences.

1 My hair isn't straight, or curly. It's _____.
2 Tom's hair isn't long, or short. It's _____-length.
3 I get _____ on my nose in the summer.
4 My grandpa eats a lot of pizza, so he's pretty _____.
5 This dress is very small. Only a _____ person can wear it.   __ / 5

I can describe people I know. (p.22)   A2

5 Reorder the dialogue.

__ **Patty** And what's she like? Is she nice?
__ **Bianca** There's a new girl in my class from Brazil.
__ **Patty** From Brazil? What does she look like?
__ **Bianca** She's slim with brown, curly hair.
__ **Bianca** Yes, she's very friendly.   __ / 5

I can ask and answer questions about famous people. (p.25)   A2

6 Complete the questions about a famous American celebrity. Then match them with the answers.

1 _____ was her name? __
2 _____ was _____ born? __
3 _____ was _____ birthday? __
4 _____ _____ she famous? __
5 _____ was _____ most famous movie? __
a *The Wizard of Oz*
b June 10th
c She was a singer and an actress.
d Judy Garland.
e Minnesota, U.S.   __ / 5

Reading, listening, and writing

	Got it?		
	Yes	I'm not sure	No
I can understand an article and answer questions about a music festival. (p.16) **A2**	☐	☐	☐
I can understand a phone conversation and answer questions about a music festival. (p.17) **A2**	☐	☐	☐
I can write a blog post about a music festival. (p.17) **A2**	☐	☐	☐
I can understand an article and answer questions about famous Americans. (p.24) **A2**	☐	☐	☐
I can understand a conversation and answer questions about a famous band. (p.25) **A2**	☐	☐	☐
I can write short profiles of famous people. (p.25) **A2**	☐	☐	☐

3 He sang all their songs

1 🔊 1.27 **Read and listen** **Who has bad news?**

Dylan It's raining again! I want to live in California! It's always hot and sunny there.

Rosie I went to California on vacation last year. The weather was beautiful. We stayed in a hotel near the beach.

Dylan Really? I went there with my family two years ago, but it rained every day!

Lewis Hey, guys!

Rosie Hi, Lewis. What's up?

Lewis I have some bad news.

Dylan Oh no … what is it?

Lewis I went to the youth center yesterday. There was a talent show and The Misfitz played.

Dylan So what?

Lewis Well, they had a new singer.

Rosie Really? Who was it?

Lewis It was Zac! He sang all their songs. He knew all the words.

Dylan Oh, no! Zac's with The Misfitz now!

Rosie And we don't have a singer!

Check it out!

Find these words and check their meaning.

What's up?   So what?

2 Comprehension **Answer the questions.**

Where was Dylan on holiday with his family?
They were in California.

1 Where was Lewis yesterday?
2 What was the bad news?
3 Who sings with The Misfitz now?

Language focus

3 Dialogue focus **There are six more mistakes in the dialogues. Find and correct the mistakes.**

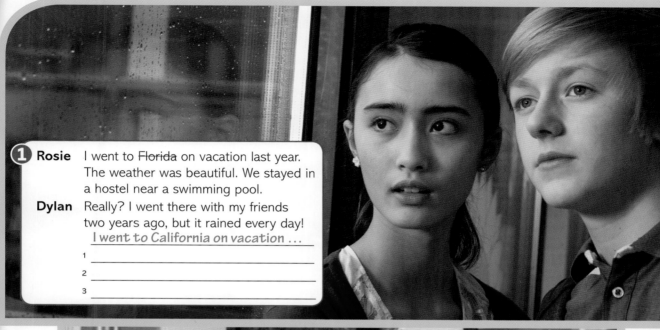

1 **Rosie** I went to ~~Florida~~ on vacation last year. The weather was beautiful. We stayed in a hostel near a swimming pool.

Dylan Really? I went there with my friends two years ago, but it rained every day!

I went to California on vacation ...

1 _____
2 _____
3 _____

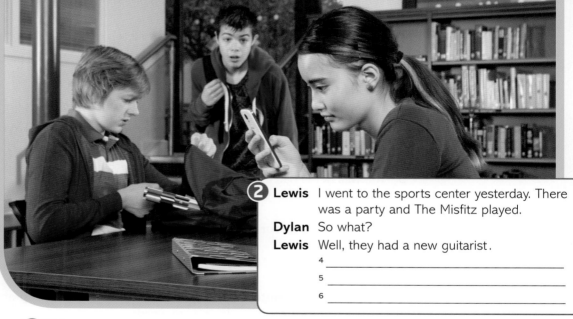

2 **Lewis** I went to the sports center yesterday. There was a party and The Misfitz played.

Dylan So what?

Lewis Well, they had a new guitarist.

4 _____
5 _____
6 _____

4 🔊 1.28 **Listen and check. Listen again and repeat.**

5 Focus on you **Read the example dialogue. Then write two similar dialogues. Use the words in the box.**

> a concert   a pizzeria   a soccer game   my grandma's house
> the movies   the sports center   the swimming pool   the youth center

A I went to my grandma's house with my brother yesterday.
B Really? I went to the movies with my friends.

6 Pairwork **Practice the dialogues in exercise 5.** 🙂

3 Vocabulary

The weather

1 🔊 1.29 **Look at the pictures and read the people's comments. Which cities are they in? Complete the sentences. Then listen and check.**

London

Paris

Seoul

Tokyo

Chicago

Seattle

"The weather here is terrible. It's **snowing** at the moment."
Quique is in <u>Paris</u>.

1 "This city is great, but the weather is horrible. It's **raining** again today!"
Paul is in _____.

2 "I'm having a great vacation. The weather is always **sunny**."
Gabriel is in _____.

3 "The city and the food are fantastic, but the weather is **cloudy**."
Claudia is in _____.

4 "Yesterday, the weather was good, but today it's very **windy**."
Jenny is in _____.

5 "The weather is bad again today! It's **foggy** and miserable."
Sam is in _____.

2 Write a sentence about the weather in each city. Use the words in bold from exercise 1.

In Paris it's snowing.

3 Look at the thermometers in the pictures in exercise 1. Complete the sentences about the cities with the temperature words.

In Chicago it's <u>cold</u>.
1 In Seattle it's _____.
2 In Paris it's _____.
3 In Tokyo it's _____.
4 In London it's _____.
5 In Seoul it's _____.

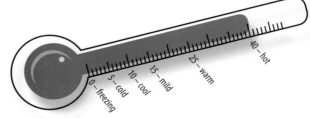

Look!

18°C = eighteen degrees Celsius
-3°C = minus three degrees Celsius

4 Pairwork Ask and answer questions about the weather and temperatures in the cities. Then ask and answer questions about the weather where you live. 😊

A What's the weather like in Seattle?
B It's mild and raining. It's 15°C.

Workbook p.16   Extra practice online

Simple past: Regular verbs

Affirmative

> We **stayed** in a hotel near the beach.
> It **rained** every day!

I / you / he / she / it / we / you / they	watch**ed**

Think!

Complete the rule.

- In English we add -_____ to the base form of regular verbs to make the simple past form.

Rules   p.W14

1 Complete the sentences with the simple past form of the verbs in parentheses.

We _visited_____ Aunt Kate last weekend. (visit)

1 The movie _____ ten minutes ago. (start)
2 We _____ baseball last Saturday. (play)
3 I _____ to the new Pitbull album yesterday. (listen)
4 You _____ a DVD after dinner. (watch)
5 Dad _____ his car on Sunday. (wash)
6 The class _____ at ten o'clock. (end)
7 My mom _____ for a year. (work)
8 The teacher _____ the window. (open)

Spelling variations

> I **loved** the beaches in Florida!
> It **stopped** raining in the afternoon.

Verbs ending in -e: + -d		
love	→	lov**ed**
use	→	us**ed**
Verbs ending with a consonant + -y: -y + -ied		
study	→	stud**ied**
tidy	→	tid**ied**
Some verbs ending with a vowel + consonant: double the consonant + -ed		
stop	→	stop**ped**
admit	→	admit**ted**
prefer	→	prefer**red**

Rules   p.W14

2 Write the verbs in the simple past.

watch _watched_____   4 hate _____
1 study _____   5 play _____
2 explore_____   6 cry _____
3 close _____   7 stop _____

3 Complete the sentences with the simple past form of the verbs in exercise 2.

Tom and Yuki _played_____ computer games after lunch.

1 We _____ the window last night.
2 The bus _____ in front of the school.
3 The baby _____ because she was cold and hungry.
4 Francisco _____ German for three years.
5 We _____ the basketball game on TV.
6 When I was a teenager, I _____ jazz.
7 We _____ the history museum.

4 🔊 1.30 **Pronunciation** Listen to the pronunciation of the words. Listen again and repeat.

/d/	/t/	/ɪd/
lived	worked	hated

We usually pronounce the simple past ending -ed as /d/.
When the base form of the verb finishes with the sounds /p/, /k/, /f/, /s/, /ʃ/, or /tʃ/, we pronounce -ed as /t/.
When the base form of the verb finishes with the sounds /d/ or /t/, we pronounce -ed as /ɪd/.

5 🔊 1.31 Listen to the verbs. Then complete the chart.

> ~~decided~~ hated ~~liked~~ ~~listened~~
> opened rained started washed watched

/d/	/t/	/ɪd/
listened	_liked_	_decided_
1 _____	3 _____	5 _____
2 _____	4 _____	6 _____

Finished?

How many sentences can you make with the words below? Remember to use the simple past.

People: Cecilia I Pedro the girls we you
Verbs: close play stop study watch work
Cecilia played the guitar.
I watched TV.

Puzzle p.105

3 Communication

Talking about vacations

1 🔊 1.32 **Listen and complete the dialogues with the words in the box. Listen again and check. Then listen and repeat.**

~~awesome~~ beautiful delicious good great

awful friendly nice terrible

1

Ana How was your vacation in Hawaii?
Jim It was _awesome_!
Ana What was the weather like?
Jim It was ¹_____. It was hot and sunny.
Ana Was the food ²_____?
Jim Yes, it was ³_____.
Ana What was your hotel like?
Jim It was ⁴_____. It had a big swimming pool.

2

Ivan How was your vacation in New York?
Lily It was ⁵_____!
Ivan What was the weather like?
Lily It was ⁶_____. It rained every day!
Ivan Were the people ⁷_____?
Lily Yes, they were. They were very ⁸_____.
Ivan What was the hotel food like?
Lily It was disgusting! Gross!

Learn it, use it!

You ask	You answer
How was your vacation in (town / country)?	It was great / awesome / OK / terrible.
What was the weather like?	It was beautiful / amazing / great / OK / miserable.
Was the food good?	Yes, it was. It was delicious. No, it wasn't. It was horrible / disgusting.
What was your hotel like?	It was great / awesome / OK / terrible / awful.
Were the people friendly?	Yes, they were. They were very nice. No, they weren't. They were unfriendly.

2 🔊 1.33 **Listen to the two conversations and complete the sentences. Listen and check.**

A Gemma went to Mexico on vacation. The weather was _great_. It was very ¹_____. The food was delicious.

B Mrs. Alonso went to ²_____ on vacation. The weather was ³_____. It was cold and windy. The people weren't ⁴_____.

3 Pairwork **Write two dialogues using the country factfiles and the dialogues in exercise 1 as a model. Then practice your dialogues.** 😊

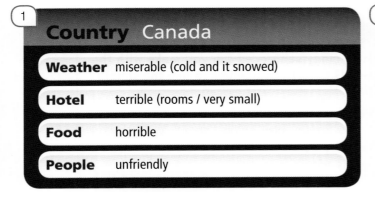

1

Country Canada

Weather	miserable (cold and it snowed)
Hotel	terrible (rooms / very small)
Food	horrible
People	unfriendly

2

Country Italy

Weather	amazing (warm and sunny)
Hotel	great (satellite TV and Internet in the rooms)
Food	delicious
People	friendly

Workbook p.18 | **Extra practice** online

Simple past: Irregular verbs

I **went** to California on vacation last year.
He **sang** all their songs.

Base form	Simple past	Base form	Simple past
do	did	read	read
eat	ate	say	said
go	went	sing	sang
make	made	take	took
Rules p.W14		**Irregular verbs list**	

1 Look at the list of irregular verbs on the inside back cover. Complete the sentences with the simple past form of the verbs in the box.

get   go   read   run   sing   swim   win

Steve _got_____ a bike for his birthday.

1 We _____ in the ocean. It was very cold!

2 We _____ to school because we were very late!

3 The first book I _____ was *Harry Potter*.

4 We _____ to Maui on vacation last year.

5 Brazil _____ the World Cup in 2002.

6 They _____ all my favorite songs at the concert.

2 Read the information. Then write sentences about what Jose did last Saturday.

Saturday

- ◯ get up early
- ◯ clean my bedroom
- ◯ play computer games
- ◯ buy some new sneakers with Mom
- ◯ have dinner with Mom and Dad
- ◯ chat online with my cousin
- ◯ go to bed late

Look!

Talking about the order of events

First, …
Then, …
Afterwards, …
Finally, …

On Saturday, Jose got up early. In the morning, he cleaned his bedroom and then he … . After that, he …

3 Complete the e-card with the simple past form of the verbs in parentheses.

A Weekend in New Orleans

Last weekend, I _visited____ (visit) New Orleans for the first time with Mom and Dad. We ¹_____ (stay) in the beautiful Roosevelt Hotel.

We ²_____ (arrive) on Friday evening and ³_____ (have) a meal in the hotel. Then, on Saturday morning, we ⁴_____ (go) on a bus tour of the city. I ⁵_____ (learn) a lot about it. The tour guide ⁶_____ (tell) me that New Orleans is the home of jazz music. And he ⁷_____ (take) us to listen to some jazz musicians.

On Sunday, we ⁸_____ (walk) around the French part of the city and ⁹_____ (see) some beautiful buildings. Then, we ¹⁰_____ (sit) by the river and ¹¹_____ (eat) a delicious picnic. We ¹²_____ (enjoy) every minute of our trip!

4 Write true sentences with past time expressions and the simple past.

go to the movies
I went to the movies last week.

1 watch my favorite TV show
_____

2 send a text message
_____

3 take a test
_____

4 go to a party
_____

5 get a present
_____

Finished?

Describe your weekend. Write five sentences using five different irregular verbs. Then tell your partner.

Puzzle p.105

The Discovery of Antarctica

Antarctica is an enormous frozen continent at the South Pole. It's very cold and windy, and there's snow and ice all year. In the 1890s, many explorers went to Antarctica, including the British explorer Ernest Shackleton, Roald Amundsen from Norway, and Nobu Shirase from Japan. Another very famous name in Antarctic history is British explorer, Captain Robert Scott.

Scott's first expedition began in 1901, but there was terrible weather, with strong winds and freezing temperatures. Scott and his men stopped their expedition before they reached the South Pole.

Between 1910 and 1912, the Japanese explorer Nobu Shirase and his men went on an expedition in Antarctica. They explored the Edward VII peninsula, but they didn't reach the South Pole.

Scott started his second expedition to the South Pole in 1910, too. There was a race between him and Roald Amundsen to reach the South Pole first. Scott and his men arrived there on January 17th 1912, but they found a Norwegian flag and a message from Amundsen. The Norwegian explorer and his men arrived at the South Pole 33 days before Scott.

Scott and his men started traveling back to camp. Again, the weather was terrible with strong winds and snow. His men were freezing and hungry, and, tragically, everyone died. They were only 18 km from their base camp.

There were many Antarctic explorers, but people admire Captain Scott for his courage and determination. He wasn't the winner of the race to the South Pole, but he helped people to understand the extreme weather, geography, and geology of Antarctica.

Check it out!

Find these words and check their meaning.

discovery
frozen
South Pole
reach

My reading skills

Scanning the text for specific information

Some questions ask you to look for specific information in a text. You don't need to read all the words to find it. Before you read the text, read the questions and underline the key words in them. This helps you to find the correct information in the text.

Reading

1 Look at the pictures. Underline the key words in the questions. Then scan the article and find the answers.

What is the <u>weather</u> like in <u>Antarctica</u>?
The weather is cold, windy, and snowing in Antarctica.
1 Who was the winner of the race to the South Pole?
2 Why do people admire Captain Scott?

2 🔊 1.34 Read and listen to the article. Then correct the mistakes in the sentences below.

Antarctica is at the North Pole.
Antarctica is at the South Pole.
1 Antarctica has mild temperatures.
2 Captain Scott traveled to Antarctica for the first time in 1890.
3 He went to Antarctica four times.
4 A German explorer wanted to get to the South Pole at the same time as Scott.
5 Scott reached the South Pole about a month before Amundsen.
6 Scott and his men died at the South Pole.

Listening

3 🔊 1.35 **Listen to the radio programme. Complete the timeline about the events in the life of the explorer Sir Edmund Hillary. Use the information in the box.**

> He arrived at the South Pole.   He died in New Zealand.
> He discovered his love of climbing.   He helped to build schools and hospitals there.
> He reached the top of Mount Everest.   ~~He was born in New Zealand.~~

1919	He was born in New Zealand.
1935	He went on a school trip to the mountains in New Zealand. ¹_____
1939	He completed his first big climb.
1951	He made his first journey to Nepal to climb the Himalayan mountains.
1953	²_____
1958	³_____
1962	He returned to Nepal. ⁴_____
2008	⁵_____

Speaking

4 Pairwork **Look at the timeline about Emilio. Describe the important events in his life with your partner. Remember to use the simple past.** 😊

2001	2006	2008	2011	2012	2013
Born in Miami	Starts elementary school	Learns to ride a bike	Travels to Uruguay on vacation	Starts junior high	Gets his first horse

A Emilio was born in Miami in 2001.
B He started elementary school in 2006.
A He …

5 Make a timeline about the important events in your life. Use it to describe the events to your partner. Use the ideas in the box, or use your own ideas.

> be born   brother / sister born   get my first …   go on vacation to …
> learn to ride a bicycle   learn to swim   lose my first tooth   meet my best friend
> say my first word   start elementary school   start junior high

I was born in …
I was born in (place) in (year). I …

Writing

6 Write a paragraph about the important events in your life.

I was born in (place) in (year). I …

4 Did you like the movie?

1 🔊 1.36 **Read and listen** Who does Kelly invite to join The Misfitz?

Kelly Did you like the movie, Zac?

Zac Yes, I did. It was good, but I didn't like the ending. Did you like it?

Kelly Yes, I did. I love science fiction movies.

Zac Science fiction movies and horror movies are my favorite types of movie.

Kelly What did you do after band practice yesterday?

Zac I went for a pizza. Did you go out?

Kelly No, I didn't. I went home. Hey, there's Rosie.

Zac Rosie? Where is she?

Kelly She's over there. Let's say hello.

Zac Good idea. Hi, Rosie. So, did you see The Misfitz last week?

Rosie Umm … no, I didn't, but Lewis saw you.

Zac Huh, Lewis and Dylan! Why do you stay with those losers?

Rosie They aren't losers. They're my friends, and we're a good band.

Zac Get real, Rosie! Supernova isn't a good band! You don't have a singer.

Kelly But you're an awesome guitarist, Rosie, and we're a great band. Why don't you join The Misfitz, too?

Check it out!

Find these words and check their meaning.

over there   losers   Get real!

2 Comprehension Complete the sentences with the names in the box.

> Dylan   Kelly   Lewis   Rosie   Zac

Zac and _Kelly_ liked the movie.

1 _____ likes science fiction movies and horror movies.

2 _____ went for a pizza after band practice.

3 _____ went home.

4 _____ saw The Misfitz last week.

5 _____ and _____ are Rosie's friends.

6 _____ is an awesome guitarist.

Language focus

3 Dialogue focus Write the sentences and questions in the correct order to form dialogues.

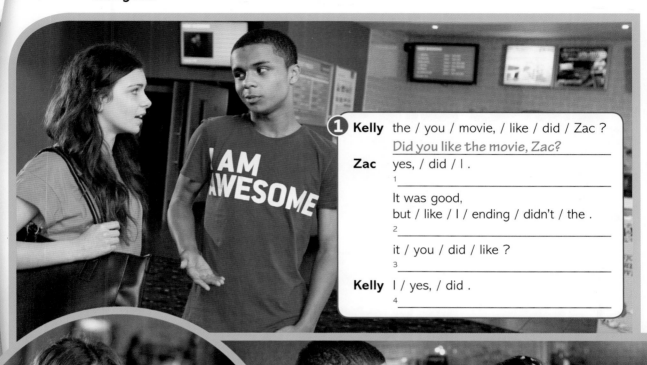

1 Kelly the / you / movie, / like / did / Zac ?
Did you like the movie, Zac?

Zac yes, / did / I .
1 _____

It was good,
but / like / I / ending / didn't / the .
2 _____

it / you / did / like ?
3 _____

Kelly I / yes, / did .
4 _____

2 Kelly did / what / you / practice / yesterday / do / band / after ? 5_____
_____

Zac I went for a pizza.
go / you / did / out ? 6_____

Kelly no, / didn't / I . 7_____

3 Zac see / so, / you / did / last / The Misfitz / week ?
8_____

Rosie didn't, / no, / umm … / I 9_____
but Lewis saw you.

4 🔊 1.37 **Listen and check. Listen again and repeat.**

5 Focus on you Read the example dialogue. Then write three similar dialogues. Use the activities in the box.

> chat with friends online   clean my bedroom   do my homework
> go shopping   go swimming   go to the movies   listen to my new CDs
> play computer games   play soccer   watch some DVDs

A What did you do yesterday?
B I went to the movies.

A Did you go swimming?
B Yes, I did. / No, I didn't.

6 Pairwork Practice the dialogues in exercise 5. 🎭

Movies

1 🔊 1.38 **Match the movie types with the pictures. Then listen and check.**

> ~~action movie~~   cartoon   comedy   fantasy movie
> horror movie   love story   musical   science fiction movie

action movie

1 _____

2 _____

3 _____

4 _____

5 _____

6 _____

7 _____

Look!

A **comedy**, a **cartoon**, a **love story**, a **musical**
but
an action **movie**, a horror **movie**, a fantasy **movie**, a science fiction **movie**

2 🔊 1.39 **Listen to the conversations about movies. Complete the chart. Then listen and check.**

Name	Type of movie
Thirty Minutes	*action movie*
1 *Animals United*	_____
2 *Dear John*	_____
3 *American Girl*	_____
4 *Dungeons and Dragons*	_____
5 *New World*	_____
6 *Silent House*	_____
7 *Secret Heart*	_____

3 Pairwork **Think of three of your favorite movies. Tell your partner the names of the movies and their movie types.** 😊

A *My favorite movies are Mamma Mia!, Shrek, and Skyfall.*
B *What type of movie is Mamma Mia!?*
A *It's a musical ...*

(Workbook p.22   **Extra practice** online)

Simple past

Negative

> I **didn't like** the ending.
> We **didn't go** out.

Full forms	Short forms
I **did not eat**	I **didn't eat**
you **did not eat**	you **didn't eat**
he / she / it **did not eat**	he / she / it **didn't eat**
we **did not eat**	we **didn't eat**
you **did not eat**	you **didn't eat**
they **did not eat**	they **didn't eat**

Think!

Choose the correct alternatives.

- In English, we form the simple past negative with *did not* (*didn't*) and the [1]**base form** / **past form** of the main verb.
- Irregular verbs [2]**follow** / **don't follow** the same rule.

Rules p.W20

1 Complete the sentences with the simple past form of the verbs in the box.

> clean   do   go   play   visit   ~~watch~~

We <u>didn't watch</u> TV last night.

1 I _____ swimming last Saturday.
2 You _____ your bedroom!
3 Shiori _____ her science homework.
4 They _____ soccer on Sunday.
5 We _____ our cousins yesterday.

2 Rewrite the sentences in the negative form.

> Tiago sent me a text yesterday.
> <u>Tiago didn't send me a text yesterday.</u>

1 My mom got up at seven o'clock.
_____

2 I went to the theater last week.
_____

3 The movie started at eight o'clock.
_____

4 Emily bought a new cell phone.
_____

5 Sam and Carlos came to the party.
_____

6 We ate pizza for dinner.
_____

3 How much do you know about Johnny Depp? Do the quiz and find out!

> Johnny Depp left school when he was ... .
> **A** 18 ___   **B** 15 ✓
> **C** 16 ___
>
> **1** He wanted to be ... .
> **A** an actor ___
> **B** a rock musician ___
> **C** a doctor ___
>
> **2** Before he was famous, he sold ... .
> **A** pens ___   **B** pencils ___   **C** cars ___
>
> **3** In *Edward Scissorhands* he starred with ... .
> **A** Keira Knightley ___   **B** Winona Ryder ___
> **C** Emma Watson ___
>
> **4** In the *Pirates of the Caribbean* films he played the part of ... .
> **A** Captain Sparrow ___   **B** Will Turner ___
> **C** Hector Barbossa ___
>
> 1 B 2 A 3 B 4 A

4 Now write sentences about Johnny Depp. Use the information in the quiz. The answers are at the bottom of the quiz.

> Johnny Depp didn't leave school when he was 18. He left school when he was 15.

5 Complete the diary page with the simple past form of the verbs in parentheses. Are the verbs affirmative or negative?

> Yesterday was a horrible day! I <u>didn't hear</u> (hear) the alarm clock, and I [1]_____ (wake up). I usually take the bus, but it [2]_____ (leave) without me, so I [3]_____ (walk). It [4]_____ (be) freezing and I [5]_____ (have) my jacket. I [6]_____ (arrive) at school miserable, late, and cold! We [7]_____ (have) a math test and I [8]_____ (know) the answers to the questions. I [9]_____ (pass) it! After school, we had an important basketball game – the final of the School Championship. We [10]_____ (play) well, and we [11]_____ (win) the cup!

Finished?

Imagine you are a movie star. What did you plan to do last weekend? Write a list of six things. Then write sentences about what you did and didn't do.

Puzzle p.105

4 Communication

Going to the movies

1 🔊 1.40 **Use the information on the movie theater poster to complete the dialogues. Listen to the dialogues and check. Then listen and repeat.**

On the phone …

Martha Let's go to watch *High Impact*.
Dan What type of movie is it?
Martha It's an <u>action</u> movie. And it's in 3D.
Dan Cool. I love action movies. Where is it playing?
Martha It's playing at the [1]_____.
Dan What time does it start?
Martha It starts at six thirty.
Dan OK. Let's go and see that then.

At the movie theater …

Martha Can I have two children's tickets for *High Impact*, please?
Clerk How old are you?
Martha We're twelve.
Clerk OK. That's [2] $_____.
Martha There you go.
Clerk Thank you. Here are your tickets and $8 change.
Martha What screen is it?
Clerk It's screen [3]_____.
Martha Thank you.

CINEMARK MOVIE THEATER

HIGH IMPACT
A new **3D** action movie!

ADULT TICKETS: $14
CHILDREN'S TICKETS: $11
TIMES: 14:45 18:30 19:45
SCREEN 7

Learn it, use it!

You ask	You answer
Let's go to …	OK.
What type of movie is it?	It's a …
Where is it playing?	It's playing at …
What time does it start?	It starts at …
Can I have … tickets, please?	That's $11.
What screen is it?	It's screen 4.

2 🔊 1.41 **Listen to three conversations and complete the movie posters. Listen and check.**

1
At the AMC movie theater tonight …
Fast Car
A new <u>action</u> movie
Adult tickets: $13.50
Children's tickets: [1] $_____
Times: 2:30 p.m. [2]_____ 8:30 p.m.
Screen: [3]_____

2
CINEMARK
Showing at the Cinemark Theater this week only!
The Music Man
A new [4]_____
Adult tickets: [5] $_____
Children's tickets: [6] $_____
Times: 2:00 p.m. [7]_____ 9:00 p.m.
Screen: [8]_____

3
Starting at the **AMC** today …!
BIRTHDAY PARTY
A new comedy
Adult tickets: [9] $_____
Children's tickets: [10] $_____
Times: 2:45 p.m. [11]_____ 8:45 p.m.
Screen: [12]_____

3 Pairwork **Choose a movie poster from exercise 2 and write a dialogue. Use the dialogues in exercise 1 as a model. Then practice your dialogue.** 😊

Workbook p.24   **Extra practice** online

Simple past

Questions and short answers

> Did you like the movie, Zac? Yes, I did.
> Did you go out? No, I didn't.

Questions	Short answers	
	Affirmative	**Negative**
Did I **eat?**	**Yes,** you **did.**	**No,** you **didn't.**
Did you **eat?**	**Yes,** I **did.**	**No,** I **didn't.**
Did he **eat?**	**Yes,** he **did.**	**No,** he **didn't.**
Did she **eat?**	**Yes,** she **did.**	**No,** she **didn't.**
Did it **eat?**	**Yes,** it **did.**	**No,** it **didn't.**
Did we **eat?**	**Yes,** you **did.**	**No,** you **didn't.**
Did you **eat?**	**Yes,** we **did.**	**No,** we **didn't.**
Did they **eat?**	**Yes,** they **did.**	**No,** they **didn't.**

Rules p.W20

1 Write the questions in the correct order. Then write short answers that are true for you.

do / your homework / you / did / yesterday ?
Did you do your homework yesterday?
Yes, I did. / No, I didn't.

1 your mom / watch TV / did / last night ?
2 your best friend / yesterday / call you / did ?
3 you / did / go to Joe's party / last night ?
4 did / last weekend / play soccer / your sister ?
5 your history teacher / give you a test / did / yesterday ?

2 **Pairwork** Look at Lucy's list of plans for yesterday. Then ask and answer questions about what she did (✓) and didn't do (**X**).

get up early (✓)   clean bedroom (**X**)
go to the gym (**X**)   take the dog for a walk (✓)
phone grandma (✓)   finish science project (**X**)

3 Complete the questions, short answers, and sentences. Use the simple past form of the verbs in parentheses.

Julia <u>Did you go out</u> (you / go out) last night?
David Yes, I [1]_____. I went to Cesar's house to watch a movie.
Julia [2]_____ (Beth / go), too?
David No, she [3]_____. She [4]_____ (not feel) well.
Julia What movie [5]_____ (you / watch)?
David *Distant Galaxies.*
Julia [6]_____ (you / like) it?
David No, I [7]_____. I [8]_____ (not enjoy) it at all!
Julia So why [9]_____ (you / watch) it?
David Cesar wanted to. He likes stupid movies!

Question words + Simple past

> **What** did you do after band practice yesterday?

What	did	you	do over the weekend?
Where	did	he	teach?
When	did	we	arrive?
What time	did	she	start work?
How	did	you	travel there?
Why	did	we	leave?

Rules p.W20

4 Look at the underlined part of the answers. Which question word do you need to use?

He got up <u>at seven o'clock</u>.   <u>What time</u>
1 She bought <u>a book</u>.   _____
2 He went to bed <u>because he was tired</u>.   _____
3 They worked <u>in a hospital</u>.   _____
4 It rained <u>on Tuesday</u>.   _____
5 He traveled across the U.S. <u>on a bike</u>.   _____

5 Write the question for each answer in exercise 4.

What time did he get up?
1 _____
2 _____
3 _____
4 _____
5 _____

Finished?

Write questions starting with *Did* and question words about what you and your classmates did last weekend. Then ask and answer them.

Puzzle p.105

Welcome to We Love Movies

a website for movie lovers!
Check out our We love ... section for information about your favorite Hollywood stars.
Follow us @welovecinema

Reese Witherspoon

Reese Witherspoon is the star of *Legally Blonde* and *This Means War*. She's the queen of Hollywood. But did you know ...? Reese isn't her first name. Her name is actually Laura Jeanne Reese Witherspoon.

She was born in New Orleans in 1976, but she lived in Germany until she was 4 years old.

She got her first part in the movie *Man In the Moon* in 1990. She was only 14!

After High School, she went to Stanford University to study English literature, but she didn't graduate. After one year, she left university and became an actress again. In 2006, she won an Oscar for her role as June Carter in the movie *Walk The Line*.

Liam Hemsworth

He's a young, good-looking Hollywood actor. But Liam Hemsworth, star of the *The Hunger Games* movies, didn't grow up in the U.S. He was born in Australia in 1990, and didn't move to the U.S. till he was 19. Liam began his acting career when he was 16. Aged 19, he auditioned for a part in the movie *Thor*, but didn't get it. But this didn't stop Liam, and eventually he started winning movie roles in Hollywood. In 2011, he won the part of Gale Hawthorne in the popular *The Hunger Games* movies. He acted opposite Jennifer Lawrence. She played Gale's best friend Katniss.

In 2010, *Details* magazine chose him as one of "The Next Generation of Hollywood's Leading Men." *We Love Movies* agrees!

Check it out!

Find these words and check their meaning.

graduate
career
magazine

My reading skills

Checking meaning: false friends

Some words in your language look like English words. But their meanings are very different. It is important to make a note of the correct meanings in your vocabulary notebook.

Reading

1 Find these false friends in the web page and choose their correct meanings.

    actually   (really) / at the moment
1 career   university degree / profession
2 eventually   in the end / for a period of time

2 🔊 1.42 Read and listen to the web page. Then answer the questions.

What is Reese Witherspoon's real name?
Her real name is Laura Jeanne Reese Witherspoon.

1 Where did Reese Witherspoon move to when she was a baby?
2 When did she first appear in a movie?
3 How long did she spend at university?
4 What did she win in 2006?
5 Where did Liam Hemsworth grow up?
6 Did Liam win a part in the movie *Thor*?
7 Who is Liam's character in *The Hunger Games*?
8 Which actress was in the movie?
9 What is Gale's relationship with Katniss in the movie?
10 Who are your favorite actors and actresses?

Listening

3 🔊 1.43 **Listen to a conversation between two friends. Check (✓) the correct answers.**

Tyler went to the ... .
A movies ✓
B sports center ☐
C swimming pool ☐

1 Raquel is Juan Carlos' ... .
A girlfriend ☐
B sister ☐
C cousin ☐

2 *The Avengers* is ... .
A an action movie ☐
B a comedy ☐
C a science fiction movie ☐

3 The stars were Mark Ruffalo and ... .
A Chris Rock ☐
B Chris O'Donnell ☐
C Chris Hemsworth ☐

4 The special effects were ... .
A good ☐
B boring ☐
C awesome ☐

5 After the movie, Tyler and his friends went ... .
A home ☐
B to a pizzeria ☐
C to a party ☐

4 🔊 1.43 **Listen again and complete the questions.**

What _did you do_____ yesterday, Tyler?
1 Who _____ with?
2 _____ did you see?
3 What type of movie _____?
4 _____ starred in it?
5 _____ think of the actors?
6 What _____ of the movie?
7 What _____ after the movie?

Speaking

5 Pairwork **Choose one of the movies in the ad. Ask and answer questions about the movie. Use the conversation in exercise 4 as a model.** 🎭

A *What did you do yesterday, Chinmae?*
B *I went to the movies.*
A *Who did you ...*

Writing

6 **Think of a movie you know well. Answer the questions below. Separate your answers by topic and plan your paragraphs. Then write a review of the movie.**

- What was the name of the movie?
- Where did you see it? (TV, tablet, movie theater)
- Who did you go with?
- When did you go?
- What type of movie was it?
- What did you like about the movie?
- Is there anything you didn't like about the movie?
- Who starred in it?
- What was your general opinion of the movie?

What's on at the movies?

AMC

Screen ❶
Oz: The Great and Powerful – A fantasy movie with James Franco and Mila Kunis
⚝⚝⚝⚝⚝

Screen ❷
The Croods – A comedy starring Nicholas Cage and Ryan Reynolds
⚝⚝⚝⚝⚝

Screen ❸
The Thing – A classic horror movie with Kurt Russell and Keith David
⚝⚝⚝⚝⚝

Screen ❹
Love and Honor – A love story starring Liam Hemsworth and Teresa Palmer
⚝⚝⚝⚝⚝

Screen ❺
Battleship – A science fiction movie starring Alexander Skarsgard and Taylor Kitsch
⚝⚝⚝⚝⚝

Vocabulary

1 Look at the information about the weather in some American cities. Write two things about the weather in each city.

It's windy and cold.

1 _____

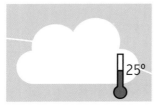 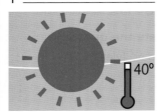

2 _____   3 _____

4 _____   5 _____
_____

2 Reorder the letters in each circle to form two movie types.

ymedicon
icviecosoi
neetmfc

1 ulesloy
mrvoai
cts

science fiction movie, comedy

2 oitaaif
saimcnnyv
etovemo

3 crireah
oronvm
otoro

3 Complete the dialogue with the words in the box.

Get real!   losers   over there
So what?   ~~What's up?~~

Ruby   What's up? You don't look very happy.
Peter   Look at those kids ¹_____. They're making a lot of noise.
Ruby   ²_____ They're only laughing at something.
Peter   I think they're ³_____.
Ruby   ⁴_____ They're having fun!

Grammar

4 Write the verbs in the simple past.

come _came_   6 get _____
1 stop _____   7 take _____
2 study _____   8 travel _____
3 try _____   9 use _____
4 watch _____   10 do _____
5 work _____   11 see _____

5 Complete the sentences with the simple past form of the verbs in the box.

clean   close   give   ~~go~~   read   run   see

We _went_ to Florida on vacation last year.
1 I _____ my bedroom last Saturday.
2 We _____ the window because it was noisy.
3 Pamela _____ her horoscope in the newspaper.
4 Henrique _____ to the bus stop.
5 They _____ a horror movie on TV last night.
6 My uncle _____ me a book for my birthday.

6 Complete the dialogues with the correct short answer and the affirmative and negative forms of the underlined verbs.

A Did Mom <u>study</u> French?
B _Yes, she did._ Mom _studied_ French at school, but she _didn't study_ German.
1 A Did you <u>write</u> an e-mail to Jo?
B ¹_____ I ²_____ an e-mail to Sam, but I ³_____ an e-mail to Jo.
2 A Did Luis <u>do</u> exercise 1?
B ⁴_____ Luis ⁵_____ exercise 1, but he ⁶_____ exercise 2.
3 A Did Anna <u>buy</u> a T-shirt?
B ⁷_____ Anna ⁸_____ a pair of jeans, but she ⁹_____ a T-shirt.

7 Look at the underlined words in the answers. Write questions for the answers with the words in the box. Use the simple past.

How   What   What time
When   Where   ~~Who~~   Why

Adrian called <u>Isabel</u>. _Who did Adrian call?_
1 Olivia and Eve went <u>to the movies</u>.
2 I ate <u>a hamburger</u> for lunch.
3 We went to Thailand on vacation <u>last year</u>.
4 The baby woke <u>up at four o'clock this morning</u>!
5 He traveled across Australia <u>on a skateboard</u>.
6 Jaime went to bed <u>because he was tired</u>.

Communication

8 🔊 1.44 **Reorder the dialogue. Then listen and check.**

_1_ **A** Where did you go on vacation last year?

___ **A** No, I didn't. I didn't choose it. But the place looked great!

___ **B** We went to Cancun in Mexico. We stayed there for two weeks.

___ **B** A movie? What type was it?

___ **B** It was very good. And the hotel was great. I took a lot of books and relaxed by the pool. Do you know Cancun?

___ **A** I know a little. I saw a movie about it a few years ago.

___ **A** Awesome! What was the weather like?

___ **B** Really? I love romantic movies! Did you enjoy it?

___ **A** It was a love story!

Pronunciation

/ʊ/ and /u/

9 🔊 1.45 **Listen to the two different sounds, /ʊ/ and /u/, in the words below. Listen again and repeat.**

/ʊ/	/u/
put	use
book	soon
could	lose
full	choose
good	who

10 🔊 1.46 **Listen to the words. Check (✓) the correct box. Then listen and repeat.**

	/ʊ/	/u/
room		✓
1 student		
2 cook		
3 took		
4 pool		
5 foot		
6 flute		
7 understood		

11 🔊 1.47 **Underline the sound /ʊ/ in the sentences and circle the sound /u/. Then listen and repeat.**

I took off my new shoes and put them in my room. Students can look for information in their books while they are doing the activity.

Listening

12 🔊 1.48 **Javier and Cristina are standing outside a movie theater. Listen to their conversation. Then check (✓) the correct answers.**

What type of movie did Javier and Cristina see?

A an action movie ☐

B a science fiction movie ✓

C a comedy ☐

1 What was the weather like when they left the movie theater?

A raining ☐

B sunny ☐

C cold ☐

2 Where did Javier have his cell phone?

A in his jacket ☐

B in his jeans ☐

C in his backpack ☐

3 Why did he take his cell phone out?

A to call his mom ☐

B to send a message ☐

C to phone Julia ☐

4 Where did the girl find Javier's cell phone?

A on his seat ☐

B near his seat ☐

C under his seat ☐

WITCHES & WIZARDS

Twelve-year-old Amy Branning is very excited. Today, she visited the Harry Potter theme park in Orlando, Florida. Amy loves the Harry Potter books and movies. But how did they all begin?

Author J.K. Rowling had the idea for Harry Potter on a train journey. But she didn't have a pen! When she got home, she started her first Harry Potter book, *Harry Potter and the Philosopher's Stone*. Five years later, in 1995, she sent the book to a lot of publishers, but they didn't like it! Finally she got a "yes" from a publisher, and in 1997, the first Harry Potter book was in bookstores. Soon it was a bestseller in the U.K., the U.S., and around the world, too. Six other Harry Potter books followed, and they became bestsellers, too.

In 2001, the first book became a movie. The movie director needed an actor for the part of Harry. In London, Daniel Radcliffe's parents heard about the movie, but they didn't tell Daniel! He was only 11 years old, and the location for the movie was Los Angeles. But the director thought Daniel was perfect for the part of Harry Potter. He changed the location from Los Angeles to London, and Daniel got the part of Harry!

The Harry Potter movies were very successful, but Harry Potter fans wanted more! In 2011, J.K. Rowling created a website, *Pottermore*. Visitors can learn to make magic spells and play interactive games.

Today, there are Harry Potter theme parks in the U.S. and Japan. Visitors watch shows, and go on rides inspired by Harry Potter. In London, fans can visit the Harry Potter movie studio. They see the movie sets and learn secrets about the special effects in the movies.

So, what's next for Amy? "I'm a very big Harry Potter fan!" she says. "Maybe I can go to the studios in London next year!"

1 **Scan the article and answer the questions.**

Who is the woman in the picture?

J.K. Rowling – the author of the Harry Potter books.

1 Where did Amy Branning go today?
2 How many Harry Potter books are there?

2 🔊 1.49 **Read and listen to the article. Then answer the questions.**

Where was J.K. Rowling when she first created Harry Potter?

She was on a train.

1 Why didn't she start writing immediately?
2 When did stores start selling the first Harry Potter book?
3 Why didn't Daniel Radcliffe's parents tell him about the movie?
4 Where did they make the Harry Potter movies?
5 What is *Pottermore*?
6 Where can fans visit the Harry Potter movie sets?
7 Do you like the Harry Potter movies / books? Why / Why not?

3 **Presentation** **Harry Potter is a very popular movie character all over the world. Think of your favorite movie character and answer the questions below. Then use your answers to prepare a short presentation.**

• What is the character's name?
• What movie is he / she in?
• Who played the part in the movie?
• What does he / she look like?
• Is he / she a good or bad character?
• Why do you like the character?

Vocabulary and speaking

I can identify weather types and temperature words (p.32) **A2**

1 Complete the sentences with the correct words.

1 It's -3°C today – it's _____!
2 It was _____ and my hat blew into the tree!
3 I hope this summer is sunny and _____!
4 When it's _____, I can't see!
5 When it's _____, the sky is gray. __ / 5

I can ask and answer questions about vacations. (p.34) **A2**

2 Match the questions and answers.

1 What was your hotel like? ___
2 What was the weather like? ___
3 What was the food like? ___
4 Were the people nice? ___
5 How was your vacation? ___

a Yes, they were. They were very friendly.
b It was warm and sunny.
c It was OK, but there wasn't a swimming pool.
d It was awesome!
e It was delicious! __ / 5

I can describe important life events. (p.37) **A2**

3 Complete the events in Jen's life with the simple past form of the irregular verbs in the box.

| go   learn   lose   say   win |

1 She _____ her first word when she was 2.
2 She _____ to swim when she was 5.
3 She _____ her first tooth in 2005.
4 She _____ her first race when she was 9.
5 She _____ on vacation in 2011. __ / 5

I can identify movie types (p.40) **A2**

4 Reorder the letters to make movie types.

1 r r r h o o   v i m e o   _____
2 d e m c o y   _____
3 v e o l   t r s y o   _____
4 t o n o r a c   _____
5 c u i s m l a   _____ __ / 5

I can use language for going to the movies. (p.42) **A2**

5 Complete the dialogue.

Raul   Let's go to the movies! *Shock* is playing.
Quique What ^{1}_____ of movie is it?
Raul   It's an action ^{2}_____.
Quique Oh, no! What about a science ^{3}_____ movie? *Project Star* is playing at the AMC.
Raul   OK. What ^{4}_____ does it start?
Quique It ^{5}_____ at 7:30 p.m.
Raul   OK. Let's go! __ / 5

I can ask and answer questions about going to the movies. (p.45) **A2**

6 Read the answers. Then complete the questions.

1 _____ did you see?
We saw *Atlantic Adventure*.
2 _____ was it?
It was an action movie.
3 _____ with?
I went with Sarah.
4 _____ it?
Nicole Kidman starred in it.
5 _____ of the movie?
I thought it was quite boring. __ / 5

Reading, listening, and writing

		Got it?	
	Yes	I'm not sure	No
I can understand an article and answer questions about the discovery of Antarctica. (p.36) **A2**	☐	☐	☐
I can understand a description of the life of an explorer and answer questions about him. (p.37) **A2**	☐	☐	☐
I can write a paragraph about the events in my life. (p.37) **A2**	☐	☐	☐
I can understand a web page and answer questions about Hollywood actors and movies. (p.44) **A2**	☐	☐	☐
I can understand a conversation and answer questions about a trip to the movie theater. (p.45) **A2**	☐	☐	☐
I can write a review of a movie I saw. (p.45) **A2**	☐	☐	☐

Vocabulary

1 Match 1–5 with a–e. Then complete the chart.

1 curly
2 classical
3 hip-
4 hot and
5 freezing and
6 love
7 blue
8 action

a eyes
b story
c sunny
d guitarist
e hair
f hop
g movie
h snowing

Physical descriptions	Music	Weather	Movies
curly hair	2 _____	4 _____	6 _____
1 _____	3 _____	5 _____	7 _____

2 How many more words can you add to the categories in the chart in two minutes?

1 word = What?!
2 words = OK
3 words = Good
4 words = Very good
5 words = Excellent!

Grammar

Simple present and present progressive

3 Complete the dialogues with the simple present or present progressive form of the verbs in parentheses.

1
A What type of music *do you like* (you / like)?
B I ¹_____ (not like) music, but I like books. I ²_____ (read) every day.
A What book ³_____ (you / read) right now?
B I ⁴_____ (read) a book by Philip Pullman.
A ⁵_____ (he / write) love stories?
B No, he ⁶_____. He ⁷_____ (write) fantasy stories!

2
A Where's Pippa? ⁸_____ (she / clean) her bedroom?
B No, she ⁹_____. She ¹⁰_____ (never / clean) her bedroom! She's in the living room with her friend Alice. They ¹¹_____ (watch) a movie.

3
A What ¹²_____ (you / do) in your free time?
B I'm in a band. I ¹³_____ (play) the guitar.
A Where ¹⁴_____ (your band / play)?
B In my house! We ¹⁵_____ (not be) very good, but we ¹⁶_____ (practice) every day!

Possessive pronouns

4 Complete the sentences with the correct possessive pronoun.

My sister doesn't have an MP3 player, so she always uses m*ine*.

1 Your PlayStation is awesome! O_____ doesn't work!
2 Whose bag is this? Is it y_____?
3 "Is that Tina's dog?" "No, h_____ is black."
4 This isn't my math book. M_____ has my name in it.
5 Give this ball to the boys. It's t_____.
6 His name is João, and h_____ is Mercedes.

Adverbs

5 Complete the sentences with the adverb form of the adjectives in parentheses.

My dad runs very *slowly*. (slow)

1 Adam plays the saxophone _____. (beautiful)
2 The children are reading _____. (happy)
3 I like his books. He writes _____. (good)
4 He's a great singer, but he acts _____. (bad)
5 I can't understand Lola. She speaks _____. (fast)
6 I cook _____. (terrible)

Simple past

6 Look at the picture. Complete the dialogue with the simple past form of *be*.

Kelly <u>Were</u> you in my class in elementary school?

Sam No, I [1]_____. I [2]_____ in your brother's class.

Kelly That's right. [3]_____ Adam and Luis in your class, too?

Sam Yes, they [4]_____. And Mrs. Novak [5]_____ our teacher.

Kelly [6]_____ she a good teacher?

Sam She [7]_____ great! We [8]_____ happy when she left!

7 Complete the past time expressions with the words in the box.

| ago | in | ~~last~~ | three | Wednesday | yesterday |

<u>last</u> week

1 two days _____
2 _____ 2011
3 last _____
4 _____ morning
5 _____ weeks ago

8 Complete the chart. Write the simple past form of the regular verbs in the correct columns.

	+ -d	+ -ed	~y + -ied	double consonant + -ed
like	liked			
1 study				
2 play				
3 stop				
4 love				
5 prefer				
6 cry				
7 want				

9 Write the simple past form of the irregular verbs.

win <u>won</u>

1 read _____
2 do _____
3 make _____
4 ride _____
5 write _____
6 speak _____

7 see _____
8 have _____
9 go _____
10 run _____
11 say _____
12 meet _____

10 Complete the chatroom messages with the simple past form of the verbs in parentheses.

<u>Did you go out</u> last night? (you / go out)

No, [1]_____.

[2]_____ your cousin? (you / see)

Yes, [3]_____. We [4]_____ (eat) pizza. We [5]_____ (watch) a movie together, too.

[6]_____? (what / you / watch)

[7]_____ to watch a horror movie – *Killer*! (Caitlin / want)

[8]_____ good? (it / be)

[9]_____ (Caitlin / enjoy) it. But I [10]_____ (not like) it. We [11]_____ (have) a good time though!

1 🔊 1.50 Read and listen Who phones Rosie?

Dad OK. Let's start. Are there any eggs in the fridge?

Rosie Yes, there are, but only a few. How many eggs do you want?

Dad Three, please. Is there any milk?

Rosie Yes, there is, but there isn't much.

Dad Hmm, how much milk is there?

Rosie There's about half a liter.

Dad Oh, that's OK. What else? Is there any cheese?

Rosie Yes, there is, but only a little. There are a lot of tomatoes.

Dad Perfect! Are you OK, Rosie?

Rosie No, I'm not. There's a problem with the band. We don't have a singer.

Dad You're kidding! What about Zac?

Rosie He left the band last week. He's with The Misfitz now. And they want me in their band, too!

The telephone rings and Rosie's dad answers.

Dad It's for you, Rosie. It's Kelly.

Rosie Kelly? From The Misfitz? Oh no! What do I do now?

Check it out!

Find these words and check their meaning.

What else?   You're kidding!

2 Comprehension Answer the questions.

What are Rosie and her dad doing?
He's cooking and Rosie is helping him.

1 What's the problem with the band?
2 When did Zac leave the band?

Language focus

3 Dialogue focus Complete the dialogues with the questions in the box.

> Are there any eggs in the fridge?   How many eggs do you want?
> How much milk is there?   Is there any cheese?   Is there any milk?

1 Dad   Are there any eggs in the fridge?
Rosie Yes, there are, but only a few.
1 _____
Dad   Three, please.

2 Dad   2 _____
Rosie Yes, there is, but there isn't much.
Dad   3 _____
Rosie There's about half a liter.
Dad   Oh, that's OK.

3 Dad   4 _____
Rosie Yes, there is, but only a little.
There are a lot of tomatoes.

4 🔊 1.51 **Listen and check. Listen again and repeat.**

5 Focus on you Read the example dialogue. Then write three similar dialogues. Use the words and phrases in the box.

> books / in your school bag   computers / in your house   cousins / in your family
> posters / on your bedroom wall   songs / MP3 player

A How many books are there in your school bag?
B There are about three. Are there any books in your school bag?
A Yes, there are. There's one.

6 Pairwork Practice the dialogues in exercise 5.

5 Vocabulary

Food and drink

1 🔊 1.52 Laura is keeping a food journal for a school science project. Label the food with the words in the box. Then listen and check.

> apple   banana   candy   carrots   cereal   cheese   chicken   chocolate
> cookies   egg   ham   ice cream   ~~milk~~   orange juice   peas
> potato chips   potatoes   soda   tea   toast   tomato   water   yogurt

Laura Jackson, 9th Grade
My food journal: day 3

Breakfast

1 _milk_
2 _____
3 _____
4 _____
5 _____
6 _____

Lunch

7 _____
8 _____
9 _____
10 _____
11 _____
12 _____
13 _____

Dinner

14 _____
15 _____
16 _____
17 _____
18 _____
19 _____

Snacks

20 _____
21 _____
22 _____
23 _____

2 Write the foods from exercise 1 in the correct groups. What other foods can you add?

1 fruit and vegetables: apple, …
2 dairy products: milk, …
3 meat and fish: ham, …
4 bread and cereal: cereal, …
5 drinks: water, …
6 other: egg, …

3 Write a food journal of the food you ate yesterday. Use the words from exercise 1.

4 Pairwork Use your food journal. Ask and answer questions about your breakfast, lunch, dinner, and snacks yesterday. Did you eat the same things? 😊

A What did you have for breakfast yesterday?
B I had coffee, toast, and fruit. What about you?

A I had tea, orange juice, and an egg. What did you have for lunch?
B I had pasta, ham, tomatoes, and a banana for lunch. And you?

Look!

have breakfast
have lunch
have dinner

Workbook p.28   **Extra practice** online

Countable / Uncountable nouns

There are three **eggs**.   There's some **milk**.

Countable		Uncountable
Singular	**Plural**	**Singular only**
a tomato	two tomatoes	milk
an egg	two eggs	pasta

Think!

Complete the rules with *countable* or *uncountable*.

- You can count <u>countable</u> nouns.
- You can't count ¹_____ nouns.
- ²_____ nouns have a singular and a plural form.
- ³_____ nouns have a singular form only.

Rules p.W26

1 Are the nouns countable (C) or uncountable (U)? Write the plural form where possible.

chicken	U
cookie	C cookies
1 bread	_____
2 egg	_____
3 cheese	_____
4 rice	_____
5 strawberry	_____
6 beef	_____
7 onion	_____
8 sugar	_____
9 mushroom	_____
10 water	_____

2 Complete the sentences with food that you like and don't like. Remember to use plural forms where possible.

I love <u>eggs, tomatoes, and cheese.</u>
I don't like <u>milk and fish.</u>
1 I love _____
2 I like _____
3 I don't like _____
4 I hate _____

3 Tell the class what you like and don't like.

some / any

There's **some** bread. There aren't **any** peas.

Countable		Uncountable
Singular	**Plural**	**Singular only**
There**'s an** egg.	There **are some** eggs.	There**'s some** bread.
There **isn't an** egg.	There **aren't any** eggs.	There **isn't any** bread.
Is there **an** egg?	**Are** there **any** eggs?	**Is** there **any** bread?

Think!

Complete the rules with *some*, *any*, and *an*.

- We use *a* and <u>an</u> with singular countable nouns.
- We use ¹_____ and ²_____ with plural countable nouns.
- We use ³_____ and ⁴_____ with uncountable nouns.
- We use ⁵_____ in affirmative sentences and ⁶_____ in questions and negative sentences.

Rules p.W26

4 Complete the sentences and questions with *a*, *an*, *some*, or *any*.

There's <u>some</u> chocolate in the kitchen.
1 There's _____ apple on the floor.
2 There aren't _____ potatoes in my bag.
3 Is there _____ cookie in my lunchbox?
4 Are there _____ carrots in the fridge?
5 There isn't _____ cereal on the table.

5 Sam is planning a picnic with his mom. Complete the dialogue with the words in the box.

> a   any   ~~are~~   Is there   some   some   there's

Sam   Mom, <u>are</u> there any apples?
Mom   Yes, and there are ¹_____ oranges, too.
Sam   OK. ²_____ any bread?
Mom   Yes, there is. And ³_____ some cheese.
Sam   Great. I need ⁴_____ tomatoes, too.
Mom   I think there's ⁵_____ tomato here.
Sam   Are there ⁶_____ cookies?
Mom   No, there aren't. You ate them all!

Finished?

Plan your own picnic and write a dialogue. Use the dialogue in exercise 5 as a model.

Puzzle p.106

5 Communication

Ordering food and drink

1 🔊 1.53 **Listen to the dialogues and choose the correct answers. Listen again and check. Then listen and repeat.**

1

A Can I help you?
B Yes, please. I'll have a baked potato with (tuna) / cheese.
A Is that for here, or to go?
B It's to go.
A OK, here you go. Anything else?
B [1] No, thanks / Yes, please. That's all.
A OK. That's [2] $5.19 / $5.99.
B Here you go.
A Thanks. And here's your change.
B Thanks.

2

A What would you like to eat?
B I'd like a ham and [3] cheese / tomato sandwich, please.
A Is that for here, or to go?
B It's for here, thanks.
A Fine.
B Can I have, some [4] water / soda, too?
A Sparkling, or still?
B A small bottle of [5] still / sparkling water, please.
A OK. That's [6] $7.65 / $7.59.
B Here you go.
A Great. Thanks.

Look!

When we make requests or offer things, we don't use *any*. We use *some*.
Can I have <u>some</u> water, please?
Would you like <u>some</u> water?

Learn it, use it!

You ask	You answer
Can I help you?	Yes, please. I'll have … / I'd like … / Can I have …?
What would you like to eat / drink?	I'd like … / I'll have …
Is that for here, or to go?	It's for here. / It's to go.
Anything else?	No, thanks. That's all. / Yes, please. I'd like …
Here's your change.	Thanks.

2 🔊 1.54 **Listen to the three conversations. Which food and drinks do the people order? Listen and check.**

　　(a chicken sandwich)　　a coffee with milk　　a cookie　　(a cup of tea)

1 a pizza　　a hamburger　　a large soda　　a small soda
2 a baked potato　　tuna　　cheese　　sparkling water　　still water

3 🔊 1.54 **Listen again and complete the chart.**

	For here, or to go?	Price
Example	for here	
1		
2		

4 Pairwork Look at the notes. Write two dialogues. Use the dialogues in exercise 1 as a model. Then practice your dialogues. 🗨

A Can I help you?
B Yes, please. I'd like a …

> Order 1
> cheese and tomato sandwich + large soda
> to go
> $8.75
>
> Order 2
> hamburger and French fries
> for here
> $7.99

Workbook p.30　　**Extra practice** online

a lot of / much / many

Countable	Uncountable
There are **a lot of** eggs.	There's **a lot of** bread.
There aren't **many** eggs.	There isn't **much** bread.
Are there **many** eggs?	Is there **much** bread?

Think!

Complete the sentences with *A lot of, Much,* or *Many.*

- ¹_____ goes before plural countable nouns, and uncountable nouns in affirmative sentences.
- ²_____ goes before plural countable nouns in negative sentences and questions.
- ³_____ goes before uncountable nouns in negative sentences and questions.

Complete the table with *a lot of, much,* or *many.*

	Plural countable	Uncountable
+	⁴_____	⁶_____
- / ?	⁵_____	⁷_____

Rules p.W26

1 Complete the sentences with *a lot of, much,* or *many.*

Do we have _much_ oil?
1 I don't drink _____ coffee.
2 We always buy _____ cheese.
3 Nick doesn't eat _____ vegetables.
4 Are there _____ strawberries in the garden?
5 Do we need _____ chicken for this recipe?

How much ...? / How many ...?

Questions	
Countable	Uncountable
How many apples are there?	**How much** sugar is there?

Think!

Complete the rules with *countable* and *uncountable.*

How much ...? + ¹_____ nouns.
How many ...? + plural ²_____ nouns.

Rules p.W27

2 Complete the questions with *How much* or *How many* and the words in the box.

bread   languages   money   people   rooms   ~~sugar~~

How much sugar does Jake put in his coffee?
1 _____ are there in the class?
2 _____ do you eat every day?
3 _____ are there in the house?
4 _____ do you have?
5 _____ do you speak?

a little / a few

Countable	Uncountable
There are **a few** eggs.	There's **a little** milk.

Rules p.W27

Note!

a few = not many
There are a few lemons.
There aren't many lemons.
a little = not much
She needs a little butter.
She doesn't need much butter.

3 Rewrite the sentences in the affirmative form. Use *a little* or *a few.*

We don't have many apples. *We have a few apples.*
There isn't much coffee. *There's a little coffee.*
1 There isn't much cheese.
2 Dad didn't cook many carrots.
3 I don't want many cookies.
4 We don't have much coffee.
5 She didn't make many sandwiches.

4 Complete the dialogue with the words in the box.

a few   a little   a lot of   any   ~~how many~~ how much   many   much   some

Lucia _How many_ onions are there?
Jorge There are ¹_____. But not ²_____. Only two or three.
Lucia OK. And ³_____ milk do we have?
Jorge Oh, not ⁴_____. But there are ⁵_____ potatoes. About 20 of them!
Lucia Well, that's OK. I only need ⁶_____ milk. But I need butter. Do we have ⁷_____?
Jorge Yes, I'm sure there's ⁸_____ in the fridge.

Finished?

Make a list of countable and uncountable food. Write a question for each item with *How much* or *How many.* Answer the questions with *a lot of / much / many / a little / a few.*

How much chocolate do you eat every day?
I don't eat much – only a little.

Puzzle p.106

A history of school lunches in the U.S.

1930s

At this time, a lot of people didn't have jobs. They didn't have much money to give their children a lot of food. A school lunch became very important for this reason, and children got at least one hot meal every day.

1940s-1950s

The National School Lunch Program began. At school, children now ate meat with two vegetables and pieces of fruit every day. They also received some bread and butter. From 1954, children also got one big cup of milk every day.

1970s

Vending machines appeared in schools. Now it was possible for children to buy soda, candy, and potato chips during school hours. Not surprisingly, not many children wanted their school lunches!

1980s

School lunches were in trouble! The government gave less money for school lunches, and fresh food became very expensive for schools. Food portions became very small. Schools started selling pizzas and burgers from private companies. These foods are full of salt and fat, and are very unhealthy.

2000s

Things are getting better! Vending machines are disappearing from schools, and some farms now sell fresh fruit and vegetables directly to schools. With less sugar, salt, and fat in school lunches, there is more fresh, healthy food for everyone!

Check it out!

Find these words and check their meaning.

piece
vending machine
less
full of

Reading

1 🔊 1.55 **Read and listen to the article. Then answer the questions.**

Why didn't parents give their children much food in the 1930s?
They didn't have jobs and didn't have much money to buy food.

1 How much milk did children get from 1954?
2 What did the vending machines in schools sell to children?
3 With new vending machines in schools, how many children wanted school lunches?
4 In the 1980s, were school lunches healthy, or unhealthy?
5 Why are pizzas and burgers unhealthy?
6 Where are some schools buying their food from now?
7 What kind of food are they buying?
8 Are school lunches a good idea? Why? / Why not?
9 What do you prefer to eat for lunch every day?

Listening

2 🔊 1.56 **Listen to a radio interview about the Okinawa diet from the Ryuku Islands in Japan. Then check (✓) the correct answers.**

My listening skills

Identifying key words

Before you listen to a recording, read the questions in the accompanying exercises. They contain important key words. These words help you to listen for the necessary information in the text. Underline the key words before you listen.

How long do the people of the Ryuku Islands live?
A They all live to over 100 years. ☐
B They don't live very long. ☐
C A lot of them live long and healthy lives. ✓

1 How important is brown rice in the diet?
A There isn't any brown rice in it. ☐
B There isn't much rice in the diet. ☐
C It's a big part of the Okinawa diet. ☐

2 What does the Okinawa diet contain?
A It contains a lot of meat. ☐
B It doesn't contain any meat. ☐
C It contains a little meat. ☐

3 How big are food portions in the Okinawa diet?
A They are very big. ☐
B They are pretty small. ☐
C They are like portions in the U.S. ☐

4 When do people on the Okinawa diet stop eating?
A They stop when they are so full, they can't move. ☐
B They stop when they are 80 years old. ☐
C They stop eating when they feel 80% full. ☐

5 Do the people of the Ryuku Islands do a lot of exercise?
A No, they don't need to exercise. ☐
B They stop exercising when they are old. ☐
C Yes, they are very active and walk a lot. ☐

Speaking

3 Pairwork **Make a list of six types of food that you like. Ask and answer questions about them.** 💬

you / like?   how much / eat?   what / eat / it with?

A Do you like French fries?   B How much fish do you eat?
B Yes, I do. I love them!   A I eat a little two or three times a week.

Writing

4 **Read the information about the American hot dog. Write a food article about it. Remember to use apostrophes in the right places!**

Hot dog	popular snack in U.S.
Origins	sausage from 13th century Germany. American Charles Feltmann sold sausage between pieces of bread in 1870
Ingredients	pork, chicken, fat, water, salt
Delicious with	mustard, ketchup, French fries

1 🔊 2.02 **Read and listen** Who is Rosie playing with in the competition on Saturday?

Zac   What are you two doing here? You aren't playing in the competition on Saturday!

Dylan   What?! Yes, we are. We're a band, too!

Zac   No, you aren't. You don't have a singer, and you don't have a guitarist now!

Rosie arrives …

Rosie   Shut up, Zac! I'm their guitarist, and I'm playing with them on Saturday! Come on guys. Let's go!

Lewis   What was that about, Rosie?

Rosie   Nothing. Forget it!

Teacher   OK, everybody. Each band is playing two songs, and you're bringing your own instruments. Then, finally, the judges make their decision!

Zac   How long does that part take?

Teacher   It doesn't usually take long, Zac, so don't worry. OK. Are there any other questions?

Everybody   No.

Teacher   Great. We're starting at 7 p.m. on Saturday, so don't be late. OK?

Everybody   Yeah.

Teacher   The competition is at the gym on Albert Street.

Lewis   How long does it take to get there from this part of town?

Teacher   It takes about 20 minutes on the subway. Good luck, everybody!

Later …

Zac   Hey, Rosie! You made the wrong decision! Your band is terrible.

Rosie   Get lost, Zac!

Check it out!

Find these words and check their meaning.

Forget it!   Good luck!   Get lost!

2 Comprehension **Answer the questions.**

When is the Battle of the Bands competition?

On Saturday

1 Who explains the rules of the competition?
2 What time is it starting?
3 Where is it?

Language focus

3 Dialogue focus There are five more mistakes in the dialogue.
Find and correct the mistakes.

① Teacher   OK, everybody. Each band is
playing ~~four~~ songs, and you're
bringing your own music.
Then, finally, the judges make
their decision!

Zac   How long does that part take?

Teacher   It doesn't usually take long,
Zac, so don't worry.

② Teacher   Great. We're starting at 8 p.m. on Saturday, so don't be late. OK?

Everybody   Yeah.

Teacher   The competition is at the movie theater on Albert Street.

Lewis   How long does it take to get there from this part of town?

Teacher   It takes about 30 minutes on the
bus. Good luck, everybody!

4 🔊 2.03 **Listen and check. Listen again and repeat.**

5 Focus on you What are you doing this weekend? Choose five activities in the box.
Write sentences about things you are doing and things you are not doing.

> clean my bedroom   do my homework   go to a concert   go to the movies
> help my parents   meet friends   play sports   stay home   visit family

I'm doing my homework. I'm not going to a concert.

6 Pairwork Ask and answer questions about your plans for the weekend. 😊

A What are you doing on Saturday?
B I'm going to the movies. What about you?
A I'm visiting my grandma. What are you doing on Sunday?

Transportation

1 🔊 2.04 **Match the words with the different forms of transportation. Then listen and check.**

~~airplane~~ bicycle / bike boat bus car helicopter motorcycle subway taxi train truck

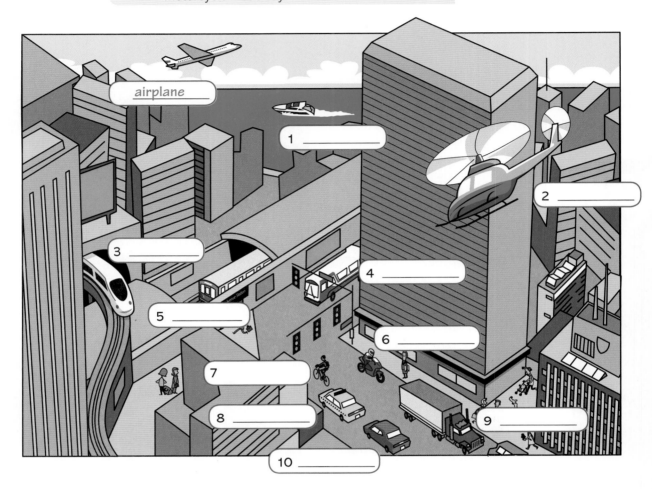

airplane

1 _____

2 _____

3 _____

4 _____

5 _____

6 _____

7 _____

8 _____

9 _____

10 _____

2 🔊 2.05 **Listen to the conversations. Complete the chart. Then listen and check.**

	Bus	Car	Train	Walk	Subway	Bike
Alejandro	✓			✓		
1 Angela						
2 Sofia						
3 Mark						
4 Fletcher						

3 Pairwork Read the model dialogue. Choose three forms of transportation from exercise 1. Make dialogues with the adverbs and expressions of frequency in the box.

often once / twice / three times a week / month / year
never rarely sometimes

A How often do you take the bus to school?
B I take the bus once or twice a week.
A How often do you walk to school?
B I rarely walk to school.

Workbook p.34 Extra practice online

Present progressive for future

> You **aren't playing** in the competition.
> We're **starting** at 7 p.m. on Saturday.

Future time expressions

this afternoon / evening, but **tonight**
on Monday / Tuesday / March 2nd
tomorrow morning / afternoon / evening / night
next Saturday / week / weekend / month / year
in May / the winter / 2016
at five o'clock / Christmas

Rules p.W33

Think!

Do the sentences describe the present (P) or the future (F)?

- [1]He's playing basketball at the moment. ☐
- [2]He's playing soccer next week. ☐
- [3]She's going to the movies tomorrow. ☐
- [4]She's watching a movie now. ☐

Rules p.W32

1 Choose the correct words.

My parents are going to Rome **at** / **(on)** Friday.

1 We're taking the train **this** / **at** six o'clock.
2 What are you doing **next** / **tomorrow** afternoon?
3 I'm going to Spain **in** / **on** August.
4 They aren't walking to the party **next** / **tomorrow** weekend.
5 Ben is taking a test **in** / **this** afternoon.
6 Are you playing tennis **next** / **at** Saturday?

2 Mary Beth and Dolly are going on a trip to Europe. Look at their travel itinerary. Write negative and affirmative sentences.

Travel itinerary
April 1st Hotel Zizzi, Rome, Italy
   airplane
April 8th Hotel San Miguel, Madrid, Spain
   train
April 16th Hotel Printemps, Paris, France

They're visiting Europe in June.
They aren't visiting Europe in June. They're visiting Europe in April.

1 They're traveling from April 1st to April 10th.
2 Mary Beth is going to Madrid by car.
3 "We're going to Germany on April 8th," says Dolly.
4 They're flying to Paris on April 16th.

3 Read Carolina's diary for next week. Write questions and answers with the words below.

Monday   play volleyball (4:30 p.m.)
Tuesday   study science at Julia's house after school
Wednesday go swimming (4:30 p.m.)
Thursday   meet Tom and Ines (4:30 p.m.)
Friday   have a pizza with Mom and Dad (8 p.m.)
Saturday   visit Uncle Ross and Aunt Sadie
Sunday   go to the movies (7 p.m.)

Carolina / play sports / on Monday?
Is Carolina playing sports on Monday?
Yes, she is. She's playing volleyball at 4:30 p.m.

1 she / stay home / after school on Tuesday?

2 what / she / do / on Wednesday afternoon?

3 she / meet Tom and Ines / before school on Thursday?

4 she / have a pizza with friends / on Friday night?

5 who / she visit / next weekend?

6 where / she go / on Sunday evening?

Finished?

Choose five future time expressions and write a question for each one in the present progressive for future. Then answer the questions.

Next weekend: What are you doing next weekend?
I'm visiting my cousins.
On Sunday: Who are you meeting on Sunday?
I'm meeting my friends.

Puzzle p.106

Inviting and making arrangements

1 🔊 2.06 **Listen to the dialogues and choose the correct answers. Listen again and check. Then listen and repeat.**

1

Asahi	Hi, Maia. Are you free on Saturday?
Maia	Yes, I am. / No, I'm not.
Asahi	Great. Let's do something together.
Maia	Good idea. What do you want to do?
Asahi	How about going ¹swimming / to the shopping mall?
Maia	OK. Where do you want to meet?
Asahi	Let's meet at the ²bus stop / subway.
Maia	Fine. At what time?
Asahi	Is ³nine / ten thirty OK?
Maia	Yes, that's fine. See you on Saturday!

2

Hugo	I'm going to ⁴the movies / a concert on Friday, Amy. Are you free?
Amy	No, I'm sorry, I'm not. I'm ⁵meeting Jack / babysitting on Friday.
Hugo	Oh, OK. How about doing something on Saturday?
Amy	No, I'm sorry, it's my ⁶dad's / brother's birthday on Saturday.
Hugo	Never mind. Let's go another time.
Amy	Yes, OK. Thanks, Hugo.

My study skills

Memorizing expressions

It's a good idea to memorize *Learn it, use it!* expressions. You can use them in a lot of different situations and they help you to sound more fluent, too. When you see an expression for the first time, think about different situations you can use it in. This helps you to memorize the new language.

Learn it, use it!

You ask	You answer
Are you free on …?	Yes, I am. / No, I'm not.
What do you want to do?	Let's go / do / play … How about doing / going …? Why don't we go / do …?
How about going / doing …?	Yes. / OK. / All right. / Good idea. / No. / No, I'm sorry, I can't. / No, I don't like …
Where do you want to meet?	Let's meet at …

2 🔊 2.07 **Listen to the conversations. Are the sentences true or false? Correct the false sentences. Listen and check.**

Carlos invites Leo to get a pizza. <u>False</u>

1 Leo says no to the invitation. _____
2 Leo is going to a football game with Ellie. _____
3 Nina invites Juan to play tennis. _____
4 Juan accepts the invitation. _____
5 They're meeting at school on Saturday morning. _____

3 **Pairwork** **Read the instructions and make dialogues. Use the activities in the box and the dialogues in exercise 1 as a model.**

> go shopping   go swimming   go to a concert   go to the movies   play tennis

1
A Invite your partner to one of the activities in the box. Say when you are doing it.
B Accept the invitation. Plan when and where to meet.
2
B Invite your partner to one of the activities in the box. Say when you are doing it.
A Refuse the invitation. Give a reason: you are babysitting / meeting a friend / going to a party, etc.

A I'm going swimming on Friday afternoon. Are you free?
B Yes, I am. Where do you want to …?

B I'm going to the movies on Saturday. Are you free?
A I'm sorry, I can't. I'm …

Workbook p.36   **Extra practice** online

How long ...? + take

How long does it take to get there from this part of town?
It takes about twenty minutes on the subway.

Think!

Read the sentences. Complete the rules with *How long*, *takes* and *take*.

How long does it **take** you to get to the gym?
It **takes** about twenty minutes.
It **doesn't take** long.

- ¹_____ does it + ²_____ + (you) + infinitive of the verb with *to*?
- It + ³_____ (me) + length of time.

Rules p.W33

1 Correct the mistakes in the sentences below.

How long ~~it takes~~ you to get to school?
How long does it take you to get to school?

1 It take three hours to travel to Georgia.
2 It me takes a long time to take a shower.
3 How long does it take walk to school?
4 She takes my mom a long time to choose the right dress.
5 How long do it take you to swim one kilometer?
6 It don't take my brother long to wake up in the morning.

2 Write questions and answers.

How long / travel / from Chicago to Las Vegas / by airplane? (six hours)
How long does it take to travel from Chicago to Las Vegas by airplane?
It takes six hours.

1 How long / walk through Central Park? (one hour)
2 How long / you / take a shower? (five minutes)
3 How long / go to Canal Street on the subway? (30 minutes)
4 How long / you / clean your bedroom? (fifteen minutes)
5 How long / you / do your homework? (two hours)
6 How long / you / bike to school? (ten minutes)

3 Complete the messages with the correct form of the verbs in the box.

decide   ~~do~~   go   have   not take
study   take   take   take

Hey, Mia, what are you doing later?

I ¹_____ math.
I ²_____ an important test tomorrow.

Oh no. How long ³_____?

Two hours!

Well, I ⁴_____ to the new shopping mall tomorrow evening. Are you free?

Yes, I am! Let's take the subway. It ⁵_____ long to get there – only 15 minutes.

OK. I need a new dress. My cousin ⁶_____ a big party on Saturday. There are a lot of nice dresses in the stores.

It always takes you a long time ⁷_____!
I ⁸_____ a book with me!

Ha ha!

Finished?

What are you doing next weekend? Write questions and answers with the words in the chart. You can use words more than once. How many can you write?

go / zoo	bus	30 minutes
have / picnic on the beach	bike	one hour
visit / the art museum	subway	15 minutes
go / to the Metro theater	walk	25 minutes
meet friend / the new café	train	45 minutes

A What are you doing next weekend?
B I'm going to the zoo.
A How are you traveling there?
B I'm taking the subway.
A How long does it take to get there?
B It takes 25 minutes.

Puzzle p.106

A very long bus ride

When Canadian student Andy Fitzpatrick left school last summer, he decided to travel to Australia. He traveled in a group from London to Sydney ... on a bus! Here are some extracts from his blog.

Week 1

We left London yesterday, and today, we're in Bruges in Belgium. Tomorrow, we're traveling to Heidelberg in Germany. The bus is very comfortable, and the other passengers are very friendly.

Week 2

A few days ago, I was in Prague in the Czech Republic. It was so beautiful! Now we're in Istanbul in Turkey, a city in both Europe and Asia! There are just two problems: 1) Ron, a student from Liverpool – he thinks he's a travel expert, but I think he's a loser! And 2) we have a different bus. It's very small!

Week 4

A new and better bus took us around Turkey, and we traveled down the coast in a boat, too. Then, we took an airplane to India. Now, we're in Delhi. It's an exciting city, but there's a lot of poverty here. Next week, we're going to Nepal.

Week 9

We visited some awesome cities: Kathmandu in Nepal, Bangkok in Thailand, and Kuala Lumpur in Malaysia. We nearly lost Ron in all of them! Now, after a very scary boat trip, we're on the island of Bali in Indonesia. I'm relaxing on the beach! We're flying to Darwin in Australia soon. I don't want to leave Asia. It's an amazing continent.

Week 13

After thirteen weeks, we're in Sydney! I'm walking a lot and exploring the city. Luckily Ron has a girlfriend, so he doesn't talk to me now! Tomorrow, I'm traveling back to London ... but I'm taking an airplane this time!

Check it out!

Find these words and check their meaning.

comfortable
expert
poverty
scary

Reading

1 Scan the article. Are the sentences true or false?

1 Andy Fitzpatrick traveled on different buses to Sydney. _True_

2 He only used buses on his trip. _____

3 He spent thirteen weeks in Australia. _____

2 🔊 2.08 Read and listen to the article. Then answer the questions.

Where is Andy from?
He's from Canada.

1 When did he finish school?

2 Why didn't Andy like Ron?

3 What was the problem with the bus in Istanbul?

4 What did Andy notice about Delhi?

5 What was the boat trip to Bali like?

6 How did he travel back to the U.K.?

7 Which countries do you want to visit? Why?

Listening

3 🔊 2.09 **Luisa is going on a vacation with her friend, Ana. Listen to their conversation. Choose the correct answers.**

Luisa **invites** / **doesn't invite** Ana to go on vacation with her.
1 The vacation is in the **spring** / **summer**.
2 Luisa is staying in a **house** / **hotel** in Mexico.
3 She's staying for **one week** / **two weeks**.
4 Luisa's brothers **are** / **aren't** going.
5 Ana **needs** / **doesn't need** to ask her parents about the vacation.
6 Luisa thinks the airplane tickets are **cheap** / **expensive**.
7 The girls arrange to meet **next weekend** / **on Tuesday evening**.

Speaking

4 Pairwork **You are making arrangements for a vacation and want to invite your partner to come with you. Complete the factfile below. Then practice your dialogue.** 😊

When	_____
Where	_____
How long	_____
Form of transportation	_____
Who else you are traveling with	_____
When you can meet your friend to plan your vacation	_____

A Hi, … I have a question for you. I'm going on vacation to … Do you want to come?
B That sounds amazing! Where are you staying?

Writing

5 **Look at your arrangements for your vacation in exercise 4. Write an itinerary for your blog about it. Use adverbs to order the events and remember to describe your feelings about your vacation.**

Vocabulary

1 Find nine more types of food and drink.

C	H	O	C	O	L	A	T	E	M
A	C	H	O	C	L	A	T	B	I
N	A	Y	O	G	U	T	T	T	L
D	X	O	K	C	A	B	E	O	K
Y	V	G	I	H	T	O	A	S	T
B	C	H	E	E	S	E	T	T	C
I	C	I	C	E	R	E	A	M	M
Y	O	G	U	R	T	F	E	G	G

2 Read the definitions. Write the correct words.

It has four wheels and carries about five people on roads. _c_ _a_ _r_

1 About four people can travel in it, and you pay the driver. __ __ __ __ __

2 It goes very fast on two wheels.
__ __ __ __ __ __ __ __ __ __

3 You see it in the sky. __ __ __ __ __ __ __ __ __

4 It's very big with a lot of wheels and carries a lot of things on the roads. __ __ __ __ __ __

5 It's a long, thin vehicle. It doesn't travel on the road. __ __ __ __ __ __

6 You travel in this on water. __ __ __ __ __

7 It has two wheels and is a healthy form of transport. __ __ __ __ __

8 You can travel under cities in this.
__ __ __ __ __ __ __

3 Complete the sentences.

We have milk and sugar. What e_lse_ do we need?

1 I heard you're doing an audition tomorrow. Good l_____!

2 You're a loser! Get l_____!

3 F_____ it. I'm not doing your homework for you!

4 You're k_____! I don't believe it.

Grammar

4 Complete the sentences with *a*, *an*, *some*, or *any*.

There isn't _any_ tea in the cupboard.

1 I eat _____ apple every day.

2 There aren't _____ cookies.

3 Is there _____ sugar in this tea?

4 There's _____ orange juice in the kitchen.

5 We need to buy _____ potatoes.

6 I always have _____ ham sandwich for lunch.

5 Choose the correct answers.

There are usually (a lot of) / many dogs in the park.

1 How much / How many coffee do you drink every day?

2 "Do we have any butter?" "Yes we do, but only a little / a few."

3 It's seven thirty in the morning. There aren't much / many students at school.

4 The children asked many / a lot of questions.

5 Do you have much / many homework today?

6 There are much / a lot of people in the restaurant.

6 Write sentences and questions in the present progressive. Do they refer to the present (P) or future (F)?

you / meet Harry / tomorrow?
Are you meeting Harry tomorrow? F

1 I / cook dinner / tonight
_____

2 What / you do / at the moment?
_____

3 Jack / not have a party / next week.
_____

4 Tina / study / now?
_____

5 We / travel to France / right now.
_____

7 Write questions and answers.

How long / your dad / drive / to work? (40 minutes)

How long does it take your dad to drive to work? It takes him 40 minutes.

1 How long / fly / Miami? (two hours)

2 How long / make / a chocolate cake? (one hour)

3 How long / your sister / do / her homework? (two hours)

4 How long / take / go / to Times Square on the subway? (one hour)

Communication

8 🔊 2.10 **Complete the dialogue with the words in the box. Then listen and check.**

> go going great have here Hi meeting
> That's There When working would

Jorge Hi_____, Sally!

Sally Jorge! ¹_____ did you start working here? It's my favorite café!

Jorge About a week ago! What ²_____ you like to eat?

Sally Can I ³_____ a cheese sandwich and a bottle of water, please?

Jorge OK. And is that for ⁴_____, or to ⁵_____?

Sally To go.

Jorge Are you ⁶_____ for a picnic?

Sally Yes. I'm ⁷_____ my friends by the river.

Jorge Lucky you! I'm ⁸_____ here all day. Here's your sandwich and water. ⁹_____ $8.49.

Sally ¹⁰_____ you go.

Jorge That's ¹¹_____, thanks. Have a great picnic!

Sally Bye!

Pronunciation

would you and *do you*

9 🔊 2.11 **We usually say the words *would you* and *do you* quickly, so the words become connected. Listen to the pronunciation of *would you* /wʊdʒu/ and *do you* /dʒu/ in these sentences. Listen again and repeat.**

1 Would you like a soda?
2 What would you like to eat?
3 What would you like on your burger?
4 What do you have to drink?
5 Do you want anything to eat?

10 🔊 2.12 **Listen to the dialogues. Practice them with a partner.**

1
A Would you like a soda?
B Yes, please. Which ones do you have?
A I only have cola. Do you want one?
B Yes, please.

2
A How would you like your burger? Do you want some cheese on it?
B No, thanks. But do you have any ketchup?
A Yes, I do. How much do you want?
B A lot, please!

Listening

11 🔊 2.13 **Max and Claudia are organizing a party. Look at their list of food and drinks. Listen to their conversation. Check (✓) the things they have and cross (✗) the things they don't have.**

bread	✓
ham	☐
cheese	☐
pizza	☐
potato chips	☐
chocolate	☐
ice cream	☐
soda	☐
orange juice	☐

12 🔊 2.14 **Listen to the conversation. What things are happening now? What things are happening in the future?**

	Now	Future
Laura is studying.	✓	
1 Laura is taking a test.		
2 Ben is relaxing.		
3 Ben is going to a party.		
4 Jessica's brother is organizing the music.		
5 A lot of Jessica's friends are going to the party.		
6 Laura is watching a movie.		
7 Laura is going to bed early.		

Junior MasterChef

Can you cook? Do your family and friends think your food is amazing? How about entering a cooking competition? There are a lot of TV cooking competitions for children these days, and they are becoming very popular.

In Australia, the cooking competition *Junior MasterChef* first appeared on TV screens in 2010. About 5,000 children entered! The show was very popular and attracted a lot of children in 2011, too. But the level of the competition was very high, and there were 50 children in the second series.

The children did a lot of different things in the 21 episodes. In one episode, they invented their own meals with two key ingredients, and in another they worked in a high school snack store for a day. They also discovered how to use ingredients like fresh herbs in their cooking, and learned how to prepare some very complicated meals.

The winner of the second series was 11-year-old Greta Yaxley. She entered the show without any hopes of winning – she simply enjoyed cooking. But each week, her excellent meals won a lot of points, and it didn't take long for the judges to see her special talent.

In the final episode of the series, Greta's first test was to prepare a dessert with only a little time. There were a few mistakes, but the result was delicious. Her second test, a seafood dish, also had a few problems, but at the end the judges thought it tasted great.

Greta's prize was AU$15,000. There was a lot of praise from the judges, too. She was very surprised and very happy. "I want to continue with food," she said. "I want to show the whole world that I love food, and that I can cook it."

MasterChef Dining

Check it out!

Find these words and check their meaning.

herbs
dessert
seafood
praise

1 Scan the article and check (✓) the correct sentence.

A Fifty children entered the competition in 2010. ☐
B Greta thought she was the best contestant on the show. ☐
C In the final episode, the judges liked her dessert. ☐

2 🔊 2.15 Read and listen to the article. Then answer the questions.

How much did people like the first series?

They liked it a lot – it was very popular.

1 How many episodes were there?

2 How much time did the contestants spend in the high school snack store?

3 What did the judges think of Greta's cooking each week?

4 Why was the dessert test in the final episode difficult?

5 What ingredient did Greta use in her second dish in the final episode?

3 Presentation There are a lot of different competitions for children on TV. Think of a competition you would like to enter, and answer the questions below. Then use your answers to prepare a short presentation.

- What type of competition is it?
- What are the judges looking for in the contestants?
- How many people enter the competition?
- How old are the contestants?
- Where does the competition take place?
- What happens during the competition?
- What is the prize?

Vocabulary and speaking

I can identify different types of food and drink. (p.54) A2

1 Choose the correct answers.

1 People usually put **milk / soda** on their cereal.
2 Juan loves chocolate **ice cream / potato chips**.
3 My favorite vegetables are **carrots / cookies**.
4 Can I have a drink of **water / toast**, please?
5 A **banana / apple** is a long, thin yellow fruit. __ / 5

I can ask and answer questions about ordering food. (p.56) A2

2 Reorder the dialogue.

A Here you go. __
B I'll have a cheese sandwich, please. __
C It's to go. __
D That's $7.50, please. __
E Is that for here, or to go? __ __ / 5

I can talk about food that I like. (p.59) A2

3 Complete the dialogue with the words in the box.

| a few   a lot   many   much   them |

Abby Do you like apples?
Sam Yes, I do. I love ¹_____!
Abby How ²_____ apples do you eat every day?
Sam I eat two or three. What about you?
Abby Oh, I only eat ³_____. I prefer chocolate.
Sam How ⁴_____ water do you drink?
Abby ⁵_____! __ / 5

I can identify forms of transportation. (p.62) A2

4 Complete the forms of transportation.

1 t __ u __ k
2 t __ __ __ n
3 a __ __ p __ __ n __
4 h __ l __ __ __ p __ __ r
5 m __ t __ __ c __ __ __ e __ / 5

I can use language for inviting and making arrangements. (p.64) A2

5 Write the sentences and questions.

1 you / Tuesday / free / are / evening / on ?
_____
2 where / you / do / meet / to / want ?
_____
3 subway / meet / the / let's / at .
_____
4 movies / going / to / the / about / how ?
_____
5 on / I'm / my cousin / Saturday / meeting .
_____ __ / 5

I can ask and answer questions about planning vacations (p.67) A2

6 Write questions and answers.

1 Where / you / go / on vacation this year?
_____
2 They / go / in August.
_____
3 Who / go / with her?
_____
4 We / stay / in a hotel.
_____
5 How long / we / stay for?
_____ __ / 5

Reading, listening, and writing

	Got it?		
	Yes	**I'm not sure**	**No**
I can understand an article and answer questions about the history of school lunches in the U.S. (p.58) A2	☐	☐	☐
I can understand a description of a special diet and answer questions about it. (p.59) A2	☐	☐	☐
I can write a food article about an item of food. (p.59) A2	☐	☐	☐
I can understand an article and answer questions about a bus trip from London to Sydney. (p.66) A2	☐	☐	☐
I can understand a conversation about plans for a vacation and answer questions about it. (p.67) A2	☐	☐	☐
I can write a blog itinerary about my plans for a vacation. (p.67) A2	☐	☐	☐

7 You're a better singer

Check it out!

Find these words and check their meaning.

No way!   I'm terrible.
How's it going?   Go for it!

1 🔊 2.16 **Read and listen** Whose voice is better?

Lewis Did you see that TV show about the Atacama Desert in Chile last night?

Dylan No. Why? Was it interesting?

Lewis It was awesome! The desert is drier than Africa. In fact, it sometimes doesn't rain for …

Rosie Guys, guys. Please stop talking about deserts. Band practice is more important. And it's late.

Lewis But geography is really interesting! It was about deserts, mountains, volcanoes …

Dylan Yeah, yeah, Lewis. Rosie's right. Let's practice.

Rosie OK. Dylan, you can sing.

Dylan Me? No way! I'm terrible. I sound worse than a cat! Listen!
La, la, la …

Rosie But my voice isn't as strong as yours. I can't sing in front of people.

Lewis Yes, you can, Rosie. You're a better singer than all of us.

Rosie's mom comes home.

Mom Hi, guys. How's it going?

Rosie Things are getting more complicated …

Lewis Rosie doesn't want to be our singer.

Mom Why not, Rosie? You have a beautiful voice.

Dylan You see, Rosie? Go for it!

2 Comprehension Write the correct names.

Who …

is interested in geography?   Lewis

1 can't sing?   _____

2 doesn't want to sing in front of people?   _____

3 arrives home?   _____

4 says that Rosie has a great voice?   _____

Language focus

3 Dialogue focus Complete the dialogues with the expressions in the box.

> Band practice is more important.
> But my voice isn't as strong as yours.   I sound worse than a cat!
> ~~The desert is drier than Africa.~~   Things are getting more complicated …
> You're a better singer than all of us.

1 Lewis Did you see that TV show about the Atacama Desert in Chile last night?
Dylan No. Why? Was it interesting?
Lewis It was awesome! The desert is drier than Africa. In fact, it sometimes doesn't rain for …
Rosie Guys, guys. Please stop talking about deserts. ¹_____ _____ And it's late.

2 Dylan Me? No way! I'm terrible. ²_____ Listen!
La, la, la …
Rosie ³_____
I can't sing in front of people.
Lewis Yes, you can, Rosie. ⁴_____ _____

3 Mom Hi, guys. How's it going?
Rosie ⁵_____
Lewis Rosie doesn't want to be our singer.
Mom Why not, Rosie? You have a beautiful voice.
Dylan You see, Rosie? Go for it!

4 🔊 2.17 **Listen and check. Listen again and repeat.**

5 Focus on you Look at the pairs of nouns in the first box. Use the adjectives in the second box to compare them. How many dialogues can you write? You can use the words more than once.

> pizza / salad   math / geography   sweatshirt / T-shirt   the U.S. / the U.K.

> better   bigger   cheaper   easier   more difficult   more expensive
> more interesting   nicer   smaller

A Which is nicer? A pizza, or a salad?
B I think a pizza is nicer.
A Yes, but a salad is better.

6 Pairwork Practice the dialogues in exercise 5.

7 Vocabulary

Geography

1 🔊 2.18 **Choose the correct answers. Then listen and check.**

The Atacama is a **mountain** / (**desert**) / **sea**.

1 Mount Everest is a **mountain** / **volcano** / **island** in the Himalayas.
2 Africa is a bigger **continent** / **country** / **island** than Europe.
3 The Atlantic **Ocean** / **Sea** / **Lake** is between Europe and Africa in the east, and the Americas in the west.
4 The Amazon is a very long **ocean** / **island** / **river** in South America.
5 Germany is a **country** / **continent** / **lake** in Europe.
6 How about going to **Desert** / **Lake** / **River** Michigan tomorrow?
7 Jamaica is a beautiful **continent** / **sea** / **island** in the Caribbean.
8 The Mauna Loa **desert** / **river** / **volcano** is in Hawaii.
9 Spain's east coast is on the Mediterranean **Country** / **River** / **Sea**.

Look!

Mount Everest
Mauna Loa
Lake Michigan
but
the Atlantic Ocean
the Mediterranean Sea
the Amazon

2 Look at the map of Iceland. Complete the description with the words in the box.

island   lake   mountains   Ocean   river   sea   volcano

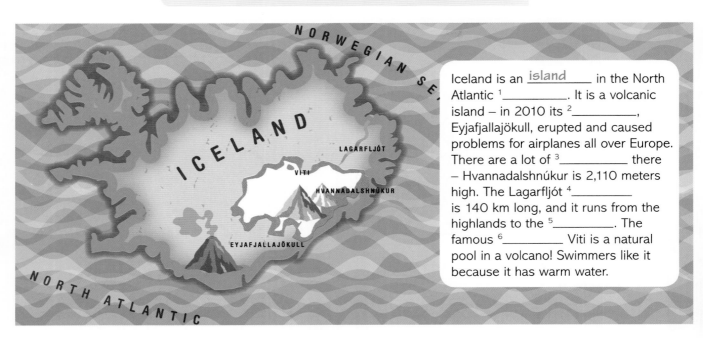

Iceland is an <u>island</u> in the North Atlantic ¹_____. It is a volcanic island – in 2010 its ²_____, Eyjafjallajökull, erupted and caused problems for airplanes all over Europe. There are a lot of ³_____ there – Hvannadalshnúkur is 2,110 meters high. The Lagarfljót ⁴_____ is 140 km long, and it runs from the highlands to the ⁵_____. The famous ⁶_____ Viti is a natural pool in a volcano! Swimmers like it because it has warm water.

3 Pairwork Complete the factfile about South America. Add two more names for each category. 😊

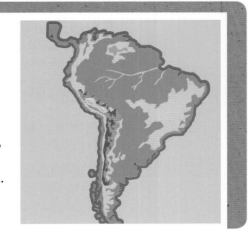

FACTFILE

South America
● Important rivers: the Amazon, Grijalva, …
● Important mountains: Aconcagua, Ojos del Salado, …
● Important lakes: Lake Maracaibo, Lake Titicaca, …
● Important islands: Grande de Tierra del Fuego, the Galapagos, …
● Important seas / oceans: the Caribbean Sea, …
● Important cities: Sao Paulo, Bogota, …

Workbook p.40   Extra practice   online

Comparative adjectives

Regular adjectives

The desert is **drier** than Africa.

Short adjectives		Comparative
slow warm	**+ -er**	slow**er** (than) warm**er** (than)
large nice	**+ -r**	large**r** (than) nice**r** (than)
thin hot	double the consonant + -er	thi**nner** (than) ho**tter** (than)
Adjectives ending with consonant + y		**Comparative**
funny heavy	**y + -ier**	funn**ier** (than) heav**ier** (than)
Long adjectives		**Comparative**
beautiful interesting	**more +** adjective	**more** beautiful (than) **more** interesting (than)

Rules p.W38

1 Complete the sentences with the comparative form of the adjectives in parentheses.

My brother is <u>older</u> than me. (old)

1 Luisa is _____ than Eva. (tall)
2 Mexico City is _____ than New York City. (big)
3 The Mississippi River is _____ than the Hudson River. (long)
4 Happiness is _____ than money. (important)
5 A walk is _____ than a run. (easy)

Think!

Choose the correct word.

• We use comparative adjectives to compare people and things.
• When a comparative adjective goes between two people or things, we write **than / of** after the adjective.

Rules p.W38

2 Read the information. Write sentences with the comparative form of the adjectives in parentheses.

The Indian elephant (6,000 kg)
African elephant (7,000 kg) (heavy)
The African elephant is heavier than the Indian elephant.
1 Seoul (population: 10.58 million)
  Tokyo (population: 13.23 million) (big)
2 The Shard tower (308 m)
  The Burj Khalifa tower (830 m) (tall)
3 The Lamborghini car ($3.9 million)
  The Ferrari car ($1.3 million) (expensive)

Irregular adjectives

I sound **worse** than a cat.

Adjective	Comparative
good	**better** (than)
bad	**worse** (than)
far	**farther / further** (than)

Rules p.W38

3 Complete Joel's blog entry. Use the comparative forms of the adjectives in the box. Use *than* in the correct places.

bad   beautiful   far   high   hungry   ~~quiet~~   thin

It's the end of my vacation in India. I'm writing my last blog post in a noisy café in Mumbai. There are <u>quieter</u> cafés, but I like it here! India is really interesting. The poverty here is
[1]_____ than in the U.S. The children are
[2]_____ than kids back home, and when they want money for food, I know that they're
[3]_____, too. But the country looks amazing. The beaches are [4]_____ than the beaches at home and the mountains are
[5]_____. I can't travel [6]_____ because I'm starting college soon. But I hope I can return one day.

Finished?

Choose two places from your vacations. Write five sentences to compare them. Use the adjectives in the box.

beautiful   big   dangerous   exciting
expensive   hot   popular   unusual

Uruguay is more expensive than Argentina.

Puzzle p.107

Asking for tourist information

1 🔊 2.19 **Listen and complete the dialogue with the questions in the box. Listen again and check. Then listen and repeat.**

> ~~Can I help you?~~ How can I get there? How much are the tickets?
> What time does it open? Where is it?

Assistant Good morning.
Can I help you?

Mario Yes, please. I want to visit the Central Park Zoo.
1 _____

Assistant They're $12 for adults, and $7 for children.

Mario 2 _____

Assistant It's open from 10 a.m. to 5 p.m. every day. It takes two hours to see all the animals.

Mario 3 _____

Assistant It's on 5th Avenue, near 65th Street.

Mario 4 _____

Assistant You can take the subway to 59th Street and then walk. Or you can take a bus, and get off between 59th and 64th Streets. The M1 and the M2 stop there.

Mario Thanks.

Assistant You're welcome. Have a nice day!

Learn it, use it!

You ask	You answer
How much are the tickets?	They're $20. / The tickets cost $20.
What time does it open / close / start / finish?	It opens / starts at … It closes / finishes at … It's open from … to …
Where is it?	It's on / near / in …
How can I get there?	You can take the subway / take a bus / walk.

2 🔊 2.20 **Listen to the conversations. Are the sentences true or false? Correct the false sentences.**

Jesse is asking about hours. _False_ _Jesse is asking about ticket prices._

1 Tickets to the Empire State Building are cheaper now. _____
2 Allison wants to know about hours at Madame Tussauds. _____
3 She knows where the museum is. _____
4 The subway goes direct to the Statue of Liberty. _____
5 Carlos asks about ticket prices to the museum. _____

3 🔊 2.20 **Listen again and complete the sentences.**

A child's ticket to the Empire State Building costs $_19_.

1 An adult's ticket costs $_____.
2 Madame Tussauds is between _____ and _____ Avenue.
3 You can take a _____ to the Statue of Liberty.
4 The Ellis Island museum opens at _____ a.m.
5 The museum closes at _____ p.m.

The Museum of Modern Art

Adult ticket: $25.00
Student ticket: $14.00

Opening times: 10:30 a.m–5:30 p.m
Location: West 53rd Street (between 5th and 6th Avenue)

Transportation: subway to 5th Avenue / 53rd Street, or bus M1, 2, 3, 4m, or 5 to 53rd Street

4 Pairwork Look at the poster for the Museum of Modern Art in New York. Use the information to write a dialogue. Then practice your dialogue.

Workbook p.42   Extra practice online

as ... as

> My voice isn't **as strong as** yours.

Affirmative	I'm **as** tall **as** my mom.
Negative	Mount K2 isn't **as** high **as** Mount Everest.
Questions	Is the Gobi Desert **as** big **as** the Sahara Desert?

Rules p.W39

1 Complete the sentences with the expressions in the box.

> is as expensive as   is as old as   isn't as deep as
> isn't as good as   ~~isn't as tall as~~   isn't as warm as

My brother is shorter than me.
My brother ___isn't as tall as___ me.

1 My aunt is 70. My grandma is 70.
My aunt _____ my grandma.

2 The book is better than the movie.
The movie _____ the book.

3 The car cost $4,000. The motorcycle cost $4,000.
The motorcycle _____ the car.

4 The Pacific Ocean is deeper than the Atlantic Ocean.
The Atlantic Ocean _____ the Pacific Ocean.

5 It's colder today than yesterday.
Today _____ yesterday.

Think!

Choose the correct alternative.

• When we use the structure *as ... as*, we **use** / **don't use** the comparative form of the adjective.

Rules p.W39

2 Rewrite the sentences using *as ... as*. Use the adjectives in parentheses.

Skiing is more difficult than swimming. (easy)
Skiing isn't as easy as swimming.

1 Fantasy movies are worse than love stories. (good)
_____

2 Art is more interesting than science. (boring)
_____

3 Lake Maracaibo is smaller than Lake Superior. (big)
_____

4 The bus is slower than the train. (fast)
_____

5 Angelina Jolie is younger than Brad Pitt. (old)
_____

less ... than

A cell phone is	**less** expensive **than**	an iPad.
Cats are	**less** intelligent **than**	people.

Rules p.W39

3 Correct the mistakes in the sentences below.

This book was ~~lesser~~ interesting than that book.
This book was less interesting than that book.

1 English is less difficult Japanese.

2 Your appearance is less important of your personality.

3 The jacket was less than expensive the dress.

4 I am less popular that my brother.

4 Write sentences giving your opinion. Use *less ... than*.

Selena Gomez / Miley Cyrus (beautiful)
Selena Gomez is less beautiful than Miley Cyrus. or
Miley Cyrus is less beautiful than Selena Gomez.

1 trains / buses (expensive)
_____

2 iPads / laptops (useful)
_____

3 Enrique Iglesias / Mark Anthony (famous)
_____

4 action movies / horror movies (exciting)
_____

5 Daniel Radcliffe / Robert Pattinson (talented)
_____

6 motorcycles / cars (dangerous)
_____

Finished?

Choose one of the categories below. Think of two nouns for that category. How many sentences can you make to compare the two things? Use *as ... as* and *less ... than*. Choose another category and repeat the activity.

> cities   countries   famous people
> food and drink   movies   music
> sports   transportation

Countries: the U.S. and Japan.
The U.S. is as exciting as Japan.
Japan isn't as big as the U.S.
The U.S. is less expensive than Japan.

Puzzle p.107

OUR CHANGING PLANET

Our planet is getting warmer. We know it changes our weather, but it changes the geography of our planet, too.

BEACHES ARE GETTING SMALLER!

When water gets warmer, it expands. And when the ice at the North and South Poles gets warmer, it melts. As a result our seas and oceans are getting bigger, and some islands are losing their beaches! The beautiful beaches of Hawaii are very popular with tourists, but they are growing smaller each year. The government is spending millions of dollars to make beaches bigger with sand from beneath the sea. But the problem is very serious.

MOUNTAINS ARE GROWING TALLER!

The surface of the Earth has two parts: the soft mantle, and the hard crust around it. The crust looks like a jigsaw puzzle, and the pieces are always colliding. They push land up, and mountains appear and grow taller. And this happens again and again! But scientists also think that with less heavy snow and ice on the mountains, it's easier for them to grow! In Patagonia, the mountains increased in height by 3.9 cm between 2003 and 2006.

VOLCANOES CAN BECOME MORE ACTIVE!

Warmer temperatures can make volcanoes on dry land more active. Melting snow and ice adds water to the oceans, and they become deeper and heavier. There is greater pressure on the ocean floor, and less pressure on dry land. This makes it easier for volcanoes to erupt. Volcanic eruptions make countries and islands larger. One example is Big Island in Hawaii. Its volcano Kilauea is very active, and its lava is forming new land. Hawaii's beaches are shrinking …, but its land is getting bigger!

Check it out!

Find these words and check their meaning.

melt
crust
jigsaw puzzle
collide

My reading skills

There are different ways you can find the meaning of new vocabulary without a dictionary.

- Decide what **part of speech** it is – a verb, noun, adjective, etc.
- Look for **cognates** – they are similar to words in your language.
- Use the **context** of a text to help you understand.

Reading

1 **Read the skills box. Then find the words in the article. Write the meanings in your language.**

1 parts of speech: serious _____ increase _____
2 cognates: expand _____ pressure _____
3 context: beneath _____ shrinking _____

2 🔊 2.21 **Read and listen to the article. Then answer the questions.**

What do warmer temperatures change?
They change our weather and the geography of our planet.

1 What is happening to beaches in Hawaii?
2 Where does the extra sand come from?
3 What is the Earth's surface made of?
4 What causes mountains to grow taller?

5 How much did the mountains in Patagonia grow in three years?
6 When do oceans become deeper and heavier?
7 What does this do to the ocean floor?
8 Why is Big Island getting bigger?

Listening

3 🔊 2.22 **Listen to a radio interview about the eruption of the Mount St. Helens volcano. Are the sentences true or false?**

The volcano erupted in 1980.	True
The volcano is in Canada.	False
1 The eruption didn't kill any people.	_____
2 Edie was a teenager at the time of the eruption.	_____
3 On the day of the eruption, the animals in her garden weren't as noisy as usual.	_____
4 The sky was a different color.	_____
5 Edie lived very near the volcano.	_____
6 Her uncle lived farther away from the volcano.	_____
7 Edie didn't feel very scared.	_____
8 The eruption wasn't as big as she expected.	_____
9 During the day, the sky got lighter.	_____
10 Edie still thinks about the people and animals who died in the eruption.	_____

4 🔊 2.22 **Listen again and correct the false sentences.**

The volcano is in Canada. *False*
The volcano is in the U.S.

Speaking

5 Pairwork **Think of a scary incident in your life. Use the adjectives in the box or your own ideas and the questions below to describe it to your partner. Whose story is more frightening? Why?** 🙂

> bad   loud   nervous   quiet   scary   terrible

- Where were you?
- Who were you with?
- What happened?
- What did you see?

- What did you hear?
- What did the incident affect / change?
- How did you feel?

A *I was at home and my parents were at a party. My sister was also out. I thought I was alone, but suddenly I heard a loud noise. I felt cold air in the room, too. Someone was in my house! Then I saw ...*

B *I was in town with two friends. It was late at night and it was cold, too. We were at the bus stop. Suddenly a man appeared and shouted at my friend ...*

A *I think your story is scarier. I felt more nervous, but ...*

Writing

6 **Write your story from exercise 5. Remember to use adjectives *also* and *too*.**

Workbook p.43   Writing builder p.95

Check it out!

Find these words and check their meaning.

so far   That sucks!   Here we come!

1 🔊 2.23 **Read and listen** **Which group wins the Battle of the Bands?**

Lewis Hey, Dylan! Sorry I'm late. Who's playing?

Dylan The Misfitz. They're the best band so far.

Lewis They aren't as good as us!

Dylan No, but Zac looks very confident up there. He's the least nervous person in this room.

Lewis Chill out! Rosie's fantastic! She has the most amazing voice of all these people.

Dylan She's an awesome singer, but she isn't a rock star.

Rosie Who isn't a rock star?

Dylan Rosie? Wow! Is that really you? You look great!

Lewis I don't believe it! You're the most beautiful girl here tonight!

Dylan And the coolest!

Rosie You look pretty good, too, guys. Come on! Let's rock!

Later …

Announcer OK, people. The top two bands are The Misfitz and Supernova. And the winner is … Supernova!

Zac What? No way! That sucks!

Rosie We won! I'm so happy!

Dylan I knew we could do it! Nice job, Rosie. I'm proud of you!

Lewis Me, too. You were amazing!

Rosie Thanks, guys. MTV, here we come!

2 Comprehension **Correct the sentences.**

Dylan is late.
Lewis is late.

1 Supernova is playing when Lewis arrives.
2 The Misfitz aren't very good.
3 Dylan is the best singer at the Battle of Bands.
4 Supernova plays before The Misfitz.
5 The Misfitz win the competition.

Language focus

3 Dialogue focus Reorder the words to complete the dialogues.

1 Dylan the / band / they're / best / so / far .
They're the best band so far.

Lewis They aren't as good as us!

Dylan No, but Zac looks very confident up there.
nervous / this / he's / least / the / person / in / room .
1_____

2 Lewis Chill out! Rosie's fantastic!
she / the / all / these / people / has / amazing / voice / of / most .
2_____
_____

3 Dylan Rosie? Wow! Is that really you? You look great!

Lewis I don't believe it!
girl / you're / most / tonight / beautiful / here / the !
3_____

Dylan and / coolest / the ! 4_____

4 🔊 2.24 **Listen and check. Listen again and repeat.**

5 Focus on you Read the example dialogue. Then write two similar dialogues. Use the words in the boxes.

> actor / Hollywood   comedy / on TV   meal / school cafeteria
> place / on the planet   soccer player / South America

> the coldest   the friendliest   the funniest
> the most delicious   the most expensive   the most talented

A *New Girl* is the funniest comedy on TV.
B No, it isn't! *The Big Bang Theory* is the funniest comedy on TV.
A Do you really think so? I think it's terrible!

6 Pairwork Practice the dialogues in exercise 5. Do you and your partner agree? 😊

Feelings and emotions

1 🔊 2.25 **Match the adjectives with the pictures. Then listen and check.**

> angry ~~annoyed~~ bored confident embarrassed excited
> fed up frightened happy nervous proud sad

annoyed

1 _____

2 _____

3 _____

4 _____

5 _____

6 _____

7 _____

8 _____

9 _____

10 _____

11 _____

My study skills

Using new vocabulary in context

When you learn new vocabulary, it is a good idea to use it in different sentences. This gives the vocabulary a context and helps you to remember it.

2 Complete the text with the words in the box.

> bored confident excited happy ~~nervous~~ proud sad

At the audition for the band, I was very __nervous__. A lot of people were there. One girl looked very ¹_____. "They didn't want me," she said. When it was finally my turn, the band seemed tired and a little ²_____. But when I started to sing, they started to listen, and I began to feel more ³_____. When I finished, the band members looked really ⁴_____. "You're perfect!" they said. Afterwards, I called my mom and she said, "I'm very ⁵_____". I'm singing in my first concert next week. I'm still a little nervous, but now I'm also ⁶_____!

3 Choose five words from exercise 1. Write two true sentences for each word.

I feel happy when I have fun with my friends.
I feel happy when Mom makes a nice dinner.
I feel angry when …

4 Pairwork Ask and answer questions about your emotions in these situations.

- It's the first day of your summer vacation.
- Your new clothes look great on you.
- Your new clothes look better on your friend.

- You argue with your best friend.
- You win a competition.
- Another student says bad things about you at school.

A *How do you feel when argue with your best friend?*
B *I usually feel sad, because I love spending time with her. How do you feel …?*

Workbook p. 46 Extra practice online

Superlative adjectives
Regular adjectives

> You're **the coolest** girl here tonight!
> You're **the most beautiful** girl here tonight!

Short adjectives		Superlative
tall	**the** + adjective + **-est**	the tall**est**
nice	**the** + adjective + **-st**	the nice**st**
sad	**the** + adjective + double consonant + **-est**	the sad**dest**
Adjectives ending with consonant + y		**Superlative**
happy	**the** + adjective -y̶ + **-iest**	the happ**iest**
Long adjectives		**Superlative**
boring important	**the most** + adjective	**the most** boring **the most** important

Rules p.W44

1 Write the superlative form of the adjectives.

small ___the smallest___

1 large _____
2 old _____
3 hot _____
4 noisy _____
5 famous _____
6 expensive _____

2 Correct the mistakes in the sentences below.

Ella is ~~most~~ popular girl in the school.
Ella is the most popular girl in the school.

1 The *Mona Lisa* is Leonardo da Vinci's famousest painting.
2 This is the most cheap hotel I can find.
3 Airplanes are safest form of transportation.
4 I think Robert Pattinson is most attractive than actor on the planet.
5 Which is the most easy language to learn?
6 Mark is the crazyest boy I know.

3 Write sentences with the superlative form of the adjectives.

Amy / young / girl in the school.
Amy is the youngest girl in the school.

1 Today / hot / day of the year so far.
_____

2 Elena's hair / long / in the class.
_____

3 London / populated / city in the U.K.
_____

4 Mount Etna / one of / active / volcanoes in the world.
_____
_____

5 This / proud / moment of my life.
_____

4 Complete the sentences with the superlative form of the adjectives in the box.

dangerous   expensive   happy
~~heavy~~   high   hot   wet

Record breakers!

Blue whales are ___the heaviest___ animals on the planet. They can weigh up to 180,000 kg!

1 _____ homes in New York cost $100 million!
2 Mount Everest is _____ in the world. And scientists think it's still growing!
3 Mawsynram in India is one of _____ places on Earth. It has 11,872 millimeters of rain every year.
4 The Australians are the _____ people in the world! Life is great there.
5 With hundreds of accidents each year, Death Road in Bolivia is _____ road in the world.
6 Death Valley in California is _____ place in the world. In 1913, temperatures reached 56.7°C!

Finished?

Write questions with the superlative form of the adjectives in the box. Then answer the questions.

attractive   easy   expensive   friendly
interesting   young

Which do you think is the most interesting subject?
I think the most interesting subject is history.
Who is the youngest person in ...

Puzzle p.107

Making a phone call

1 🔊 2.26 **Reorder the sentences to form two dialogues. Listen and check. Then listen and repeat.**

1

____ Hi! It's Mercedes here. Is this Carla?

____ That's (212)-555-0371. OK. Bye.

____ Hello?

____ Yes, please. Can you ask her to return my call by eight o'clock at the latest? My number is (212)-555-0371.

____ No, it isn't. It's her sister, Becca. Carla isn't here right now. She's at the library. Do you want to leave a message?

____ Bye.

2

____ Hello. Can I speak with Diego please?

____ It's Ben, Diego's best friend.

____ Yes, of course. Who's calling?

____ Hello?

____ Oh, hi, Ben! Hang on a minute. Diego! It's for you. It's Ben.

Learn it, use it!

You ask	You answer
Can I speak with …?	Yes, of course. Sorry, (Julia / Simon) isn't here right now.
Who's calling?	It's (Julia / Simon).
Is this …?	Yes, it is. / No, it isn't.
Do you want to leave a message?	Yes, please. Can you tell him / her …? / Can you ask him / her to return my call? No, thanks.

2 🔊 2.27 **Listen and complete the dialogues. Listen again and check.**

1

A Hello?

B Oh, hi. Is this Amelia? _____

A No, it isn't. It's her cousin, Laura. [1]_____
She's at the movies. [2]_____

B No, thanks. I can call again tomorrow.

A OK. Bye.

B [3]_____

2

A Hello. [4]_____

B Is this Julian?

A [5]_____

B Oh, hi, Julian. Cesar, [6]_____ It's Julian! Oh …
hang on a minute. Julian, Cesar is taking a shower at the moment. Do you
want to leave a message?

A Yes, please. Can you ask him to[7]_____
There's something important I need to tell him! [8]_____

B That's (212)-555-9235. OK. Bye.

A Bye.

3 Pairwork Make dialogues with a partner. Use the dialogues in exercises 1 and 2 as a model. 💬

Workbook p.48　　Extra practice　online

Superlative adjectives

Irregular adjectives

They're **the best** band so far.

Adjective	Superlative
good	**the best**
bad	**the worst**
far	**the furthest / farthest**

Rules p.W45

1 Complete the sentences with the superlative form of *good*, *bad*, or *far*.

I love Fridays. They're _the best_____ day of the week.

1 _____ place from the North Pole is the South Pole.

2 Rain is _____ thing for a picnic!

3 This song is awesome! It's _____ one on the album.

4 With his old-fashioned clothes, Dad wears _____ things in our family!

Comparative / Superlative

Think!

Read the sentences. Then choose the correct word.

The Yangtze is **longer than** the Mississippi.
The Nile is **the longest** river in the world.

- We use the [1] comparative / superlative to compare two people or things.
- We use the [2] comparative / superlative to compare something with more than two people or things.

Rules p.W45

2 Write sentences with the comparative and superlative forms of the adjectives in parentheses.

Pia (1.68 m) / Ali (1.62 m) / Pat (1.57 m) (tall)
Ali is taller than Pat. Pia is the tallest.

1 Chile (756,096 km^2) / Argentina (2,780,400 km^2) / Paraguay (406,752 km^2) (big)

2 iPhone (€549) / Samsung (€473) / BlackBerry (€619.53) (expensive)

3 Pacific (10,911 m) / Atlantic (8,605 m) / Arctic (5,441 m) (deep)

4 horse (70.76 km/hour) / kangaroo (71 km/hour) / dolphin (65 km/hour) (fast)

the least

He's **the least** nervous person here.

Adjective	Superlative
boring	**the least** boring
important	**the least** important
interesting	**the least** interesting

Rules p.W45

3 Rewrite the sentences with *the least* and one of the adjectives in the box.

confident   dangerous   ~~expensive~~   noisy

My mom bought me the cheapest phone in the store.
My mom bought me _the least expensive_ phone in the store.

1 Lizzie is the most nervous girl in the competition.
Lizzie is _____ girl in the competition.

2 My grandparents live in the safest part of town.
My grandparents live in _____ part of town.

3 Our bathroom is the quietest room in the house!
Our bathroom is _____ room in the house!

4 Game! Complete the sentences with the adjectives in parentheses. Use comparative and superlative forms. More than one answer is possible. Are the sentences true (T) or false (F)? Who got the most correct answers?

With great prices, trains are _the least expensive_ form of transportation in the U.S. (expensive) _F_

1 Airplanes are _____ trains for the environment. (bad) ___

2 With a lot of fruit and vegetables, the Okinawan diet is _____ in the world. (healthy) ___

3 At 206 cm, Elisany da Cruz Silva is _____ woman in the world. (tall) ___

4 The Yellow River is _____ the Mississippi. (long) ___

5 With only fifty inhabitants, the Cook Islands are _____ islands in the world. (populated) ___

Finished?

Write three more sentences for the quiz. Ask your classmates if they are true or false.

Seoul is the biggest city in South Korea.

Puzzle p.107

THE '-EST' MOMENT OF YOUR LIFE!

Tell us about the '-est' moment of your life. Was it the best? The funniest? The proudest? We want to know!

Ana

Last year, a note turned up in my bag. It said, "Do you want to go on a date?" and had a cell phone number at the bottom. It was from Pablo, a boy in my class. I was very excited because I thought he was the coolest boy in school! I called the number but, guess what? Pablo didn't know about the note. His friends played a joke on me – it was the worst day of my life and I was so embarrassed. Now Pablo always ignores me. I'm still embarrassed, and my friends and I think he and his friends are idiots!

Naomi
elevator.jpg attached

My scariest moment was in an elevator – I needed to go to the twentieth floor. It was just me and a man I didn't know in there, and suddenly the elevator stopped and the lights went out. I was really frightened, and I started screaming and shouting. We got out after about twenty minutes. That poor guy – I don't know what was scarier for him – the problem with the elevator, or me!

David
party.jpg attached

My younger brother, João, has problems with his legs. Last year, he started elementary school. I felt nervous for him, and I was very annoyed when the other kids asked why he wasn't as fast as they were. But João just laughed – he didn't care, and his first day turned out fine. Now he's very popular and on his seventh birthday, all the class came to his party. That was the proudest day of my life.

Reading

1 Find the phrasal verbs *turn up*, *go out*, *get out*, and *turn out* in the website. Then choose the correct answers.

   OK, guys. When the lights **go out** / **turn out**, you stop talking and go to sleep!

   1 We put the dog in the kitchen and closed the door, so it can't **go out** / **get out**.
   2 I'm worried because I've lost my cell phone. I hope it **turns up** / **turns out** soon.
   3 I was worried about the weather. But it **went out** / **turned out** OK in the end.

2 🔊 2.28 **Read and listen** to the website. Then write *João*, *Naomi*, or *Pablo* next to the sentences.

   1 Who is the least worried about his situation? _João_
   2 Who was in the darkest location? _____
   3 Who is less popular than before? _____

3 Answer the questions.

   Where did Pablo's friends put the note? *They put it in Ana's bag.*

   1 How did Ana feel when she discovered the joke?
   2 How did Ana's opinion of Pablo change?
   3 Who was in the elevator with Naomi?
   4 What was it like in the elevator when it stopped?
   5 How long were they in the elevator together?
   6 Who was David worried about?
   7 Why isn't João as fast as the other kids?
   8 How did David feel on the day of his brother's party?

Listening

4 🔊 2.29 **Listen to a radio interview about a survey. Choose the correct answers.**

Australia is the (happiest) / **richest** / **safest** country in the world.

1 Jodie thinks that the Australian **lifestyle** / **food** / **culture** makes Australians happy.

2 The survey shows that Australians' lives are often **longer than** / **shorter than** / **as long as** other people's lives.

3 Americans and Norwegians are **healthier** / **poorer** / **richer** than Australians.

4 Jodie believes that money is less important than **free time** / **good health** / **good weather** .

5 Jodie agrees that Australians have a lot of **negative** / **normal** / **positive** feelings.

6 She feels proud of **her country** / **her lifestyle** / **the result of the survey**.

Speaking

5 Pairwork **Ask and answer questions about your country with the comparative and superlative forms of the adjectives in the box.** 😀

> beautiful   cheap   expensive   happy   healthy   proud   rich   safe   warm

A Do you think our country is a happy country?

B Yes, but I think other countries are happier. We have problems with …

A Is our country the safest in the world?

B It isn't the safest, but it's safer than …

6 **Prepare a short presentation about your country with your partner. Use your answers from exercise 5.**

Writing

7 **Write a report about your country. Use your presentation from exercise 6.**

Vocabulary

1 Reorder the letters to form geography words.

t i n c n o n t e   _continent_

1 k e l a   _____

2 a e s   _____

3 d l s a i n   _____

4 c o n u t y r   _____

5 v e r i r   _____

6 n t m u a o n i   _____

2 Complete the sentences with an adjective of feeling or emotion.

Fabio was e_mbarrassed_ because his cell phone rang in the movie theater.

1 I get f_____ if I hear a noise at night.

2 Mom's very a_____! The dog ate our dinner!

3 Sam is f_____ u_____ because he can't go out with his friends.

4 We're very p_____ of our dad. He got a fantastic new job last week.

5 The girls are e_____ about their vacation.

6 Are you n_____ about your audition?

3 Complete the dialogue with the words in the box.

come   go   ~~going~~   so   sucks   terrible   way

Nick   How's it _going_?

Ryo   I'm running in a race tomorrow! Do you want to do it too?

Nick   No ¹_____! I'm ²_____ at running. Are you ready?

Ryo   No, I'm not! I have a bad leg again.

Nick   Not again. That ³_____.

Ryo   But we're collecting money for the hospital. We have about $80 ⁴_____ far.

Nick   That's awesome. ⁵_____ for it!

Ryo   Thanks. Tokyo 2020, here I ⁶_____!

Grammar

4 Choose the correct answers.

It's (warmer) / more warm today than yesterday.

1 I think Beyoncé is **better** / **gooder** than Shakira.

2 Venezuela is **larger** / **largger** than Uruguay.

3 My cell phone was **more expensive** / **expensiver** than my brother's.

4 Blue whales are **heavier** / **heavyer** than elephants.

5 Summer is **hoter** / **hotter** than spring.

5 Complete the sentences with as … as, less … than, and the adjectives in parentheses.

price: $499.00
weight: 652 g
popularity rating: ★★★★★

price: $649.00
weight: 112 g
popularity rating: ★★★★★

The cell phone isn't _as big as the tablet_____. (big)

1 The tablet is _____. (expensive)

2 The cell phone is _____. (popular)

3 The cell phone is _____. (heavy)

6 Complete the dialogue with the superlative form of the adjectives in the box.

bad   ~~cool~~   funny   unfriendly   unlucky

Eva   You know Miguel, _the coolest_____ boy in class?

Maria   And ¹_____. He makes me laugh!

Eva   I dropped my lunch on his pants!

Maria   Oh, no!

Eva   But that wasn't ²_____ thing. When I apologized, he just ignored me.

Maria   He's ³_____ boy in the class!

Eva   But also ⁴_____, too. He didn't have any other pants!

7 Write sentences comparing the singers. Use the comparative and superlative forms of the adjectives in the box.

old   popular   short   talented   tall   young

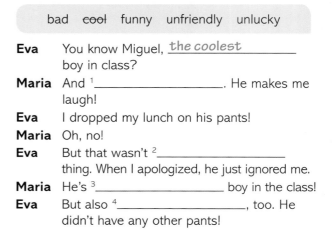

Name:	Name:	Name:
Connor Maynard	Ed Sheeran	Bruno Mars
Birth date:	Birth date:	Birth date:
Nov 21, 1994	Feb 17, 1991	Oct 8, 1985
Height: 179 cm	Height: 178 cm	Height: 165 cm

Ed Sheeran is taller than Bruno Mars. Connor Maynard is the tallest. Bruno Mars is the shortest.

Communication

8 🔊 2.30 **Complete the dialogue. Then listen and check.**

Yesul Hi, is _____ Clara?

Sonia No, it isn't. ¹_____ her sister, Sonia. Who's ²_____?

Yesul It's Yesul.

Sonia Oh, hi, Yesul. ³_____ on a minute. Clara! It's for you! It's Yesul.

Clara Hi, Yesul. How are you?

Yesul Great, thanks. Do you want to go to the new science museum tomorrow morning?

Clara ⁴_____ is it?

Yesul It's on Main Street.

Clara ⁵_____ do I get ⁶_____?

Yesul You can get the number 30 bus.

Clara And ⁷_____ much are the tickets?

Yesul ⁸_____ $8.

Clara OK. When do you want to meet?

Yesul 10 a.m.?

Clara Great! See you there tomorrow!

Yesul OK. Bye!

Pronunciation

/h/

9 🔊 2.31 **Read the explanations. Then listen to the words.**

• In spoken English, we usually pronounce the *h* as /h/ at the beginning of a word. A few words beginning with *wh* also have the /h/ sound.

> have   head   house   who   whole

• However, some words beginning with *wh* don't have the /h/ sound. We pronounce these words with a /w/.

> what   where   while   why

10 🔊 2.32 **Listen to the words. Check (✓) the words that start with the /h/ sound. Then listen and repeat.**

what	X	3 hat	___
1 when	___	4 white	___
2 home	___	5 whose	___

11 🔊 2.33 **Underline the /h/ sounds in the dialogue. Then listen and repeat.**

Mom Where are you? <u>Who</u> are you with? How are you getting home?

Bianca I'm with Harry. He's having hamburgers for his dinner. Can I stay another hour? His house is near ours.

Mom OK. Call me when you finish.

Listening

12 🔊 2.34 **Listen to Bella and Andres talking about their vacation in Wales. Are the sentences true or false?**

Bella and Andres went to Wales last winter.   _False_

1 The weather was sunny at the beach.   _____

2 The weather was bad every day.   _____

3 Bella doesn't like walking.   _____

4 Andres climbed a mountain.   _____

5 Bella never worries about things.   _____

13 🔊 2.34 **Listen again and answer the questions.**

What does Bella call the vacation?

She calls it the worst time of her life.

1 How did Andres feel on the beach?

_____

2 How often did it rain during their vacation?

_____

3 How did Bella feel when the weather was bad?

_____

4 Why was Andres proud?

_____

5 Why was Bella frightened?

_____

6 Where are Bella and Andres going on vacation next year?

_____

GUINNESS WORLD RECORDS

Guinness World Records is a famous book of world records about people, animals, and the natural world. It started in 1951, and there is a new edition every year. Today, the book is one of the best-selling books in the world!

THE OLDEST PERSON IN HISTORY

The oldest person in history was Jeanne Calment, a French woman. She was born in 1875, and died in 1997 aged 122 years and 164 days. Jeanne never needed to work because her husband was rich. But she was a very active person and enjoyed playing sports. She rode a bike till the age of 100 and said her long life was because of olive oil, wine, and chocolate.

THE WORLD'S MOST FLEXIBLE FACE

Some people can make very strange expressions with their faces. This sport is called gurning – and it is in the Guinness World Records! The current record holder is Tommy Mattinson from the U.K. He is the only person to win the World Gurning Championship twelve times!

THE WORLD'S MOST EXPENSIVE HAMBURGER

Feeling hungry? Why not visit the restaurant Serendipity 3 in New York? There you can eat a delicious hamburger made with meat from Japan. It comes with cheese, expensive mushrooms, and an egg, and sits on a bread roll with butter. This delicious meal only costs $295! Go on – why are you waiting?!

THE WORLD'S FASTEST-TALKING WOMAN

The world's fastest-talking woman is Fran Capo, from New York. She first got the title in 1986, and can say 603.32 words in 54.2 seconds. Fran appears on a lot of TV talk shows to show people her talent. She was always a fast talker, but she doesn't know why. However, she definitely has a lot to say!

Check it out!

Find these words and check their meaning.

edition
record holder
title

1 🔊 2.35 **Read and listen** to the article. Then answer the questions.

When did the *Guinness World Records* book first arrive in stores?
It first arrived in stores in 1951.

1 How old was Jeanne Calment when she died?
2 When did she stop riding a bike?
3 What do you do with your face in gurning?
4 Where can you eat the world's most expensive burger?
5 Name four of the ingredients of the burger.
6 When did Fran Capo first become the world's fastest talking woman?
7 Where can you see Fran demonstrate her talent?

2 Presentation Find out about a world record holder from your country. Use the *Guinness World Records* book, or the website (www.guinessworldrecords.com). Then use your answers to prepare a short presentation.

- What is the name of the person?
- How old is he / she?
- Where is he / she from?
- What record does he / she have?

Vocabulary and speaking

I can identify geography words. (p.74)   A2

1 Complete the geography words.

1 v __ l __ __ n __
2 __ o n __ __ n __ n t
3 i __ l __ __ d
4 m __ __ n __ a __ n
5 __ i __ e __

__ / 5

I can ask for tourist information. (p.76)   A2

2 Write the sentences in the correct order to form a dialogue.

A help / can / you / I ?
1 _____

B I want to visit the zoo.
   open / time / does / what / it ?
2 _____

A open / it's / 9 a.m. / from / 5 p.m. / to .
3 _____

B I / get / how / there / can ?
4 _____

A bus / number 3 / take / you / the / can .
5 _____

__ / 5

I can use language to tell a scary story. (p.79)   A2

3 Complete the story with the comparative form of the adjectives in parentheses.

When everybody left the house, it seemed
¹_____ (quiet). Then night arrived and the sky grew ²_____ (dark), too. Alone in the house, I started to feel more and ³_____ (nervous). Then suddenly I heard a noise. It wasn't the cat – it was ⁴_____ (loud) than that. A person – or something horrible – was in the house. Then suddenly I saw it … it was ⁵_____ (terrible) than anything you can imagine … !

__ / 5

I can identify feelings and emotions. (p.82)   A2

4 Complete the sentences.

1 When I go on vacation, I'm e_____.
2 When I make a mistake, I feel e_____.
3 I was very n_____ before the math test.
4 My parents are p_____ of me.
5 A s_____ person sometimes cries.

__ / 5

I can make and answer a phone call. (p.84)   A2

5 Choose the correct answers.

A Hello. Is ¹**than / this** Jaime?
B No, it isn't. It's Diego. Who's ²**calling / talking**?
A It's Mark.
B Oh, ³**bye / hi**, Mark. Do you want to leave ⁴**a message / an answer**?
A No, ⁵**problem / thanks**. Bye.

__ / 5

I can use comparatives and superlatives to compare countries. (p.87)   A2

6 Find and correct the mistakes in the sentences.

1 Suriname is the small country in Latin America.
_____
_____

2 I think Peru is more exciting Argentina.
_____

3 Our country isn't the richest the world.
_____

4 Our country isn't the safer, but it's safest than some.
_____
_____

5 South America is the more beautiful continent in the world!
_____
_____

__ / 5

Reading, listening, and writing

	Got it?		
	Yes	I'm not sure	No
I can understand a text about the changing geography of our planet. (p.78) A2	☐	☐	☐
I can understand an interview about a volcanic eruption. (p.79) A2	☐	☐	☐
I can write a short story about a scary incident. (p.79) A2	☐	☐	☐
I can understand a text about events in people's lives. (p.86) A2	☐	☐	☐
I can understand an interview about Australia. (p.87) A2	☐	☐	☐
I can write a report about my country. (p.87) A2	☐	☐	☐

1 A blog

1 Read the rules for using pronouns.

Using pronouns

a We use pronouns to replace the names of people, places, and things. With pronouns our language isn't repetitive.
*I know **Paul**. I know **him** from school.* ✓
*I know **Paul**. I know **Paul** from school.* ✗

b There are different kinds of pronoun: subject, object, and possessive.
***We** go to junior high school.* (subject pronoun)
*Mom always gives **me** great birthday presents.* (object pronoun)
*That isn't Ellen's pizza. **Hers** is on the table.* (possessive pronoun)

2 Look at the pronouns in the sentences. Write *S* (subject), *O* (object), or *P* (possessive) next to each sentence.

At the moment, **she** is on vacation. _S_
1 I hate carrots. I never eat **them**! ____
2 **We** are running for the bus. ____
3 I have **mine**, but where are yours? ____
4 I can hear **him**, but I can't see **him**. ____

3 Complete the sentences with the correct pronouns.

Tom and I have homework. I'm doing mine here. Tom is doing _his_ in the kitchen.
1 This book is fantastic. I'm really enjoying ____.
2 Where are my friends? I'm waiting for _____!
3 Give us that chocolate. It's _____!
4 The children are happy. _____ are playing.
5 Our grandma lives in Chicago. We visit _____ every summer.

4 Complete the blog post with the correct pronouns.

Hello friends,
It's me, Joe! This week _I_'m at my favorite music festival, the Bonnaroo festival in Tennessee. This year [1]____ starts on June 13th. I'm here with my cousin Alicia. I go with [2]____ every year. [3]____ always have fun.
Right now, [4]_'m having a guitar lesson with a really cool teacher called Eric. My guitar is only a cheap one, but [5]____ is awesome. This evening The xx are on stage. Alicia is excited because she really likes [6]_____. What's [7]_____ favorite festival?

More news soon,
Joe

5 Now do exercise 6 on page 17.

2 A famous actor

1 Read the rules for positions of adjectives.

Position of adjectives

a Adjectives describe nouns. They can go immediately before a noun.
*a **heavy** bag*
***blue** eyes*
***new** sneakers*

b They can also go after a verb.
*Her hair is **long**.*
*The food tastes **horrible**.*
*You don't look **happy**.*

2 Where does the adjective go in the sentence? Check (✓) the correct position.

My ____ sister ____ has ✓ hair ____. (blond)
1 This ____ TV ____ show ____ is ____. (awesome)
2 Your ____ vacation ____ sounds ____. (great)
3 It's ____ a ____ party ____. (terrible)
4 Jack ____ can't ____ find ____ his ____ jacket ____. (blue)
5 Do ____ you ____ feel ____ about ____ the ____ test ____? (nervous)

3 Reorder the words to make sentences.

is / blue / Polly / dress / a / wearing .
Polly is wearing a blue dress.
1 curly / teacher / our / hair / has .
_____
2 sneakers / cool / look / your .
_____
3 gray / Grandpa's / are / eyes .
_____
4 city / lives / in / Diego / a / big .
_____
5 day / long / it / a / was .
_____

4 Complete the profile of Katharine Hepburn with the words in parentheses. Remember to use *was* and *were*.

Katharine Hepburn _was a famous actress._ (actress / be / famous). She was born in Hartford, Connecticut in 1907. Her movie *Little Women* [1]_____ (be / popular / very). She [2]_____ (be / beautiful / woman). Her [3]_____ (be / brown / hair), and her [4]_____ (be / blue / eyes). She died on May 12th, 2003.

5 Now do exercise 5 on page 25.

3 Life events

1 Read the spelling rules.

Spelling rules

a Remember the spelling rules for regular simple past verbs, e.g.:

learn + **ed** = learned

cry -~~y~~ + **ied** = cried

stop + p + **ed** = stopped

b Remember the spelling rules for regular plural nouns, too, e.g.:

bike + **s** = bikes

glass + **es** = glasses

party -~~y~~ + **ies** = parties

shelf -~~f~~ + **ves** = shelves

2 Choose the correct answers.

Yesterday my mom **tuck** / **took** me to a birthday party.

1 My sister goes to extra math **classes** / **classis** on Tuesdays.

2 How many **computeres** / **computers** do you have?

3 I **sleept** / **slept** very badly last night.

4 They spent their **lifes** / **lives** in Canada.

3 Write the correct past or plural forms of the verbs in parentheses.

Last year, my sister <u>grew</u> her hair long. (grow)

1 We need to move these _____. (box)

2 My brother _____ elementary school yesterday. (start)

3 Jack _____ jeans and a T-shirt to the party. (wear)

4 I _____ my first tooth when I was six. (lose)

5 Sofia didn't eat her _____. (potato)

4 Use the prompts to write sentences. Write the plural form of the nouns.

In 2000, / my cousin and I / be / baby

In 2000, my cousin and I were babies.

1 Last year, / my parents / move / to Washington

2 In 2012, / Luis / start / class in two languages

3 Last month, / she / travel / around Australia / with her brother

4 Jack / go / to three different elementary school

5 Sir Hillary / become / one of my hero

5 Now do exercise 6 on page 37.

4 A review

1 Read the rules for using paragraphs.

Using paragraphs

Use paragraphs to divide a longer piece of writing into clear points or topics.

a Before you start writing, plan what you want to say in separate points. Then group them together by topic, e.g.:

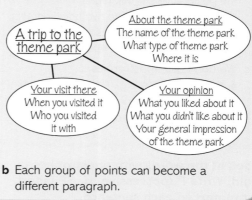

b Each group of points can become a different paragraph.

2 Read the notes about a trip to a new burger restaurant. Write A, B, or C.

A about the restaurant

B about your visit there

C your opinion of the restaurant

The Shack – new restaurant in my town <u>A</u>

1 invitation from cousin ___

2 can order burgers, Mexican food, pizza, soda, milkshakes, etc. ___

3 friendly waiters, great atmosphere ___

4 my burger didn't taste nice ___

5 delicious ice cream ___

6 went last Saturday ___

7 on Penn Avenue ___

8 long wait for food ___

3 Use the notes in exercise 2 to write full sentences. Put them in the correct paragraphs.

Paragraph A

There's a new restaurant in my town called The Shack …

_____

Paragraph B

_____

_____

Paragraph C

_____

_____

4 Now do exercise 6 on page 45.

5 A food article

1 Read the rules for using apostrophes.

Using apostrophes

a We use apostrophes to show possession or relationships.
The apostrophe goes before the possessive *s* if the person or thing is singular, and after the possessive *s* if it is plural.
Carmen's house.   The two boys' parents.

b We also use apostrophes for short forms.
*I **don't** have my bag. **We're** waiting for you!*

c We don't use apostrophes …
- to show plurals, e.g., *I have two pencils.*
- in possessive pronouns, e.g., *hers.*
- in the possessive adjective *its*, e.g., *The cat broke its leg.*

2 Look at the words with apostrophes in bold. Write P (possessive) or SF (short form) next to each sentence.

1 **Lucy's** parents eat a lot of meat. ____
2 **Mario's** having a birthday party tomorrow. ____
3 **Who's** cooking dinner? ____
4 The **teacher's** ruler is on the table. ____

3 Circle the correct answers.

Mom's / Moms leaving **her's** / **hers** on the table.

1 **You're** / **Your** with **you're** / **your** friends.
2 This **café's** / **cafés** **burger's** / **burgers** are awesome.
3 The dog wants **it's** / **its** dinner because **it's** / **its** very hungry.
4 **They're** / **Theyre** my **dad's** / **dads** new **car's** / **cars**.

4 Read the text. Add apostrophes in the correct places.

The history of the hamburger
The hamburger is one of America's favorite foods, but theres a lot of discussion about its origins. The round piece of meat probably first appeared in Germany in the 19th century. But it wasnt till 1904 that an American restaurant owner decided to sell it between two pieces of bread. That mans name was Louis Lassen and he was possibly the first person to make the famous hamburger we know today. The hamburgers ingredients are usually beef, eggs and onions. Theyre delicious!

5 Now do exercise 4 on page 59.

6 An itinerary

1 Read the rules for ordering events.

Ordering events

a We use adverbs to order events. This helps the reader to understand the text because it has a clear structure. We can use words like *first, next, then, after, after that, lastly,* and *finally.*

b We can also separate events with commas and *and.*
*First we visited the museum, then we had lunch in a restaurant, **and** lastly we went for a walk along the river.*

2 Choose the correct answers.

After / **Next** the concert, I'm going to a party and **finally** / **first** we're going home about midnight.

1 **Finally** / **First**, we're flying to Miami and **first** / **then**, we're traveling to Tampa.
2 Jorge is going to Spain next week. **First** / **Then** he's staying in Madrid, and **finally** / **first**, he's traveling south to Malaga.

3 Order the events with adverbs, commas, and *and*. More than one answer is possible.

I went to school. I played sports. I did my homework. I watched TV. I went to bed.

First I went to school, then I played sports, next I did my homework, and lastly I went to bed.

1 We have breakfast at eight o'clock. We have a snack at about eleven o'clock. Lunch is usually at one o'clock and we eat dinner at about seven o'clock. We have another snack at about ten o'clock.
2 I'm flying to Berlin. I'm spending a day in Weimar. I'm taking a train to Trier. I'm visiting some friends in Bonn. I'm flying home.

4 Put the events in the correct order. Then add adverbs to each sentence to order the events. Sometimes more than one answer is possible.

A He's arriving in New York late at night. _1_
B He's spending his last day at Ellis Island and the Statue of Liberty. __
C He's going to the tourist office for a map. __
D He's visiting the Empire State Building and the Guggenheim Museum, and going to the theater on Broadway. __
E He's spending his first night in the city. __
F He's flying home. __

5 Now do exercise 5 on page 67.

7 A story

1 Read the rules for using *also* and *too*.

> **also and too**
>
> *Also* and *too* have the same meaning. We use the words to link two similar or related points. However, they go in different parts of a sentence.
> **a** *Also* usually goes after the verb *be* or before other verbs.
> *I also thought the movie was scary.*
> *But it was also pretty funny.*
> **b** *Too* usually goes at the end of a sentence, after a comma.
> *I thought the movie was scary, too.*

2 Reorder the words to complete the sentences. Sometimes more than one answer is possible.

are / but / dangerous / are / beautiful, / also / they

Volcanoes <u>are beautiful, but they are also dangerous</u>.

1 to climb / Iceland / like / , too / I'd / like / to visit / , and / its mountains

I'd _____

_____.

2 are / getting / also / are / they / and / getting / warmer, / deeper

Our oceans _____

_____.

3 , too / was / it / sunny, / very cold / but / was

The weather _____

_____.

3 Look at the sentences of a story below. Put them into pairs. Write a short story using the sentences and use *also* and *too*. More than one combination is possible.

The night was dark.
I felt alone.
She looked very old.
I started to run.
I was a little scared.
I noticed that we were the only people on the street.
It was cold.
She was very thin.
Then she started to run.
I saw a woman.

The night was dark. It was cold, too. ...

4 Now do exercise 6 on page 79.

8 A report

1 Read the rules for using *however* and *although*.

> **however and although**
>
> We use *however* and *although* to compare and contrast two points.
> **a** *However* often goes at the beginning of a sentence or paragraph.
> **b** We always put a comma after *however*.
> *It was a beautiful, sunny day.* **However**, *Nuria looked very sad.*
> **c** We usually use *although* in one sentence with two contrasting points. *Although* can go at the beginning of the sentence, or between the two points.
> *Although it's colder than yesterday, it's sunny.*
> *Eva never seems tired, although she always goes to bed late.*

2 Choose the correct answers.

However / (**Although**) it's a hot day, it's very cloudy.

1 Selma eats a lot. **However, / although** she's very slim.

2 Costa Rica isn't the richest country in the world. **Although / However,** it's one of the happiest.

3 I was fed up yesterday, **although / however** I feel happier today.

4 **Although / However** it was a horror movie, it wasn't scary at all.

5 In Ecuador, you can find high mountains, beautiful beaches, pretty towns, and beautiful cities. **Although / However,** it is only a small country.

3 Write matching sentences with *however* and *although*. Use commas in the correct places.

There's a lot of poverty in Indian cities. However, ... *they are also very beautiful and exciting.*

1 Sao Paulo is one of the most expensive cities in South America. However ...

2 Although Chile is one of the richest countries in South America ...

3 Some people think life in the countryside is safer than in the cities. However ...

4 I think Ecuador has the best weather in South America. However ...

5 Although Australia is officially the happiest country in the world ...

4 Now do exercise 7 on page 87.

The Suzuki Method

1 **A** We sometimes see video clips of young children playing instruments. The children are so small that their violins, pianos, and other instruments appear
5 enormous next to them, but they play like expert musicians. Their little fingers move rapidly, and their bodies move in time to the music. But how can these very young children play so well? They
10 are learning with the Suzuki method.

B The Suzuki method of learning musical instruments comes from Japan, and was the idea of a man called Shinichi Suzuki (1898–1998), a violin teacher from
15 Nagoya. His belief was that all children can play musical instruments well. He also believed that children can learn to play a musical instrument in the same way that they learn to speak a language.

20 **C** As babies, we learn a new word when we hear it hundreds of times. With the Suzuki method, children learn a new piece of music through listening.
25 Constant repetition of the music helps them learn.

D We learn to talk first, and then to read. In the same way, the Suzuki method teaches children to play their
30 instrument, and then to read music.

E We learn from our parents and teachers, and from other children, too. For this reason, children have individual music lessons, but also learn in groups with
35 other children. In groups, children can motivate and encourage each other.

F Shinichi Suzuki also believed it is better when children learn their instrument from a very young age. Therefore with
40 the Suzuki method, there are a lot of music students as young as three or four.

G Some people don't like the Suzuki method. They think it creates robots,
45 not musicians because the children are only repeating what they hear. Others believe it can only work with ambitious parents who make their children work very hard.

50 **H** There are different opinions, but it is difficult not to admire these children. For this reason the Suzuki method is now popular all over the world.

Check it out!

Find these words and check their meaning.

enormous adj line 5
encourage v line 36

1 Read the article. Where is the Suzuki method from?

2 Read the article again. Write the letter of the paragraph.

Which paragraph mentions the students' age? Paragraph <u>F</u>

1 Which paragraph says that students don't always study alone? Paragraph ___
2 Which paragraph says that children learn music when they hear it again and again? ___
3 Which paragraph says that children from many different countries learn with the Suzuki method? ___

3 Complete the sentences.

Shinichi Suzuki was <u>a violin teacher</u>.

1 Children learn to play instruments in the same way as they learn _____.
2 Suzuki students _____ music many times to learn it.
3 First they learn to play, and then they learn to _____.
4 Children learn to play well in _____ of other children.
5 It's normal for Suzuki students to start music lessons when _____.
6 Some people think the _____ only works for children with ambitious parents.

4 Which pictures give false information? Correct the information.

<u>a</u> is false. _____.
___ is false. _____.
___ is false. _____.

Shinichi Suzuki
1898–1998

Mama

Suzuki School

Project

What is your favorite instrument? Write an article about it. Include the following information:

- A piece of music where you can hear the instrument.
- A famous musician who plays the instrument.
- Is it easy or difficult to learn?
- Are you learning it? Do you want to learn it?

Why We Have Seasons

1 When you look at Planet Earth's journey around the sun, you can see that our planet isn't straight. It's tilted, at 23.5 degrees. Scientists
5 aren't completely sure why it is like this. But some believe that about 4.5 billion years ago, a collision with an enormous object, like an asteroid, pushed Earth into a new position. As
10 a result our planet was tilted, and the collision created our seasons, too.

The Earth's journey around the sun takes one year. For six months of the year, the North Pole tilts towards the sun. Therefore,
15 the top part of our planet, or northern hemisphere, experiences summer time. At the same time, the South Pole tilts away from the sun, and the southern hemisphere is in winter time. For the other six months
20 of the year, the South Pole tilts towards the sun, the North Pole tilts away, and the seasons reverse. So, maybe it's snowing on Christmas Day in Canada, but in Uruguay people are celebrating in hot, sunny weather!

summer   fall

25 The middle of Planet Earth, the equator, is always near the sun and countries in this region, such as Brazil, Colombia, and Northern Australia have tropical weather. Temperatures there are usually warm, above eighteen degrees, and
30 there are no seasons. But it gets very rainy, too. That's why the equator has a lot of rainforests. Constant, hot, wet weather is a perfect place for them.

Nevertheless, seasons are very important for
35 animal and plant life. Imagine our planet without its tilt, and without the seasons. In this situation, near the North and South Poles it's always dark and freezing, so plants and animals in those regions can't survive. Most plants and animals
40 live near the equator because it's warm and sunny there, but this is bad for essential plants like wheat, corn, and potatoes. These plants also need cold winter weather to grow well. The result is that we have great weather, but
45 we don't have sufficient food. How can we live on our planet like this?

The collision 4.5 billion years ago created the seasons, with their temperature variations and beautiful changes of color. But most importantly,
50 it created enormous possibilities for life on our planet.

winter   spring

k it out!

ese words and
their meaning.

	adj	line 3
	adj	line 4
	adj	line 28
st	n	line 31
eless	adv	line 34
	n	line 42
	n	line 42

1 Read the article. Then label the parts of Planet Earth.

1 _____

2 _____

3 _____

4 _____

5 _____

6 _____

2 Read the article again. Correct the mistakes in sentences below.

Some scientists believe that ~~the seasons~~ caused the Earth's tilt.

Some scientists believe that a collision caused the Earth's tilt.

1 Our planet needs six months to travel around the sun.

_____

2 When the South Pole points away from the sun, it's summer in the southern hemisphere.

_____

3 The equator always has cold weather.

_____

4 Rainforests need hot, dry weather.

_____

5 Essential plants like wheat grow better when it's always warm.

_____

3 Answer the questions.

When do some scientists think the collision happened?

They think it happened about 4.5 billion years ago.

1 During the Earth's journey around the sun, how long does the North Pole tilt towards the sun?

_____

2 When it's spring in Uruguay, what season is it in Canada?

_____

3 Why are there no seasons on the equator?

_____

4 In a world with no seasons, what is it like in northern and southern countries?

_____

5 In a world with no seasons, what happens to plants and animals on our planet?

_____

Project

What is your favorite season? Write an article about it. Include the following information:

- When the season occurs.
- Festivals and celebrations during the season.
- The temperature – do you like it?
- The activities you can do at that time of year.
- The different things you can see at that time of year.

A HISTORY OF AIR TRAVEL

1485

1 In about 1485, Leonardo da Vinci began studying birds and how they fly. He drew a series of detailed pictures of flying machines. One, called the *ornithopter*, copied the movement of birds' wings.

1903

5 On December 17th 1903, Orville Wright flew 36 meters in an airplane. It was probably the first flight in a flying machine to stay in the air under the control of a pilot, and lasted twelve seconds!

1914

At the beginning of the First World War (1914–1918),
10 airplanes were very simple. Pilots only used them to follow the movements of enemy soldiers. But at the end of the war, they were pretty sophisticated and pilots used them to fight the enemy.

1937

Amelia Earhart was the first woman to fly alone across
15 the Atlantic Ocean. In 1937, she tried to fly around the world. Sadly, on July 2nd, her airplane disappeared over the Pacific Ocean. Today, we still don't know the location of Amelia's airplane, or her body.

1957

In 1957, the Russians completed the first successful
20 flights into space. In the same year, a dog called Laika became the first animal in space. The first astronaut traveled into space in 1961.

1976

In 1976, Concorde airplanes became the world's first supersonic commercial airplanes to carry passengers.
25 But the Concorde planes were very expensive because they used a lot of fuel. The last Concorde flight was in 2003.

2005

In 2005, the world's largest passenger airplane appeared in the skies. The Airbus A380 can fly over
30 15,000 km without stopping, and can carry 555 passengers! People ask why an enormous airplane is a good idea. Its designers say it only uses a little fuel for its size, and doesn't make much noise.

2014

In January 2014, the Virgin Galactic SpaceShipTwo
35 completed its third test flight and reached more than 21 km above the Earth. It prepared to carry a group of tourists above the Earth's atmosphere for a two-and-a-half-hour journey. But this trip is very expensive – tickets cost about $250,000!

Check it out!

Find these words and check their meaning.

wing	n	line 4
flight	n	line 6
alone	adv	line 14
passenger	n	line 24
largest	adj	line 28

40 This timeline shows the enormous changes in air travel in 100 years. And it is still changing very fast! Where are we going next? The future is very exciting!

1 Read the timeline. Which forms of air travel are for tourists?

_____

2 Read the timeline. Write the correct year next to each picture.

<u>1957</u>

1 _____

2 _____

3 _____

4 _____

3 Complete the sentences with the simple past form of the verbs in the box.

be   cost   ~~do~~   keep   know   pay   think

Leonardo da Vinci _did___ a lot of drawings of birds.

1 Orville Wright _____ his airplane in the air for twelve seconds.

2 When Amelia Earhart disappeared, nobody _____ exactly where she was.

3 Laika _____ the first animal to travel into space.

4 The Concorde airplane _____ a lot of money to maintain.

5 Some people _____ that the Airbus A380 was too big.

6 Reports say that tourists _____ a lot of money to be the first tourists in space.

4 Answer the questions.

Did Leonardo da Vinci design, or build his flying machines?

_He designed them._____

1 What was the distance of Orville Wright's first controlled flight?

_____

2 When did Amelia Earhart disappear?

_____

3 Which animal did the Russians send into space?

_____

4 How fast was Concorde?

_____

5 What distance can the Airbus A380 stay in the air for?

_____

6 How far above the Earth did the Virgin Galactic SpaceShipTwo go in January 2014?

_____

Project

Think about a recent flight on a plane, or imagine one. Write a story about it. Include the following information:

- Where was the flight to?
- How long was it?
- How did it feel when you took off?
- Was the flight comfortable?

- What were the views from the plane like?
- What was the weather like during the flight?
- Did you enjoy it?

The Rules of Behavior in **Different Countries**

1 Every country is proud of its rules of polite and acceptable behavior. However, they are different in each country. In the U.S., for example, there are some forms of behavior that Americans think are polite. But in South
5 Korea, these forms are rude and can make local people embarrassed. And there are South Korean customs that are difficult for Americans to understand!

BODY LANGUAGE

Some countries are more relaxed in their body language than others.
10 In South American countries in general, people stand closer to each other than in English-speaking countries. Some parts of the body can offend people, too. In Asia,
15 people think the feet are the dirtiest part of the body, so showing the soles of your feet can make people very angry. There are different rules about blowing your nose: never
20 blow it in Japan, where people think it's absolutely disgusting!

TABLE MANNERS

When you are visiting another country, it is important to try to eat in the same way as local people. In some parts of India and Africa, people eat whole meals with their hand. In
25 the U.S., it's normal to eat some things (but not everything!) with your hands, and across the ocean in the U.K. the same is true. In South Korea, it is polite to eat all the food on your plate at a dinner party. But in China, an empty plate indicates that your host didn't give you sufficient food!

GREETINGS

30 First impressions are important wherever you go, so it's important to greet a new person in the correct way. In the U.S., people generally
35 appear more relaxed and confident than in other countries, and it's normal to tell a new person your name. However, in Korea, people
40 always wait until another person does this for them. In many parts of Europe, people offer their hand to greet someone for the first time, but
45 in Asian countries, people bow.

A GENERAL RULE

For people who are traveling to another country, it's a good idea to learn a few of the local rules of behavior. But most people
50 understand when a visitor makes a cultural mistake. And there is always one thing people can do which helps in all situations: smile!

Check it out!

Find these words and check their meaning.

behavior	n	line 4
polite	adj	line 4
rude	adj	line 5
sole	n	line 16
blow	v	line 19
disgusting	adj	line 21

1 **Read the article quickly. Check the correct answer.**

The article tells you …

A how to behave politely in other countries. ☐

B what to wear in other countries. ☐

C what time to eat in other countries. ☐

2 **Read the article again. Write the correct country or continent.**

Don't do this in …

1 _____   2 _____   3 _____

3 **Answer the questions.**

Why is it difficult to learn the correct behavior in different countries?

The rules are different in every country.

1 Why do people in Asia think it's rude to show the soles of your feet?

_____

2 How do many people in some parts of India and Africa eat their meals?

_____

3 Where is it polite to finish your meal?

_____

4 What is the normal way to greet a person in many parts of Europe?

_____

5 How do people in Asia usually greet each other?

_____

Project

Think about polite behavior in your country. Write a magazine article for visitors to your country. Include the following information:

- How close people stand to each other.
- Parts of the body you don't show.
- Nose blowing!
- Polite eating habits.

- How people greet each other?
- What snacks do they eat?
- How often do they eat snacks?

Got it! Puzzles 1-2

1A Break the code and write the musical genres and instruments.

4	5	6	7	8	9	10	11	12	13	14	15	16
A	B	C	D	E	F	G	H	I	J	K	L	M
17	18	19	20	21	22	23	24	25	26	1	2	3
N	O	P	Q	R	S	T	U	V	W	X	Y	Z

22 4 1 18 19 11 18 17 8 _saxophone_ ____

1 6 15 4 22 22 12 6 4 15 _____

2 21 8 6 18 21 7 8 21 _____

3 11 12 19 - 11 18 19 _____

4 9 15 24 23 8 _____

5 25 12 18 15 12 17 _____

1B Draw lines to connect the words and make sentences.

——— ✔ | ✔ ＼ ✘ ／ ✘

He	listen	saxophone	2. I	is	late	are	a
is	play	sing	am	singing	she	5. He	is
playing	the	flute	singer	a	heavy metal song	terrible	a
1. She	happy	plays	3. You	playing	noisily	guitarist	terribly
is	listening	bad	play	good	my	not	mine
listen	to	reggae	the drums	4. This	yours	is	trumpet
badly	singer	slow	well	hip-hop CD	is	yours	6. That

2A Complete the sentences. Use the letters in the gray boxes to complete the mystery sentence.

Kelly's birthday was last [m][o][n][t][h].

1 Her party was a week [ ][ ][ ].

2 She was at the movies [ ][ ][ ][ ][ ][ ][ ][ ] evening.

3 She [ ][ ][ ][ ]'[ ] happy about the extra math homework last week.

4 [ ][ ][ ][ ][ ] was she this morning?

Mystery sentence: Kelly was ____

2B Copy the words with the same color. Reorder the words to make sentences.

very	your	isn't	like?	is
very	my	does	friendly	teacher
brother	like?	student	new	what
she	strict	what's	look	the

____

____

____

3A Find five more weather words. Then complete the sentences.

C	S	D	W	G	V	I	W	X	E
L	D	Y	I	S	I	N	D	A	H
O	U	L	G	G	H	S	Y	K	S
D	W	F	O	Y	G	W	F	W	D
I	N	F	I	D	I	N	A	S	U
A	I	H	S	S	W	G	E	N	N
R	N	G	E	N	O	W	I	Y	G

The sun disappears when it's _cloudy_____.

1 It's difficult to see things in front of you when it's _____.

2 My hair is wet because it's _____.

3 We spent a beautiful hot and _____ day on the beach.

4 Yesterday was very _____ and my newspaper blew away!

5 It's cold and it's _____ – a typical winter's day.

3B Use some of the letters in each group to make the missing irregular verbs in the simple past. Use the extra letters to make a secret message.

1 Yesterday, I _____ a new dress.
   H B A T O M U A G N

2 I _____ my new sneakers under the bed.
   F N S O T U O D

3 Toby _____ all the answers to the questions.
   L E E N W M Y K

4 Anna _____ an SMS message to her friend.
   B N I K E S E T

Secret message: _____

4A Read the sentences. Write the correct movie types in the puzzle. What's the mystery movie type?

The two men drove their cars very fast in the _action_____ movie.

1 The singers in the _____ were awesome.

2 I find all _____ movies very scary!

3 A _____ movie shows things that can't happen in real life.

4 The _____ made us laugh.

5 Boy meets girl in the _____ story of the year!

6 My brother watches a lot of science _____ movies.

(crossword grid: A C T I O N across the top, clues numbered 1–6)

The mystery movie type is _____.

4B Complete the negative form of the sentences. Use the letters in the gray boxes to find out what kind of movie Carla and Jorge saw.

They met outside the movie theater.
They didn't [m][e][e][t] outside the movie theater.

1 The tickets cost $18.
   The tickets didn't [ ][ ][ ][ ][ ] $18.

2 Jorge forgot to bring his money.
   Jorge didn't [ ][ ][ ][ ][ ][ ][ ] to bring his money.

3 They saw the horror movie.
   They didn't [ ][ ][ ] the horror movie.

4 Carla enjoyed the movie.
   Carla didn't [ ][ ][ ][ ][ ][ ] the movie.

5 Jorge ate all the popcorn.
   Jorge didn't [ ][ ][ ] all the popcorn.

6 Carla drank all the cola.
   Carla didn't [ ][ ][ ][ ][ ][ ] all the cola.

Type of movie: _____

Got it! Puzzles 5-6

5A

Reorder the letters to make food and drink words. Write them next to the correct pictures.

~~draeb~~

ootamt

ncikhec

cei macre

trwae   rgneoa jcuei

gegs

bread

 1 _____

 2 _____

 3 _____

 4 _____

 5 _____

 6 _____

5B

Complete the sentences. Write the missing words in the crossword.

Down

We have _a lot of_____ milk — ten litres of it.

1 I need _____ eggs.

2 How _____ apples do you need?

5 Is there _____ milk?

Across

3 I don't eat _____ candy.

4 I eat _____ chocolate every day: not much.

5 There aren't many tomatoes — only _____.

Crossword: A L O T O F

6A

Match the letters to make different forms of transportation.

hel	ai	ic	ain	to	ay
cle	tr	ck	opt	bw	rpl
tru	su	er	mo	ane	rcy

helicopter

1 _____

2 _____

3 _____

4 _____

5 _____

6B

The verbs are in the wrong sentences. Write the correct verbs.

I'm ~~going~~ a mountain tomorrow. _climbing_____

1 We're starting a movie tonight. _____

2 They're meeting on vacation in August. _____

3 She's climbing a birthday party next weekend.

_____

4 I'm having college soon. _____

5 He's watching his friends in a café this evening.

_____

Got it! Puzzles 7-8

7A Break the code and write the geography words.

D	E	F	G	H	I	J	K	L	M	N	O	P
a	b	c	d	e	f	g	h	i	j	k	l	m

Q	R	S	T	U	V	W	X	Y	Z	A	B	C
n	o	p	q	r	s	t	u	v	w	x	y	z

LVODQG   _island_

1 YROFDQR   _____

2 RFHDQ   _____

3 GHVHUW   _____

4 FRQWLQHQW   _____

5 ODNH   _____

6 PRXQWDLQ   _____

7 FRXQWUB   _____

8 ULYHU   _____

7B Use some of the letters in each group to make the missing comparative adjectives. Use the extra letters to make a secret sentence.

The Pacific Ocean is _deeper_ than the Atlantic.
ADENEEPELRE

1 Mount Everest is _____ than Mount K2.
PHHIGAHNETR

2 Australia is _____ than Japan.
BIISGHGEER

3 Venezuela is _____ than the U.K.
AHVOITETERR

4 The Arctic Ocean is _____ than the Mediterranean Sea.
TCOHLDAERN

5 The Mississippi River is _____ than the Ganges.
ALOCNAGETR

Secret sentence: _____

8A Find seven more feelings and emotions. Match them to the correct faces.

E	S	C	I	T	O	H	A	P	P	Y
M	V	F	R	C	S	G	Y	F	S	C
B	F	R	I	G	H	T	E	N	E	D
A	R	W	P	V	F	F	T	P	R	E
R	H	G	A	W	N	E	F	Z	S	X
R	C	O	N	F	I	D	E	N	T	C
A	W	C	G	N	V	U	S	P	M	I
S	Y	P	R	S	W	P	N	H	V	T
S	M	Z	Y	Y	Y	K	Y	G	M	E
E	Y	V	N	E	R	V	O	U	S	D
D	S	N	W	R	S	A	D	M	R	H

embarrassed   1 _____   2 _____   3 _____

4 _____   5 _____   6 _____   7 _____

8B Look at the code. Complete the words in the questions. Answer the questions.

a = @   e = *   i = $ o = %   u = !

Wh@t w@s th* b*st d@y %f y%!r l$f*?

What was the best day of your life?

1 Wh% $s th* m%st $mp%rt@nt p*rs%n $n y%!r l$f*?

2 Wh@t $s y%!r w%rst sch%%l s!bj*ct?

3 Wh% $s th* m%st f@m%!s p*rs%n y%! kn%w?

4 Wh@t $s th* m%st $nt*r*st$ng th$ng $n y%!r sch%%l b@g?

5 Wh% $s th* t@ll*st p*rs%n $n y%!r f@m$ly?

6 Wh@t w@s y%!r sc@r$*st j%!rn*y?

Unit 1

Musical genres
classical /'klæsɪkl/
heavy metal /hɛvi 'mɛtl/
hip-hop /'hɪp hɑp/
pop /pɑp/
reggae /'rɛgeɪ/
rock /rɑk/

Musical instruments
drums /drʌmz/
flute /flut/
guitar /gɪ'tɑr/
piano /pi'ænoʊ/
recorder /rɪ'kɔrdər/
saxophone /'sæksəfoʊn/
trumpet /'trʌmpət/
violin /vaɪə'lɪn/

Other nouns
atmosphere /'ætməsfɪr/
attraction /ə'trækʃn/
bass /beɪs/
beach volleyball /bitʃ 'vɑlibɔl/
concert /'kɑnsərt/
dictionary /'dɪkʃənɛri/
eraser /ɪ'reɪsər/
fan /fæn/
festival /'fɛstəvl/
free /fri/
girlfriend /'gərlfrɛnd/
key /ki/
living room /'lɪvɪŋ rum/
musician /myu'zɪʃn/
singer /'sɪŋər/
stage /steɪdʒ/
test /tɛst/
zone /zoʊn/

Verbs
borrow /'bɑroʊ/
copy /'kɑpi/
ring /rɪŋ/

Other adjectives
busy /'bɪzi/
impossible /ɪm'pɑsəbl/
serious /'sɪriəs/

Adverbs
badly /'bædli/
beautifully /'byuţəfli/
early /'ərli/
fast /fæst/
happily /'hæpəli/
impossibly /ɪm'pɑsəbli/
neatly /'nitli/
late /leɪt/
terribly /'tɛrəbli/
well /wɛl/

Unit 2

Physical descriptions
average height /ævrɪdʒ 'haɪt/
average weight /ævrɪdʒ 'weɪt/
beard /bɪrd/
blue /blu/
braces /'breɪsɪz/
eyes /aɪz/
freckles /'frɛklz/

glasses /'glæsɪz/
green /grin/
height /haɪt/
middle-aged /mɪdl'eɪdʒəd/
mustache /'mʌstæʃ/
old /oʊld/
overweight /oʊvər'weɪt/
short /ʃɔrt/
slim /slɪm/
tall /tɔl/
weight /weɪt/
young /yʌŋ/

Hair
bald /bɔld/
black /blæk/
blond /blɑnd/
brown /braʊn/
curly /'kərli/
gray /greɪ/
long /lɔŋ/
red /rɛd/
short /ʃɔrt/
shoulder-length /'ʃoʊldər lɛŋkθ/
straight /streɪt/
wavy /'weɪvi/

Other nouns
actress /'æktrəs/
character /'kærəktər/
desk /dɛsk/
guy /gaɪ/
keyboard /'kibɔrd/
leader /'lidər/
nickname /'nɪkneɪm/
painting /'peɪntɪŋ/
poem /'poʊəm/
president /'prɛzədənt/
rule /rul/
series /'sɪriz/
songwriter /'sɔŋraɪţər/
star /stɑr/
writer /'raɪţər/

Verbs
assassinate /ə'sæsəneɪt/

Other adjectives
cool /kul/
crazy /'kreɪzi/
friendly /'frɛndli/
imaginary /ɪ'mædʒənɛri/
nice /naɪs/
popular /'pɑpyələr/
strict /strɪkt/
strong /strɔŋ/
tough /tʌf/
typical /'tɪpɪkl/

Review A

Nouns
magazine /'mægəzin/
member /'mɛmbər/
ticket /'tɪkət/

Adjectives
common /'kɑmən/
good-looking /gʊd'lʊkɪŋ/
priceless /'praɪsləs/

Culture club A

Nouns
action /'ækʃn/
boycott /'bɔɪkɑt/
decision /dɪ'sɪʒn/
incident /'ɪnsədənt/
law /lɔ/
right /raɪt/
seat /sit/
solution /sə'luʃn/
support /sə'pɔrt/

Verbs
imagine /ɪ'mædʒən/

Adjectives
angry /'æŋgri/
clear /klɪr/
equal /'ikwəl/
ordinary /'ɔrdnɛri/
typical /'tɪpɪkl/

Unit 3

The weather
cloudy /'klaʊdi/
cold /koʊld/
cool /kul/
foggy /'fɔgi/
freezing /'frizɪŋ/
hot /hɑt/
mild /maɪld/
museum /myu'ziəm/
raining /'reɪnɪŋ/
snowing /'snoʊɪŋ/
sunny /'sʌni/
warm /wɔrm/
windy /'wɪndi/

Nouns
album /'ælbəm/
Antarctica /æn'tɑrkţɪkə/
base camp /'beɪs kæmp/
beach /bitʃ/
courage /'kərɪdʒ/
determination /dɪtərmə'neɪʃn/
discovery /dɪ'skʌvəri/
expedition /ɛkspə'dɪʃn/
explorer /ɪk'splɔrər/
flag /flæg/
geology /dʒi'ɑlədʒi/
ice /aɪs/
jazz /dʒæz/
peninsula /pə'nɪnsələ/
picnic /'pɪknɪk/
race /reɪs/
satellite TV /sæţlaɪt ti 'vi/
talent show /'tælənt ʃoʊ/
tour /tʊr/
winner /'wɪnər/
youth center /'yuθ sɛntər/

Verbs
admire /əd'maɪər/
build /bɪld/
reach /ritʃ/

Other adjectives

delicious /dɪˈlɪʃəs/
disgusting /dɪsˈgʌstɪŋ/
extreme /ɪkˈstrim/
miserable /ˈmɪzərəbl/

Adverbs

tragically /ˈtrædʒɪkli/

Unit 4

Movies

action movie /ˈækʃn muvi/
cartoon /kɑrˈtun/
comedy /ˈkɑmədi/
fantasy movie /ˈfæntəsi muvi/
horror movie /ˈhɔrər muvi /
love story /ˈlʌv stɔri/
musical /ˈmyuzɪkl/
science fiction movie /saɪəns ˈfɪkʃn muvi/

Other nouns

actress /ˈæktrəs/
career /kəˈrɪr/
choose /tʃuz/
ending /ˈɛndɪŋ/
guitarist /gɪˈtɑrɪst/
loser /ˈluzər/
part /pɑrt/
queen /kwin/
relationship /rɪˈleɪʃnʃɪp/
swimming pool /ˈswɪmɪŋ pul/

Verbs

audition /ɔˈdɪʃn/
graduate /ˈgrædʒueɪt/

Adverbs

actually /ˈæktʃuəli/
eventually /ɪˈvɛntʃuəli/

Review B

Nouns

backpack /ˈbækpæk/
horoscope /ˈhɔrəskoup/
kid /kɪd/
pair /pɛr/

Verbs

relax /rɪˈlæks/

Culture club B

Nouns

bestseller /bɛstˈsɛlər/
bookstore /ˈbʊkstɔr/
director /dəˈrɛktər/
fan /fæn/
location /louˈkeɪʃn/
publisher /ˈpʌblɪʃər/
ride /raɪd/
special effects /spɛʃl ɪˈfɛkts/
spell /spɛl/
studio /ˈstudiou/
witch /wɪtʃ/
wizard /ˈwɪzərd/

Verbs

inspire /ɪnˈspaɪər/

Adjectives

interactive /ɪntərˈæktɪv/
perfect /ˈpərfɪkt/

Adverbs

immediately /ɪˈmidiətli/

Unit 5

Food and drink

apple /ˈæpl/
banana /bəˈnænə/
candy /ˈkændi/
carrots /ˈkærəts/
cereal /ˈsɪriəl/
cheese /tʃiz/
chicken /ˈtʃɪkən/
chocolate /ˈtʃɑklət/
cookies /ˈkʊkiz/
egg /ɛg/
ham /hæm/
ice cream /ˈaɪs krim/
milk /mɪlk/
orange juice /ˈɑrɪndʒ dʒus/
peas /piz/
potato chips /pəˈteɪt̮ou tʃɪps/
potatoes /pəˈteɪt̮ouz/
soda /ˈsoudə/
tea /ti/
toast /toust/
tomato /təˈmeɪt̮ou/
water /ˈwɔt̮ər/
yogurt /ˈyougərt/

Other nouns

baked potato /beɪkt pəˈteɪt̮ə/
beef /bif/
butter /ˈbʌt̮ər/
change /tʃeɪndʒ/
coffee /ˈkɑfi/
company /ˈkʌmpəni/
farm /fɑrm/
fat /fæt/
fresh /frɛʃ/
full /fʊl/
job /dʒɑb/
ketchup /ˈkɛtʃəp/
lemon /ˈlɛmən/
liter /ˈlit̮ər/
lunchbox /ˈlʌntʃbɑks/
meat /mit/
mushroom /ˈmʌʃrum/
mustard /ˈmʌstərd/
oil /ɔɪl/
onion /ˈʌnyən/
pork /pɔrk/
portion /ˈpɔrʃn/
recipe /ˈrɛsəpi/
rice /raɪs/
salt /sɔlt/
sandwich /ˈsænwɪtʃ/
sparkling /ˈspɑrklɪŋ/
strawberry /ˈstrɔbɛri/
still /stɪl/
sugar /ˈʃʊgər/
tuna /ˈtunə/
vegetable /ˈvɛdʒtəbl/
vending machine /ˈvɛndɪŋ məʃin/

Adverbs

surprisingly /sərˈpraɪzɪŋli/

Unit 6

Transportation

airplane /ˈɛrpleɪn/
bicycle /ˈbaɪsɪkl/
bike /baɪk/
boat /bout/
bus /bʌs/
car /kɑr/
helicopter /ˈhɛləkɑptər/
motorcycle /ˈmout̮ərsaɪkl/
subway /ˈsʌbweɪ/
taxi /ˈtæksi/
train /treɪn/
truck /trʌk/

Other nouns

bus stop /ˈbʌs stɑp/
competition /kɑmpəˈtɪʃn/
coast /koust/
decision /dɪˈsɪʒn/
expert /ˈɛkspərt/
extract /ˈɛkstrækt/
gym /dʒɪm/
invitation /ɪnvəˈteɪʃn/
judge /dʒʌdʒ/
part /pɑrt/
poverty /ˈpɑvərt̮i/
ride /raɪd/
shopping mall /ˈʃɑpɪŋ mɔl/
zoo /zu/

Verbs

babysit /ˈbeɪbisɪt/
bring /brɪŋ/
help /hɛlp/
refuse /rɪˈfyuz/
worry /ˈwəri/

Adjectives

comfortable /ˈkʌmftərbl/

Adverbs

rarely /ˈrɛrli/

Review C

Nouns

audition /ɔˈdɪʃn/
sky /skaɪ/
wheel /wil/

Culture club C

Nouns

contestant /kənˈtɛstənt/
dessert /dɪˈzərt/
dish /dɪʃ/
episode /ˈɛpəsoud/
judge /dʒʌdʒ/
level /ˈlɛvl/
praise /preɪz/
result /rɪˈzʌlt/
seafood /ˈsifud/
series /ˈsɪriz/
snack store /ˈsnæk stɔr/

Verbs

attract /əˈtrækt/
invent /ɪnˈvɛnt/

Adjectives

complicated /ˈkɑmpləkeɪt̮əd/

Word list

Unit 7

Geography
continent /ˈkɑntənənt/
country /ˈkʌntri/
desert /ˈdɛzərt/
island /ˈaɪlənd/
lake /leɪk/
mountain /ˈmaʊntn/
ocean /ˈoʊʃn/
river /ˈrɪvər/
sea /si/
volcano /vɑlˈkeɪnoʊ/

Other nouns
appearance /əˈpɪrəns/
crust /krʌst/
eruption /ɪˈrʌpʃn/
highlands /ˈhaɪləndz/
Iceland /ˈaɪslənd/
mantle /ˈmæntl/
Patagonia /pæt̬əˈgoʊniə/
personality /pərsəˈnæləti/
pressure /ˈprɛʃər/

Verbs
cause /kɔz/
erupt /ɪˈrʌpt/
expand /ɪkˈspænd/
increase /ɪnˈkris/
melt /mɛlt/
shrink /ʃrɪŋk/
spend /spɛnd/

Adjectives
complicated /ˈkɑmpləkeɪt̬əd/
strong /strɔŋ/
volcanic /vɑlˈkænɪk/

Adverbs
direct /dəˈrɛkt/

Unit 8

Feelings and emotions
angry /ˈæŋgri/
annoyed /əˈnɔɪd/
bored /bɔrd/
confident /ˈkɑnfədənt/
embarrassed /ɪmˈbærəst/
excited /ɪkˈsaɪt̬əd/
fed up /fɛdˈʌp/
frightened /ˈfraɪtnd/
happy /ˈhæpi/
nervous /ˈnərvəs/
proud /praʊd/
sad /sæd/

Nouns
culture /ˈkʌltʃər/
date /deɪt/
dolphin /ˈdɑlfən/
elevator /ˈɛləveɪt̬ər/
idiot /ˈɪdiət/
inhabitant /ɪnˈhæbət̬ənt/
joke /dʒoʊk/
kangaroo /kæŋgəˈru/
lifestyle /ˈlaɪfstaɪl/
message /ˈmɛsɪdʒ/
millimeter /ˈmɪləmit̬ər/
moment /ˈmoʊmənt/

Verbs
miss /mɪs/
weigh /weɪ/

Adjectives
attractive /əˈtræktɪv/
crazy /ˈkreɪzi/
old-fashioned /oʊld ˈfæʃnd/

Review D

Nouns
audition /ɔˈdɪʃn/
hospital /ˈhɑspɪtl/
noise /nɔɪz/
whale /weɪl/

Culture club D

Nouns
expression /ɪkˈsprɛʃn/
gurning /ˈgərnɪŋ/
natural world /ˈnætʃrəl wərld/
olive oil /ˈɑlɪv ɔɪl/
record holder /ˈrɛkərd hoʊldər/

Verbs
demonstrate /ˈdɛmənstreɪt/

Adjectives
best-selling /bestˈsɛlɪŋ/
current /ˈkərənt/
rich /rɪtʃ/
strange /streɪndʒ/

Adverbs
definitely /ˈdɛfənətli/

Curriculum extra A

Nouns
body /ˈbɑdi/
expert /ˈɛkspərt/
finger /ˈfɪŋgər/
repetition /rɛpəˈtɪʃn/
video clip /ˈvɪdioʊ klɪp/

Verbs
encourage /ɪnˈkərɪdʒ/
motivate /ˈmoʊt̬əveɪt/

Adjectives
constant /ˈkɑnstənt/
enormous /ɪˈnɔrməs/

Adverbs
rapidly /ˈræpədli/

Curriculum extra B

Nouns
asteroid /ˈæstərɔɪd/
collision /kəˈlɪʒn/
corn /kɔrn/
rainforest /ˈreɪnfɑrəst/
variation /vɛriˈeɪʃn/
wheat /wit/

Verbs
reverse /rɪˈvərs/

Adjectives
enormous /ɪˈnɔrməs/
straight /streɪt/
tilted /ˈtɪltəd/
tropical /ˈtrɑpɪkl/

Adverbs
nevertheless /nɛvərðəˈlɛs/

Curriculum extra C

Nouns
astronaut /ˈæstrənɔt/
enemy /ˈɛnəmi/
fuel /ˈfyuəl/
movement /ˈmuvmənt/
passenger /ˈpæsəndʒər/
pilot /ˈpaɪlət/
soldier /ˈsoʊldʒər/
space /speɪs/
wing /wɪŋ/

Adjectives
sophisticated /səˈfɪstəkeɪt̬əd/

Curriculum extra D

Nouns
host /hoʊst/
plate /pleɪt/
sole /soʊl/
sufficient /səˈfɪʃnt/

Verbs
blow /bloʊ/
bow /baʊ/

Adjectives
acceptable /əkˈsɛptəbl/
behavior /bɪˈheɪvyər/
customs /ˈkʌstəmz/

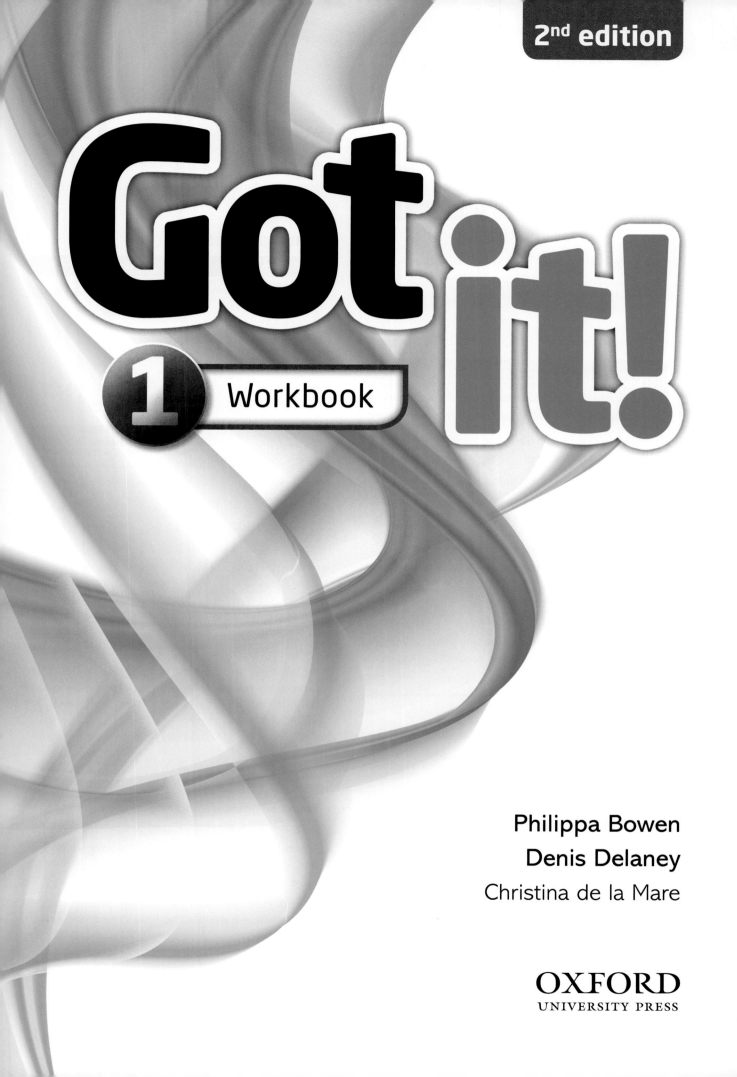

2ND edition

Got it!

1 Workbook

Philippa Bowen
Denis Delaney
Christina de la Mare

OXFORD
UNIVERSITY PRESS

1 Grammar rules

Simple present / Present progressive

Simple present

Affirmative	Negative
I play	I do not (don't) play
you play	you do not (don't) play
he / she / it plays	he / she / it does not (doesn't) play
we / you / they play	we / you / they do not (don't) play

Questions	Short answers	
	Affirmative	Negative
Do I play?	Yes, you do.	No, you don't.
Do you play?	Yes, I do.	No, I don't.
Does he / she / it play?	Yes, he / she / it does.	No, he / she / it doesn't.
Do we / you / they play?	Yes, we / you / they do.	No, we / you / they don't.

1 We use the simple present to talk about:
   habits and daily routines.
   – I **get up** at half past seven.
   permanent situations.
   – They **live** in Milford, and they **work** in Tysoe.

2 We often use the simple present with adverbs of frequency to say how often something happens.

100%   0%

always   usually   often   sometimes   rarely   never

I **usually** do my homework in the afternoon.

Other expressions of frequency are:
every day / week   twice a day / week
once a day / week   three times a day / week

Spelling variations

1 We make the third person singular with the base form of the verb + -s.
   like + **-s**   likes

2 We use the base form of the verb + -es when the verb ends in -ch, -s, -sh, -x, -z, or -o.
   he teach**es**   she go**es**   it wash**es**

3 When the verb ends in a consonant + -y, we change the -y to -i and add -es.
   she stud**ies**   he fl**ies**

4 When the verb ends in a vowel + -y, we add -s.
   he play**s**

Present progressive

Affirmative	Negative
I am ('m) playing	I am not ('m not) playing
you are ('re) playing	you are not (aren't) playing
he / she / it is ('s) playing	he / she / it is not (isn't) playing
we / you / they are ('re) playing	we / you / they are not (aren't) playing

Questions	Short answers	
	Affirmative	Negative
Am I playing?	Yes, you are.	No, you aren't.
Are you playing?	Yes, I am.	No, I'm not.
Is he / she / it playing?	Yes, he / she / it is.	No, he / she / it isn't.
Are we / you / they playing?	Yes, we / you / they are.	No, we / you / they aren't.

1 We use the present progressive to talk about something that is happening now.
   Marisol **is talking** to her mom at the moment.

2 We also use the present progressive to describe temporary events that are happening during a definite period, for example, today, this week, this month, etc.
   Yuki's concert is in June, so he**'s practicing** a lot this month.

Spelling variations

1 For most verbs, we add -ing to the base form.
   play + -ing = playing   walk + -ing = walking

2 When the verb ends in -e, we drop the -e and add -ing.
   have ➤ having

3 For short verbs ending in a vowel plus a consonant, we double the final consonant and add -ing.
   sit ➤ sitting

4 *Travel* is irregular.
   travel ➤ traveling

Possessive pronouns

Possessive adjectives	Possessive pronouns
my	mine
your	yours
his / her / its	his / hers / –
our	ours
your	yours
their	theirs

1 Possessive adjectives come before a noun.
my iPad   **your** cell phone

2 Possessive pronouns substitute a possessive adjective and a noun.
It's **my** violin. = It's **mine**.

3 We often use possessive pronouns to avoid repeating.
This is **my book**. That's **yours**.

Adverbs of manner
Regular adverbs

Adjective		Adverb
quick	+ -ly	quickly
quiet		quietly
beautiful		beautifully
easy	-y to -i + -ly	easily
fantastic	+ -ally	fantastically

1 We use adverbs of manner to talk about how we do something. They change what the verb means.
Pablo plays guitar **beautifully**.

2 Adverbs of manner always come after a verb or after an object.
subject + verb + (object) + adverb of manner
Maria speaks (to him) **quietly**.

3 We make adverbs of manner by adding -ly to the adjective.
bad ➜ bad**ly**
slow ➜ slow**ly**

Spelling variations

1 When the adjective ends in a -y, we change the -y to -i and add -ly.
easy ➜ eas**ily**
noisy ➜ nois**ily**

2 When the adjective ends in -ic, we add -ally.
fantastic ➜ fantastic**ally**

Irregular adverbs

Adjective	Adverb
good	well
early	early
late	late
fast	fast

- Irregular adjectives do not follow any rules. You have to learn each form separately.
Tina plays the guitar **well**.

(**Student Book** p.15

Word list

Review the Vocabulary. Write your own study notes (or translation) for each word.

Musical genres
classical _____
heavy metal _____
hip-hop _____
pop _____
reggae _____
rock _____

Musical instruments
drums _____
flute _____
guitar _____
piano _____
recorder _____
saxophone _____
trumpet _____
violin _____

Musicians
drummer _____
guitarist _____
pianist _____
singer _____
trumpeter _____

Check it out!
I give up! _____
Let's rock! _____

Learn it, use it!
Can I open the window, please? _____
Yes, you can. / Yes, OK. _____
Can I borrow (your pen), please? _____
Not now. / You can borrow (it) later. _____
Can I use an English dictionary? _____
No, you can't. _____

(**Student Book** pp.12, 10, 14

Vocabulary

Musical genres and instruments

1 **Find the names of five more musical genres in the puzzle.**

E	T	A	H	O	C	K	R	A	E
R	O	C	A	L	S	H	O	C	K
E	C	L	A	S	S	I	C	A	L
G	G	A	P	O	L	P	K	M	E
G	E	V	Y	S	S	H	C	T	O
A	C	K	E	I	P	O	P	H	P
E	S	I	P	C	L	P	I	C	O
H	E	A	V	Y	M	E	T	A	L

2 **Find the musical instruments in the squares.**

dr	pia	vio
no	lin	ums

1 _drums_____,
_____,
_____

re	one	cor
sax	der	oph

2 _____,
_____

pet	tar	trum
te	flu	gui

3 _____,
_____,
_____

Grammar

Simple present / Present progressive

3 **Choose the correct answers.**

Jenny **reads** / **is reading** a book at the moment.

1 I **use** / **am using** my computer every day.
2 Juan **doesn't talk** / **isn't talking** to his girlfriend at the moment.
3 **Do you get up** / **Are you getting up** early on Sundays?
4 We **don't play** / **aren't playing** sports in the afternoons.
5 I **write** / **am writing** my blog at the moment.
6 He usually **plays** / **is playing** the piano every day.

4 **Complete the dialogues with the correct form of the verbs in parentheses.**

A How often _do you practice_ the recorder? (you / practice)
B I _practice_____ the recorder twice a week. (practice)

1
A What _____ to at the moment? (you / listen)
B I _____ to reggae. (listen)

2
A When _____ to the gym? (Jack / go)
B He usually _____ to the gym on Mondays and Wednesdays. (go)

3
A Miwa is on the phone. Who _____ to? (she / talk)
B She _____ to her friend, Eva. (talk)

4
A How often _____ guitar lessons? (you / have)
B I _____ guitar lessons once a week. (have)

5 **Complete the paragraph about Juana with the simple present or present progressive form of the verbs in the boxes.**

give   not go   teach   work

Juana is a classical music teacher. She _teaches_____ students to play the piano and the violin. She usually ¹_____ in a school, but she ²_____ to the school on Wednesdays. She ³_____ classes at home.

decide   not play   practice   not talk

In her free time, Juana ⁴_____ classical music – she plays guitar in a rock band! Right now, the band members ⁵_____ for a concert and they are very excited. But they ⁶_____ about the music. They ⁷_____ what clothes to wear for the concert!

Student Book pp.12-13

Extra practice online

Possessive pronouns

6 **Complete the chart with possessive adjectives and possessive pronouns.**

Possessive adjectives	Possessive pronouns
_____ my _____	mine
your	3 _____
1 _____	his
her	4 _____
its	–
our	5 _____
your	6 _____
2 _____	theirs

7 **Complete the sentences with the possessive adjectives and possessive pronouns in the box.**

its	mine	~~my~~	ours	their	your	yours

I love rock music.
_My_____ favorite band is Paramore.

1 Is this your pen, Sara? No, _____ is in my bag.

2 Matthew and Dom are American. _____ parents are from Colorado.

3 You can have this DVD. It's _____ now.

4 Ana, finish _____ breakfast before you go to school.

5 We can't play soccer. This ball isn't _____.

6 The house is horrible, but _____ garden is beautiful.

Adverbs of manner

8 **Complete the chart with adverbs of manner.**

Adjective	Adverb
quiet	_____ quietly _____
slow	1 _____
fantastic	2 _____
fast	3 _____
late	4 _____
noisy	5 _____
good	6 _____

9 **Complete the sentences with the words from exercise 8.**

I can't hear you. Why are you talking so _quietly_____?

1 Javier is a fantastic runner. He runs very _____.

2 Grandpa is old and walks very _____.

3 Weekends are great because we can get up _____.

4 Young children don't usually write very _____.

5 The library is a place for quiet study. But the students are chatting _____.

6 Your sister is a talented pianist. She plays _____.

Round-up

10 **Choose the correct answers.**

Lollapalooza is a (fantastic) / fantastically music festival.

1 Adrian is practicing the saxophone **every Friday / at the moment.**

2 "Is that your drink, Miguel?" "Yes, it's **my / mine.**"

3 The school soccer team usually plays **good / well.**

4 How often **are you going / do you go** to concerts?

5 Are these **your / yours** sneakers?

6 I take a shower **now / every morning.**

11 **Choose the correct answers.**

January 23rd   Clear window • Report

Hi, Luisa!

How are you? I'm at orchestra practice today, but the violins (**aren't practicing**) / **don't practice** at the moment. The flutes [1]**are playing / play** and they sound great! It's really fun here.

We have a big school concert in November, so we [2]**practice / 're practicing** a lot this month. Usually we only [3]**are meeting / meet** once a week. I need a new violin. [4]**Mine / My friend** Carrie has a new one and [5]**her / hers** sounds awesome. But [6]**mine / my** makes a funny noise every time I play it! Carrie always plays [7]**fantastic / fantastically.** She's an [8]**amazing / amazingly** player. I don't play very [9]**good / well**! Oh! The saxophones are stopping now.

Talk soon!

Sofia

1 Communication

Making requests

1 Complete the dialogues with the phrases in the box.

> Can I borrow   ~~Can I open~~   Can I use
> I'm listening   Not now   you can   you can't

1

A <u>Can I open</u> the window, please?
B Yes, ¹_____. It's hot today.
A Thank you.

2

A ²_____ a pencil for this exercise?
B No, ³_____! You can use a pen.

3

A ⁴_____ your MP3 player, Adam?
B ⁵_____. ⁶_____ to my new album. You can borrow it later.

2 Match the questions with the answers.

1 Can I go to Quique's house, Mom?   <u>b</u>
2 Can I use your pen, please?   ___
3 Can I borrow your book?   ___
4 Can I watch the game on TV?   ___
5 Can I play on your phone, Dad?   ___
6 Can I have a drink?   ___

a Yes, you can. What time does it start?
b ~~No, you can't. You have homework!~~
c Yes, you can. But I only have water.
d Not now. I need it to write a story.
e Yes, you can. Here you are.
f Not now! I need to call Mom!

3 Reorder the dialogues.

<u>2</u>   No, you can't!
<u>1</u>   Can I wear your red shoes to the party, Claudia?
<u>3</u>   But you can wear my white ones.

1
___   You can watch it later.
___   Not now. Grandpa is watching the basketball.
___   Can I watch a DVD, please?

2
___   Can I use your bathroom, please?
___   It's at the top of the stairs.
___   Yes, you can.

3
___   Thank you.
___   Yes, you can. Here's a chair.
___   Can I sit down, please?

4 Use the prompts to write requests and answers.

use / a dictionary?
<u>Can I use a dictionary?</u>
Yes
<u>Yes, you can.</u>

1 copy / your homework?
_____
No
_____

2 borrow / your book?
_____
No / read / moment.
_____

3 have / some water?
_____
Yes
_____

4 use / your pen?
_____
No / can / later.
_____

5 Use the instructions to write dialogues.

You need to borrow a history book for a school project. You ask your friend if you can borrow his. He says that you can't because he needs it for the same project!
You   <u>Can I borrow your history book?</u>
Your friend   <u>No, you can't. I need it for the same project!</u>

1 You are at the movie theater. A woman is sitting next to an empty seat, but it has her bag on it. You ask her if you can sit there. She agrees.
You   _____
_____
Woman   _____
_____

2 You want to play soccer with your friends. Your mom says that you can't because dinner is ready, but that you can play later.
You   _____
_____
Your mom   _____
_____

Student Book p.14   Extra practice online

SCHOOL OF ROCK

In a school in Vista, California, the students are studying hard. But they aren't reading their books quietly. They're playing noisily! Because this is not an ordinary school, and its students are not ordinary students. It's the School of Rock, and the students are the rock stars of the future!

The School of Rock in Vista is one of 86 Schools of Rock (SOR) in the U.S. and Mexico. At SOR, children aged 7 to 18 learn to play guitar, drums, and piano, and they learn to sing, too. They also study the music genres of bands and musicians like The Beatles, The Rolling Stones, Jimi Hendrix, and many others.

All the teachers at SOR schools are professional musicians. They teach the children how to play their instruments. But they also teach them how to perform in front of a big crowd, and how to work well in a group. For this reason students have one private lesson a week, but they also practice with other students in bands, and prepare for big concerts. SOR gives students the chance to perform in big concert buildings, and also at music festivals like Lollapalooza.

Alex Kasvikis is one of SOR's stars of the future. It's his dream to be a professional musician. He loves the school for its music, but he really likes the students, too. Alex thinks the school offers some fantastic experiences. But most importantly, he thinks it helps students to see their futures as musicians.

Reading

1 Read the article. Then answer the questions.

What subject are the students studying at SOR Vista?

They're studying music.

1 In which two countries can you find the Schools of Rock?

_____

2 Can 6-year-old children study at a SOR?

_____

3 What do the teachers teach children to do?

_____

_____

4 What do the students do at Lollapalooza?

_____

5 What does Alex Kasvikis want to be in the future?

_____

6 What two things does he like about SOR?

_____

Writing

2 Imagine you are a student at a music school. Write a blog entry about it. Remember to include subject, object, and possessive pronouns in your blog. Include the following information:

- Where is the school?
- Which instrument are you learning to play?
- Which musical genres are you studying?
- How often do you have lessons?
- What are you practicing at the moment?
- When is your next concert?
- Are the other students friendly?
- What are your dreams for the future?

I'm a student at a music school in ...

2 Grammar rules

be: Simple past
Affirmative

Affirmative
I **was**
you **were**
he **was**
she **was**
it **was**
we **were**
you **were**
they **were**

1 We use *was* with singular pronouns and singular nouns. We use *were* with plural pronouns and plural nouns.
2 We do not contract *was* and *were*.
3 We use the simple past to talk about situations in the past.
  It **was** sunny on Sunday.
  We **were** at band practice yesterday.
  Luis **was** overweight when he was young.

Negative

| Negative ||
Long form	Short form
I was not	I wasn't
you were not	you weren't
he was not	he wasn't
she was not	she wasn't
it was not	it wasn't
we were not	we weren't
you were not	you weren't
they were not	they weren't

1 We make the negative with *was* / *were* + *not*.
  I **wasn't** at home.
  You **weren't** at band practice.
2 We can use the short forms *wasn't* and *weren't*.
  I **wasn't** at home.
  You **weren't** at band practice.
3 We usually use the short forms *wasn't* and *weren't* in spoken English, and when we write e-mails, messages, and letters to friends.

Past time expressions

Past time expressions
yesterday morning / afternoon / evening
last night / Monday / week / month / summer / Christmas / year
a year / a month / a week / two days / twenty minutes **ago**
in 2013 / June / the 1990s / the twentieth century

1 We use these time expressions to say when something happened in the past.
  Yesterday morning, I was late for school.
  Last month, we were in Spain.
  We were at school **twenty minutes ago**.
2 We can put the time expressions at the start or end of the sentence. The meaning does not change.
  Yesterday, there was a concert at our school.
  There was a concert at our school **yesterday**.

be: Simple past
Questions and short answers

Questions	Short answers	
	Affirmative	**Negative**
Was I?	Yes, you were.	No, you weren't.
Were you?	Yes, I was.	No, I wasn't.
Was he?	Yes, he was.	No, he wasn't.
Was she?	Yes, she was.	No, she wasn't.
Was it?	Yes, it was.	No, it wasn't.
Were we?	Yes, you were.	No, you weren't.
Were you?	Yes, we were.	No, we weren't.
Were they?	Yes, they were.	No, they weren't.

1 We put *was* or *were* before the subject to make a question.

Was it on TV last night?

Were you at band practice yesterday?

2 We answer questions with *Yes* + subject pronoun + *was* or *were*. The affirmative short answer has no short form.

Were you at the concert? **Yes, I was.**

Was he friendly? **Yes, he was.**

3 We answer questions with *No* + subject pronoun + *wasn't* or *weren't*. The negative short answer has a short form.

Was she American? **No, she wasn't.**

Were they in the classroom? **No, they weren't.**

Question words + *was / were*

Question word	*was / were*
When	were you born?
Why	was he late for practice?
Where	were you yesterday?
Who	was the blond woman?
How old	were you last year?

• We make questions with question word + simple past of *be*.

When was the movie on TV?

Where were you yesterday?

Watch out!

was / were born
We use *was / were* + *born* to talk about birth.
When **were** you **born**?
NOT ~~When are you born?~~

Student Book p.23

Word list

Review the Vocabulary. Write your own study notes (or translation) for each word.

Physical description

average height _____

average weight _____

beard _____

blue _____

braces _____

eyes _____

freckles _____

glasses _____

green _____

height _____

middle-aged _____

mustache _____

old _____

overweight _____

short _____

slim _____

tall _____

weight _____

young _____

Hair

bald _____

black _____

blond _____

brown _____

curly _____

gray _____

long _____

red _____

short _____

shoulder-length _____

straight _____

wavy _____

Check it out!

Calm down. _____

Who cares about …? _____

Learn it, use it!

What's (she) like? _____

(She)'s nice. _____

(She)'s friendly. _____

(She)'s OK. _____

(She's) strict. _____

What does (he) look like?

_____

(He)'s tall and (he) has …

_____

Student Book pp.20, 18, 22

Vocabulary
Physical descriptions

1 Write two more words for each category.

1 height: tall, <u>average height</u>, _____

2 weight: slim, _____, _____

3 hair length: long, _____, _____

4 hair color: brown, _____, _____

5 hair style: wavy, _____, _____

6 eyes: brown, _____, _____

7 age: young, _____, _____

8 other: beard, _____, _____

2 Complete the sentences with the words in the box.

> bald   braces   eyes   glasses
> hair   red   straight

My dad wears <u>glasses</u>.

1 Mateo has blond _____.

2 Tina has green _____ and freckles.

3 Bruno doesn't have any hair. He's _____.

4 I have short, _____, wavy hair.

5 My sister has _____ on her teeth.

6 Norie's hair isn't curly. It's _____.

Grammar
be: Simple past
Affirmative

3 Choose the correct answers.

Cesar **was** / were at Silvia's party.

1 The school bus **was** / **were** late.

2 The concert tickets **was** / **were** free!

3 I **was** / **were** 13 on January 2nd.

4 We **was** / **were** at home last night.

5 My elementary school **was** / **were** small.

6 My grandparents **was** / **were** teachers.

7 The movie **was** / **were** awesome!

8 The science lessons **was** / **were** very interesting.

Negative

4 Rewrite the sentences in exercise 3 in the negative form.

<u>Cesar wasn't at Silvia's party.</u>

1 _____

2 _____

3 _____

4 _____

5 _____

6 _____

7 _____

8 _____

Past time expressions

5 Choose the correct words.

last evening / (yesterday morning)

1 ago Wednesday / in August

2 two years last / three months ago

3 yesterday afternoon / last ten minutes

4 in May / June ago

5 last summer / in Christmas

6 yesterday evening / in night

6 Put the sentences in chronological order.

___ Tom was at school yesterday afternoon.

___ Tom was in the kitchen ten minutes ago.

___ Tom was at his grandma's house last week.

_1_ Tom was in 8th grade in 2012.

___ Tom was in France two months ago.

___ Tom was at home last night.

7 Rewrite the sentences in the simple past. Use the past time expressions in parentheses.

I'm not in the school musical. (last year)

<u>I wasn't in the school musical last year.</u>

1 My hair is long. (a year ago)

_____

2 The boys aren't in the park. (yesterday morning)

_____

3 Mr. Wilson is my English teacher. (last year)

_____

4 You're in tenth grade. (in 2013)

_____

5 I'm not at school. (last Friday)

_____

be: Simple past
Questions and short answers

8 Write questions and affirmative (✓) or negative (✗) short answers. Use the words in parentheses to give extra information.

it / Rosa's birthday / yesterday? (✗ Bastian's birthday)

<u>Was it Rosa's birthday yesterday?</u>
<u>No, it wasn't. It was Bastian's birthday.</u>

1 you / at the concert / last night? (✓ music / cool)

_____

_____

2 the math test / difficult? (✗ easy)

_____

_____

3 the movie / good? (✓ fantastic)

_____

_____

4 you / born in 1998? (✗ 1997)

_____

_____

Question words + *was* / *were*

9 Read the information about Muhammad Ali. Write the questions in the correct order. Then answer the questions.

BORN: January 17th, 1942, in Kentucky, U.S.
TITLES: Olympic champion in Rome in 1960 World Champion in 1964, 1974, and 1978
MOTTO: "I am the greatest."

when / born / he / was ?
<u>When was he born?</u>
<u>He was born on January 17th, 1942.</u>

1 born / he / was / where ?

_____

_____

2 he / when / Olympic / was / champion ?

_____

_____

3 in / 1960 / he / was / how / old ?

_____

_____

4 his / what / was / motto ?

_____

_____

10 Complete the messages with the words in the box.

the evening   Saturday   six o'clock   was
was   Was   wasn't   wasn't   were   were
~~weren't~~   where   Who

1

Hi Daniel,
You <u>weren't</u>_____ at band practice yesterday. It was at ¹_____, and we ²_____ all there, but ³_____ were you?
Ana ⁴_____ very happy with you … The next practice is on Sunday at 4 p.m. Don't forget!
Jorge

2

✉

Help! I can't find my French homework! It was on the desk in class this morning, but it ⁵_____ in my bag in ⁶_____. You ⁷_____ next to me in French. Do you have it?
Elizabeth

3

A   Thanks for the party on
    ⁸_____. It was great!
B   Thanks! But I ⁹_____ very tired the next day!
A   ¹⁰_____ was the tall girl with wavy blond hair?
B   That was Lydia.
A   She was very friendly.
    ¹¹_____ she there with your cousin?
B   Yes, she ¹²_____ – why? Do you want her phone number?!

☺

2 Communication

Describing people

1 Match the questions with the answers.

A

1 Who's Carlos? _c_

2 What does he look like? ___

3 What's he like? ___

a He's tall and he has brown hair.

b He's nice. He's very friendly.

c ~~He's a new boy in my class.~~

B

4 Who's Miss Lewis? ___

5 What's she like? ___

6 What does she look like? ___

d She's short and she has black hair. She wears glasses.

e She's our new math teacher.

f She's OK, but she's pretty strict.

2 Read about a young actress. Then answer the questions.

ABC talent agency

Actor profile

Name: Jasmine Thomas

Age: 16

Description: average height, slim, blue eyes, blond hair

Personality: friendly

What's her name?
Her name's Jasmine Thomas.

1 How old is she?

_____

2 What does she look like?

_____

_____

3 What's she like?

_____

3 Read the answers about a young actor. Write the questions.

What's his name?

It's Ryan O'Leary.

1 _____

He's nice. He's very friendly.

2 _____

He's 17 years old.

3 _____

He isn't very tall, but he's slim. He has green eyes and brown hair.

4 Imagine that you know the people below. One of your friends is asking you questions about the people. Read the information about them and complete the dialogues.

Factfile

Mrs. Adamska

Who: your piano teacher

From: Poland

Personality: OK, very strict

Description: short and slim; red, curly hair; blue eyes

1

Your friend _Who's Mrs. Adamska?_

You _She's my_ ¹ _____

Your friend Where ² _____

You ³ _____

Your friend What's ⁴ _____

You ⁵ _____

Your friend What does ⁶ _____

You ⁷ _____

_____

Factfile

Thiago Costa

Who: your basketball coach

From: Brazil

Personality: nice, friendly

Description: very tall; short, black hair; brown eyes, glasses

2

Your friend _Who's_ ⁸ _____

You _He's my_ ⁹ _____

Your friend ¹⁰ _____

You ¹¹ _____

Your friend ¹² _____

You ¹³ _____

Your friend ¹⁴ _____

You ¹⁵ _____

_____

Emma

Hi, Emma here!

Today, I'm looking at pictures of my mom and her brother and sister over the years. Physical appearance is important to them and they always look good. But they look different in every picture!

When my mom was a young girl, she was short and overweight with dark brown, curly hair, and glasses. When she was eighteen, she was tall and slim. Her hair was different, too. It was short, red, and wavy!

Mom's brother, my Uncle Joe, was also overweight when he was a boy. His hair was short, brown, and straight. When he was a teenager, his hair was shoulder-length and blond, and he was slim.

Their big sister, Rachel, was always very tall and slim. As a child, her hair was long, dark brown, and very curly. But as a teenager, it was straight!

Today, they look very different. Mom and Aunt Rachel have long, blond straight hair, and Uncle Joe is bald! Mom and Uncle Joe aren't very slim now, and Uncle Joe wears glasses, too. Aunt Rachel is still very slim.

My physical appearance is important to me, too. Sometimes I don't feel happy about it – I have braces and I don't like them very much. But there are good things, too. I'm pretty slim and I like my big, brown eyes. Mom, Uncle Joe, and Aunt Rachel always tell me that personality is important, and I hope I'm nice and friendly, like them.

Emma

Reading

1 Read the blog. Then write the correct name next to the pictures.

> Emma   Emma's mom   Uncle Joe
> Aunt Rachel

1  _____

2  _____

3  _____

4  _____

2 Answer the questions.

What was Emma's mom's hair like when she was a girl?

It was dark brown and curly.

1 Was Emma's mom overweight when she was a teenager?

_____

2 What color was Joe's hair when he was a boy?

_____

3 Are Emma's mom and Uncle Joe very slim now?

_____

4 What does Emma look like?

_____

5 What are Emma's mom, brother, and sister like?

_____

Writing

3 Think of a friend or family member. What does he / she look like? What is he / she like?

• Make notes about his or her appearance and personality.

• Write a description of the person with your notes.

• Remember to put the adjectives in the correct places in the sentences.

My dad is tall and slim. He has short
black hair . . .

3 Grammar rules

Simple past: Regular verbs
Affirmative

Affirmative
I walked
you walked
he walked
she walked
it walked
we walked
you walked
they walked

1 We make the simple past with the base form of the verb + -ed.

walk ➜ walked

2 The simple past regular verbs have the same ending for all people.

3 We use the simple past to describe an action that started and finished in the past.

We played tennis yesterday.

Spelling variations

1 We usually form the simple past by adding -ed to the base verb.

2 However, there are some spelling variations:

- Verbs ending in -e. Add -d.
  like ➜ liked
  arrive ➜ arrived

- Verbs ending with a consonant + -y. Change -y to -i and add -ed.
  tidy ➜ tidied
  hurry ➜ hurried
  study ➜ studied
  try ➜ tried
  cry ➜ cried

- Short verbs ending in a vowel plus a consonant. Double the consonant and add -ed.
  stop ➜ stopped
  rob ➜ robbed
  plan ➜ planned
  prefer ➜ preferred

Pronunciation

1 When the base form of the verb ends with a voiced (hard) sound, -ed is pronounced /d/.

rained	/reɪnd/
loved	/lʌvd/
played	/pleɪd/

2 When the base form of the verb ends with an unvoiced (soft) sound, -ed is pronounced /t/.

watched	/wɑtʃt/
liked	/laɪkt/
stopped	/stɑpt/

3 When the base form of the verb ends with sound /d/ or /t/, -ed is pronounced /ɪd/.

started	/stɑrtɪd/
hated	/heɪtɪd/
decided	/dɪsaɪdɪd/

Simple past: Irregular verbs

1 Irregular verbs don't follow a pattern. You need to learn them.

I go to the movie theater every night.
➜ I went to the movie theater last night.

2 We can put irregular verbs into groups with the same sound or spelling. This can help us to remember them.

Base form	Simple past
run	ran
drink	drank
sing	sang
sit	sat
begin	began

Base form	Simple past
buy	bought
catch	caught
teach	taught

Base form	Simple past
break	broke
choose	chose
speak	spoke

Student Book pp.33, 35

Base form	Simple past
cut	cut
hit	hit
put	put

Base form	Simple past
tell	told
sell	sold

Base form	Simple past
come	came
become	became

Base form	Simple past
give	gave
forgive	forgave

Base form	Simple past
blow	blew
know	knew
grow	grew

3 The simple past irregular verbs have the same ending for all people.

I **ate** a sandwich.

He **ate** a sandwich.

They **ate** a sandwich.

4 There is a list of irregular verbs on the inside back cover.

Student Book p.35

Word list

Review the Vocabulary. Write your own study notes (or translation) for each word.

The weather

cloudy _____

cold _____

cool _____

foggy _____

freezing _____

hot _____

mild _____

raining _____

snowing _____

sunny _____

warm _____

windy _____

Check it out!

So what? _____

What's up? _____

Learn it, use it!

How was your vacation in (town / country)? _____

It was great / awesome / OK / terrible. _____

What was the weather like? _____

It was beautiful / amazing / great / OK / miserable. _____

Was the food good? _____

Yes, it was. It was delicious. _____

No, it wasn't. It was horrible / disgusting. _____

What was your hotel like? _____

It was great / awesome / OK / terrible / awful. _____

Were the people friendly? _____

Yes, they were. They were very nice. _____

No, they weren't. They were unfriendly. _____

Student Book pp.32, 30, 34

Vocabulary

The weather

1 Reorder the letters to form weather words and complete the sentences.

It was <u>hot</u> (t o h) and <u>sunny</u> (n u y s n) yesterday.

1 It's _____ (g i n a i r n). Do you have an umbrella?

2 It was very _____ (d o l c) and _____ (d i y n w) last week.

3 Is it _____ (w o n g i n s)? Yes, it is. The garden is all white!

4 Last December, it was _____ (m r a w), but this year it's _____ (z e e f r i n g)!

5 It's very _____ (g o y f g) today. I can't see very well.

6 Yesterday, it was _____ (d i l m), but it was _____ (d o u l c y).

2 Look at the weather report. Complete the sentences.

World Weather			
Rio de Janeiro	39°C	London	3°C
San Francisco	18°C FOG	Hong Kong	14°C
Toronto	−5°C	Paris	9°C

In Rio it's h <u>o</u> <u>t</u>. The temperature is 39°C, and it's <u>cloudy</u>.

1 In San Francisco it's w __ __ __ . The temperature is 18°C, but it's _____.

2 In Toronto it's f __ __ __ __ __ __ __ and it's _____.

3 In London it's c __ __ __. The temperature is 3°C, but it's _____.

4 In Hong Kong it's m __ __ __. The temperature is 14°C and it's _____.

5 In Paris it's c __ __ __. The temperature is 9°C and it's _____.

Grammar

Simple past: Regular verbs
Affirmative

3 Rewrite the sentences in the simple past.

I walk to school.
<u>I walked to school</u> yesterday.

1 We play volleyball.
_____ last Friday.

2 My dad works in a hospital.
_____ two years ago.

3 I watch a lot of TV.
_____ last week.

4 The store opens at 9 a.m.
_____ yesterday.

5 They listen to Radio Deejay.
_____ yesterday evening.

6 It rains a lot.
_____ in March.

7 You finish school early.
_____ yesterday.

Spelling variations

4 Complete the chart with the correct form of the verbs.

Base form	Simple past
close	<u>closed</u>
<u>stop</u>	stopped
1 _____	cried
like	4 _____
try	5 _____
2 _____	decided
3 _____	preferred
travel	6 _____

5 Complete the sentences with the simple past form of the verbs in the box.

arrive   clean   love   stop   study   travel   ~~use~~

The students <u>used</u> dictionaries in the test.

1 It was an amazing movie. I _____ it!

2 The car _____ at the red light.

3 My mom _____ French at school.

4 We _____ to Houston by bus.

5 Raquel _____ her room yesterday.

6 I _____ in Las Vegas at 2 p.m.

Simple past: Irregular verbs

6 Find three irregular simple past verbs in each word square. Then write the simple past verbs and their corresponding base forms from the box.

drink fall feel get know put
say send sing take tell write

d	e	t	o
k	n	t	s
l	e	n	w

1 told – tell _____ ,
_____ ,
_____

f	w	e	t
o	t	e	g
l	r	o	t

2 _____ ,
_____ ,
_____

s	a	k	n
d	o	i	t
g	a	o	s

3 _____ ,
_____ ,
_____

n	p	l	r
e	d	f	k
u	l	a	t

4 _____ ,
_____ ,
_____

7 Complete the diary entry with the simple past form of the verbs in parentheses.

February 19th

Dad won _____ *(win) $200 with a lottery ticket yesterday and he* 1_____ *(give) me $50!*

February 20th

This morning, I 2_____ *(go) shopping with Mom. I* 3_____ *(buy) a new top with my $50. It's perfect for Alicia's birthday party.*

February 21st

Min soo 4_____ *(come) to visit me yesterday afternoon. We* 5_____ *(do) our geography homework, and then we* 6_____ *(make) a cake for Alicia. It's her birthday today!*

February 22nd

Alicia's party was awesome! I 7_____ *(see) a lot of friends from school and I* 8_____ *(meet) Alicia's brother, Jose Luis. He's really nice … Oh, and I* 9_____ *(wear) my new top! All my friends* 10_____ *(think) it was cool!*

8 Read about Emerson's day. Then use the information to complete the description of yesterday. Use the simple past.

6:30 a.m.	wake up
6:45 a.m.	get up and take a shower
7:00 a.m.	have breakfast then prepare school bag
7:20 a.m.	leave home and walk to school
7:30 a.m.	arrive at school
2:30 p.m.	finish school and go to basketball practice
4:30 p.m.	get home, do homework, study for test
6:00 p.m.	have dinner
6:30 p.m.	clean bedroom
6:45 p.m.	play soccer outside with my friends
9:00 p.m.	watch TV
10:00 p.m.	go to bed

Yesterday, Emerson woke up _____ at six thirty. He stayed in bed for fifteen minutes, then he 1_____ and he 2_____ a shower before breakfast. After breakfast, he 3_____ his school bag. Then he 4_____ home at seven twenty. He 5_____ to school and he 6_____ at seven thirty. When school 7_____ at two thirty, Emerson 8_____ to basketball practice. He 9_____ home at four thirty, 10_____ his homework, and 11_____ for a history test. At six o'clock, he 12_____ dinner with his mom and dad and his sister, Daniela. After dinner, Emerson 13_____ his bedroom, and then 14_____ soccer outside with his friends. At nine o'clock, he 15_____ TV. Finally, he 16_____ to bed at ten o'clock. It was a typical school day.

9 Write about your day yesterday. Use the description in exercise 8 as a model.

Yesterday, I woke up at … In the morning, I …

3 Communication

Talking about vacations

1 Use the prompts to write questions and answers in the dialogues. Use the dialogues on page 34 of the Student Book as a model.

1

A How was your vacation in Sydney?
  <u>It was amazing!</u>
  (amazing)
B ¹_____
  (weather / like?)
A ²_____
  (great / warm / sunny.)
B ³_____
  (food / good?)
  Yes, it was delicious.

2

A ⁴_____?
  (your vacation / Chicago?)
B Not very good!
A What was the weather like?
B ⁵_____
  (pretty bad / very cold / windy.)
A Were the people nice?
B ⁶_____
  (yes / very friendly.)

2 Write the sentences in the correct order.

___ Bye, Sophie! See you soon!
___ Really? It was sunny here. What was your hotel like?
___ Paris was great! It's a fantastic place!
___ I like Paris, too. There are some great places to visit. What was the weather like?
_1_ Hi, Ellie! How are you?
___ Umm … It was very small, but it had a restaurant and it was near the city center.
___ Oh yes, Paris! What was it like?
___ It wasn't very good. It rained a lot.
___ What was the food in the hotel restaurant like?
___ Hi, Sophie. I'm OK, thanks. I returned from Paris yesterday.
___ Mmm! I love French food! Oh, here's my bus. Bye, Ellie!
___ Umm … the food was OK, but we only had breakfast at the hotel. We usually ate in cafés and restaurants.

3 Match the questions with the answers.

1 What was the food like?   _b_
2 Were the people friendly?   ___
3 What was the hotel like?   ___
4 What was your vacation in Thailand like? ___
5 Was the weather nice?   ___

a It was OK, but it was a bit small. Our room had a nice balcony.
b It was delicious! I love Thai food.
c It was fantastic! Thailand is a beautiful country.
d Yes, they were. They were very friendly.
e It was great! It was hot and sunny every day.

4 Complete the dialogue with the missing questions. Use the questions in exercise 3 as a model.

Max   Hi, Paul! <u>What was your school trip to Yellowstone National Park like?</u>
Paul It was great.
Max   ¹_____
Paul Umm … It wasn't great. It rained on two of the days, but on the last day it was sunny.
Max   ²_____
Paul It was OK. I was in a room with two friends. We had a bathroom and a TV.
Max   ³_____
Paul It was horrible. We had pasta with tomato sauce every day!
Max   What about the people at Yellowstone?
      ⁴_____
Paul Yes, they were. The workers in the park were cool.

5 You are talking with a friend about your last vacation. Answer the questions. Invent additional information.

Your friend What was your vacation like?
You   _____
             _____

Your friend What was the weather like?
You   _____

Your friend Was the hotel nice?
You   _____

Your friend What was the food like?
You   _____

Your friend Were the people friendly?
You   _____
             _____

The Schoolhouse Blizzard of January 12th, 1888

In the 21st century, with accurate weather reports, it's easy to plan for bad weather. But in the 19th century, things were different. For many people, only the sky gave any indication of weather changes.

One winter's morning in January 1888, the weather in the American mid-west was pretty mild. The sky appeared normal and gave no indication of bad weather.

But suddenly, at about two o'clock, cold air arrived from the north and it became very windy and started to snow. The wind and snow created a blizzard, and it became impossible to see. Soon the snow was over one meter deep.

A lot of people were at work or school when the blizzard started. As a result, 235 people died trying to get home. Three of them were Lois Royce's pupils at a school in Nebraska. Her house was only a short distance away and she wanted to take

them there. But in the freezing weather, she and the children became lost. All three children died.

But others were lucky. Teacher Seymour Dopp, also from Nebraska, chose to stay with his seventeen pupils at school. They slept there that night and made fires to keep warm. The next day, their parents walked through the deep snow to collect them.

Weather events like the schoolhouse blizzard are terrible, but they are an important part of history. Those 235 people didn't survive that day in 1888, but they are still in our memories.

Reading

1 Read the article. Then answer the questions.

Why is it easy for us to find out about weather changes?
We have accurate weather reports.

1 In the 19th century, where did a lot of people look to find out about weather changes?

_____

2 Why didn't people know about the blizzard?

_____

3 Where did the bad weather come from?

_____

4 Which two types of weather created the blizzard?

_____

5 Why weren't most people at home when the blizzard started?

_____

6 Where did Lois Royce try to take her pupils?

_____

7 Where did Seymour Dopp and his pupils sleep on the night of the blizzard?

_____

8 Who came to the school to collect the children the next day?

_____

Writing

2 Complete the questionnaire about an unforgettable day in your life. Then write a paragraph about the day. Remember to check your spelling, especially any spelling variations in simple past verbs.

What year was it?

How old were you?

Who were you with?

Where were you?

What was the place like?

What was the weather like?

What happened?

4 Grammar rules

Simple past
Negative

Negative	
Full forms	**Short forms**
I did not work	I didn't work
you did not work	you didn't work
he did not work	he didn't work
she did not work	she didn't work
it did not work	it didn't work
we did not work	we didn't work
you did not work	you didn't work
they did not work	they didn't work

1 We make the negative form of the simple past with *did not* + base form of the verb.
   I **did not** study.

2 We make short forms with *did* + *n't*. We use short forms more often than long forms.
   You **didn't** call Victoria.

3 The simple past negative is the same for all people. It doesn't change.
   I **didn't see** the movie.
   He **didn't play** his guitar at the concert.
   We **didn't study** for the test.

4 We form the simple past in the same way with regular and irregular verbs.

   Regular verbs
   They **watched** the soccer game on TV.
   They **didn't watch** the soccer game on TV.

   Irregular verbs
   We **saw** a musical at the movie theater.
   We **didn't see** a musical at the movie theater.
   NOT ~~We didn't saw a musical at the movie theater.~~

Questions and short answers

Questions	Short answers	
	Affirmative	**Negative**
Did I work?	Yes, you **did**.	No, you **didn't**.
Did you work?	Yes, I **did**.	No, I **didn't**.
Did he work?	Yes, he **did**.	No, he **didn't**.
Did she work?	Yes, she **did**.	No, she **didn't**.
Did it work?	Yes, it **did**.	No, it **didn't**.
Did we work?	Yes, you **did**.	No, you **didn't**.
Did you work?	Yes, we **did**.	No, we **didn't**.
Did they work?	Yes, they **did**.	No, they **didn't**.

1 We make the question form of the simple past with *Did* + base form of the verb.
   Did she / we / they **enjoy** the comedy?

2 We make short answers with *Yes* / *No* + subject pronoun + *did* / *didn't*.
   Did she remember the tickets? **Yes, she did.**
   Did you buy a DVD yesterday? **No, I didn't.**

3 We form the simple past question in the same way with regular and irregular verbs.

   Regular verbs
   Did you **like** the actors?
   Yes, I **did**. / **No**, I **didn't**.

   Irregular verbs
   Did they **eat** all the popcorn?
   Yes, they **did**. / **No**, they **didn't**.

Question words + Simple past

Question word	Simple past
What	did you do last weekend?
Where	did he teach?
When	did we arrive?
What time	did the movie start?
How	did you travel here?
Why	did she go?

• Question word + *did* + subject + base form of the verb.
   What time did you **send** the e-mail?
   When did the movie **start**?

Simple past summary
Regular verbs

Affirmative
Subject + base form of the verb + *-ed*
I + play**ed**

Negative
Subject + *didn't* + base form of the verb
I + **didn't** + **play**

Questions
Did + subject + base form of the verb
Did + **you** + **play**?

Short answers
Affirmative
Yes, + subject pronoun + *did*.
Negative
No, + subject pronoun + *didn't*.

Irregular verbs

Affirmative
Subject + simple past form of the verb
I + **went**

Negative
Subject + *didn't* + base form of the verb
He + **didn't** + **go**

Questions
Did + subject + base form of the verb
Did + **you** + **go**?

Short answers
Affirmative
Yes, + subject pronoun + *did*.
Negative
No, + subject pronoun + *didn't*.

Student Book pp.33, 35, 41, 43

Word list

Review the Vocabulary. Write your own study notes (or translation) for each word.

Movies

action movie _____

cartoon _____

comedy _____

fantasy movie _____

horror movie _____

love story _____

musical _____

science fiction movie _____

Check it out!

Get real! _____

losers _____

over there _____

Learn it, use it!

Let's go to … _____

OK. _____

What type of movie is it? _____

It's a … _____

Where is it playing? _____

It's playing at … _____

What time does it start? _____

It starts at … _____

Can I have … tickets, please? _____

That's $11. _____

Which screen is it? _____

It's screen 4. _____

Student Book pp.40, 38, 42

4 Exercises

Vocabulary
Movies

1 Read the sentences. Then complete the different types of movie.

My favorite movie is *Titanic*.
It's a l_love_____ s_tory_____.

1 *Avatar* was on TV last night. It's a great
  s_____ f_____ movie.
2 Aslan, the lion, is my favorite character in the
  f_____ movie, *The Chronicles of Narnia*.
3 Dracula is a famous vampire. He's in
  h_____ movies!
4 My favorite song from the m_____
  Grease is *Summer Nights*.
5 *The Muppets* movie is a fantastic
  c_____y.
6 *Toy Story III* is my favorite c_____n.
7 Tom Cruise was the star of the *Mission:
  Impossible* a_____ movies.

2 Read the dialogues. Then choose the correct movie type for each one.

> **Tom** You're my life, Kate! Don't go!
> **Kate** I love you, Tom, but I can't stay …

cartoon / (love story)

1
> **Agent 005** Oh, no! It's a bomb!
> **Agent 006** You're right! Let's go! Quick!

action movie / horror movie

2
> **Android** Where does the alien come from?
> **Robo** It comes from Kepler, a planet in a distant galaxy.

love story / science fiction movie

3
> **Woman** Is that you, Max? Max?
> It's so dark and scary here!

action movie / horror movie

4
> **Goran** The gold is in a cave in the Magic Forest. A dragon protects it.
> **Boy** I can ask the forest animals for help.

musical / fantasy movie

5
> **Mom** What were the exam questions like?
> **Boy** Oh, the exam questions were easy … it was just the answers that were difficult!

comedy / science fiction movie

Grammar
Simple past
Negative

3 Complete the chart with the correct form of the verbs.

Simple past	
Affirmative	**Negative**
went	_didn't go_
came	1 _____
took	2 _____
played	3 _____
bought	4 _____
rained	5 _____
won	6 _____
got up	7 _____
clean	8 _____

4 Complete the sentences with the simple past negative form of the verbs in exercise 3.

He _didn't go_____
to the movies yesterday.

1 It was sunny yesterday.
  It _____.
2 They _____
  volleyball yesterday.
3 Tina _____
  to Sally's birthday party.
  She wasn't well.
4 Mom _____ the jeans.
  They were very expensive.
5 I _____ a shower this
  morning because I woke up late!
6 We _____ the basketball
  game. The other team was very good.
7 Ella _____ her bedroom
  at the weekend. It's a mess!
8 Sam _____ early.
  He was tired.

Student Book pp.40-41 Extra practice online

Questions and short answers

5 Look at the questionnaire about Mark and Emma's weekend. Use the words to write questions and short answers in the simple past.

Last weekend, I …	Mark	Emma
1 watched TV	✓	✓
2 listened to music	✗	✓
3 went online	✓	✗
4 studied for a test	✓	✓
5 played sports	✗	✗

Mark and Emma / watch TV / last weekend?
Did Mark and Emma watch TV last weekend?
Yes, they did.

1 Mark / listen to music / last weekend?
_____
_____

2 you / listen to music / last weekend
_____, Emma?
_____

3 Emma / go online / last weekend?
_____
_____

4 Mark / go online / last weekend?
_____
_____

5 Mark and Emma / study for a test / last weekend?
_____
_____

6 you / play sports / last weekend
_____, Mark and Emma?
_____

Question words + Simple past

6 Write questions for the answers.

Where did you stay?
We stayed in a hotel.

1 _____
I bought a new T-shirt.

2 _____
He went last year.

3 _____
They went to Greece on vacation.

4 _____
She got up at eight o'clock.

5 _____
He traveled on the bus.

Round-up

7 Complete the text with the simple past form of the verbs in parentheses.

Gabe's blog

Last April, my friend Yuki and I _entered_ a movie competition for high school students.

At first, we [1]_____ (not / know) what type of movie to make. But one lunchtime, we [2]_____ (have) a great idea. We [3]_____ (decide) to make a comedy! We started writing our story, and soon we [4]_____ (know) exactly what our movie was about! We didn't have money for professional actors, but that [5]_____ (not / be) a problem. Hundreds of students [6]_____ (want) to be in our movie and were really excited about it.

When we entered the competition, we [7]_____ (not / expect) to win a prize. To be honest, I [8]_____ (not / think) our movie was very good. But the competition judges [9]_____ (not / feel) the same way – they loved it! We [10]_____ (not / win) first prize, but we [11]_____ (win) some money to study movies – we both want to study movie making in college!

8 Imagine you are talking to Gabe. Complete the dialogue with the missing words.

You   What competition *did you enter*?
Gabe   I entered *a movie competition* with my friend Yuki.
You   [1]_____ type of movie did you make? [2]_____ a horror, or an action movie?
Gabe   No. We made a comedy in our high school!
You   Did you know immediately what kind of movie you wanted to make?
Gabe   [3]_____. We weren't sure at first.
You   [4]_____ as actors in your movie?
Gabe   We used students in the school.
You   Did you and Yuki expect to win a prize?
Gabe   [5]_____ – we didn't think our movie was very good!
You   Did the judges like it?
Gabe   [6]_____. They thought it was great. We won a prize, too!
You   [7]_____ win?
Gabe   We won some money to study movies.
You   [8]_____ making the movie?
Gabe   Yes, we really enjoyed it. It was awesome.

4 Communication

Going to the movies

1 Complete the dialogue with the phrases in the box.

> How old are you?   What time does it start?
> ~~What type of movie is it?~~   Where is it playing?
> Which screen is it?

On the phone …

Matt	Let's go to watch *The Music Man*.
Charlie	*What type of movie is it?*
Matt	It's a musical. And it's in 3D.
Charlie	Cool. I love musicals.
	¹_____
Matt	It's playing at the Cinemark movie theater.
Charlie	²_____
Matt	It starts at seven o'clock.
Charlie	OK. Let's go and see that then.

At the movie theater …

Matt	Can I have two children's tickets for *The Music Man*, please?
Clerk	³_____
Matt	We're 13.
Clerk	OK. That's $22.
Matt	There you go.
Clerk	Thank you. Here are your tickets, and $8 change.
Matt	⁴_____
Clerk	It's screen 7.
Matt	Thank you.

2 Match the questions with the answers.

1 What type of movie is it?   _d_
2 Is it in 3D?   ___
3 Where is it playing?   ___
4 What time does it start?   ___
5 Which screen is it?   ___

a It's playing at the Rio movie theater.
b It's screen 4.
c Yes, it is.
d ~~It's a fantasy movie.~~
e It starts at eight thirty.

3 Use the information to complete the dialogue at the movie theater.

Movie: **The Avengers**
Tickets: adults $14; children (under 14) $11.50
Screen: 3

Robbie	Can I have two children's tickets for *The Avengers*_____, please?
Man	¹_____?
Robbie	We're 12.
Man	OK. That's ²_____.
Robbie	There you go.
Man	Thank you. Here are your tickets, and $7 change.
Robbie	Which screen is it?
Man:	³_____.

Movie: **Adventure Time**
Tickets: Adults $13, Children (under 10) $10.50
Screen: 6

Kate	Can I have one adult ticket, and one child ticket for ⁴_____ _____, please?
Woman	Yes, of course. ⁵_____ the child?
Kate	He's 8 years old.
Woman	OK. That's ⁶_____.
Kate	There you go.
Woman	Thank you.
Kate	Which screen ⁷_____?
Woman	⁸_____.

4 You and your friend agree to go to the movies. Read the instructions and write a dialogue.

1 You are talking on the phone to your friend Nick. Suggest going to the movies and tell him about one of the three movies in the list below. Nick asks what genre the movie is. He agrees to see the movie with you. He asks where and when the movie is. Answer his questions.

2 Arrive at the movie theater. Buy two children's tickets and ask what screen it is.

The Odeon Cinema		
Screen 1	**Monsters University**	
3D Animated cartoon Tickets: Adults $14, Children: $11	**Starts: 6:30 p.m.**	
Screen 2	**The Prince and Me 4**	
Love story Tickets: Adults $14, Children: $11	**Starts: 8:00 p.m.**	
Screen 3	**Skyfall**	
Action movie Tickets: Adults $14, Children: $11	**Starts: 8:30 p.m.**	

A Multimedia Superhero

When Wolverine first appeared in a Marvel comic book in 1974, he didn't play an important part in the story. But readers liked the superhero. He was nearly 200 years old, but had the body of a young man, spoke ten languages, and was an expert in martial arts. He was part human, part animal, and part machine. Soon Wolverine appeared in another comic book series. This time, he was in a series of science fiction stories about the X-Men, a group of mutants with superhuman powers.

Wolverine and the X-Men were very popular, and they moved to TV in the 1990s and to video games, too. Then, in 2000, the first *X-Men* movie arrived in movie theaters. Wolverine appeared in this movie and in two more *X-Men* movies, in 2003 and in 2006. But 2009 saw the first movie with Wolverine as its star. By now, movie viewers wanted to know more about him: Where did he come from? Why did he become a mutant? This movie, *X-Men Origins: Wolverine*, with the popular Australian actor Hugh Jackman playing the superhero, answered their questions.

In 2013, a second Wolverine movie arrived in movie theaters. It told the story of Wolverine's fight with old enemies, and the loss of his super powers.

Today, Wolverine's story continues in comic books and video games. Fans are also waiting excitedly for another movie in the future. Wolverine is a true multimedia superhero!

Reading

1 **Read the article. Then answer the questions.**

Where did readers first see Wolverine?
<u>In a Marvel comic book.</u>

1 How many languages does he speak?
_____

2 Which comic book series was Wolverine in?
_____

3 What genre were the stories?
_____

4 When was the first *X-Men* movie?
_____

5 In which movie did viewers learn more about Wolverine's past?
_____

6 Who played Wolverine in the movie?
_____

7 What did Wolverine lose in the 2013 movie?
_____

Writing

2 **Write a short essay about your favorite movie star. Include the following information:**

Paragraph 1:
Your favorite movie star
Some of the movies he / she appears in
The genre of the movies

Paragraph 2:
A description of one of their movies

Paragraph 3:
Reasons why you like this movie star and his / her movies

5 Grammar rules

Countable / Uncountable nouns

Countable		Uncountable
Singular	Plural	Singular only
an egg	eggs	milk
a book	books	water

1 We use countable nouns to describe things we can count. Countable nouns can be singular or plural.

a pen → (five) pens

2 We can use *a / an* with singular countable nouns in affirmative and negative sentences.

I have **a** book, but I don't have **a** pen.

3 We use uncountable nouns to describe things we cannot count. Uncountable nouns can only be singular.

bread NOT ~~a bread, two breads~~

4 Expressions such as *a carton of*, *a bottle of*, *a glass of*, etc. make uncountable nouns countable.

milk (= uncountable)

BUT **a carton** of milk / **three cartons** of milk (= countable)

some / any

Countable	Uncountable
Affirmative	
There are **some** eggs.	There is **some** milk.
Negative	
There aren't **any** eggs.	There isn't **any** milk.
Questions	
Are there **any** eggs?	Is there **any** milk?

1 We can use *some* with plural countable nouns and uncountable nouns. We use *some* in affirmative sentences.

We have **some** milk.

I bought **some** apples at the market.

2 We use *any* with plural countable nouns and uncountable nouns. We use *any*:

– in negative sentences.

I didn't buy **any** bananas.

I didn't buy **any** milk.

– in questions.

Did you buy **any** bananas?

Did you buy **any** milk?

3 We use *some* with polite requests and offers.

Can I have ...? or *Would you like ...?*

Can I have some juice, please?

Would you like some cheese?

a lot of / much / many

Countable	Uncountable
Affirmative	
There are **a lot of** eggs.	There is **a lot of** cheese.
Negative	
There aren't **many** eggs.	There isn't **much** cheese.
Questions	
Are there **many** eggs?	Is there **much** cheese?

1 *A lot of*, *much*, and *many* are all expressions which mean "a large quantity".

2 We use *a lot of* in affirmative sentences. We use *a lot of* with plural countable and uncountable nouns.

There are **a lot of** students in my school.

I bought **a lot of** paper.

3 We use *much* in negative sentences and questions. We use *much* with uncountable nouns.

I don't have **much** time.

Do you do **much** sport at school?

4 We use *many* in negative sentences and questions. We use *many* with plural countable nouns.

I don't have **many** DVDs.

Do you have **many** friends?

Student Book pp.55, 57

How much ...? / How many ...?

Countable	Uncountable
How many eggs are there?	How much cheese is there?

1 We use *How much ...?* and *How many ...?* to ask about quantities.

2 We use *How much ...?* to ask about uncountable nouns.
How much coffee do we have?

3 We use *How many ...?* to ask about plural countable nouns.
How many children are there?

a little / a few

Countable	Uncountable
There are **a few** eggs.	There is **a little** cheese.

1 *A little* and *a few* are expressions which mean "a small quantity".

2 We use *a little* with uncountable nouns.
I have **a little** sugar in my coffee.

3 *A little* means the same as *not much*.
There's **a little** milk in the cup.
There **isn't much** milk in the cup.

4 We use *a few* with plural countable nouns.
There are **a few** CDs on the table.

5 *A few* means the same as *not many*.
I know **a few** foreign students.
I **don't** know **many** foreign students.

(**Student Book** p.57

Summary chart:

Expressions of quantity

We can use these with countable nouns:
a / an, *some / any*, *How many...?*, *a lot of*, *many*, *a few*.

We can use these with uncountable nouns:
some / any, *How much...?*, *a lot of*, *much*, *a little*.

Word list

Review the Vocabulary. Write your own study notes (or translation) for each word.

Food and drink
apple _____
banana _____
candy _____
carrots _____
cereal _____
cheese _____
chicken _____
chocolate _____
cookies _____
egg _____
ham _____
ice cream _____
milk _____
orange juice _____
peas _____
potato chips _____
potatoes _____
soda _____
tea _____
toast _____
tomato _____
water _____
yogurt _____

Check it out!
What else? _____
You're kidding! _____

Learn it, use it!
Can I help you? _____
Yes, please. I'll have ... / I'd like ... / Can I have ...?
_____
What would you like to eat / drink? _____
_____
I'd like ... / I'll have ... _____
Is that for here, or to go? _____
It's for here. / It's to go. / Anything else? _____
_____
No, thanks. That's all. _____
Yes, please. _____
I'd like ... _____
Here's your change. _____
Thanks. _____

(**Student Book** pp.54, 52, 56

5 Exercises

Vocabulary
Food and drink

1 Circle the incorrect word in each group.

	orange juice	(carrots)	water	tea
1	ice cream	carrots	potato	peas
2	candy	chocolate	tomato	cookies
3	apple	orange	banana	toast
4	milk	yogurt	cheese	potato chips
5	soda	tea	chocolate	orange juice

2 Complete the word puzzle. What is the mystery food?

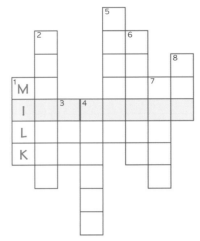

1 This drink comes from a cow.
2 This meat comes from a bird.
3 This comes from a chicken.
4 You eat it for breakfast with milk.
5 It's plain, or with fruit.
6 It's yellow and you put it on pasta.
7 This drink doesn't have a color.
8 It's a popular meat on a pizza.
Mystery food: _____

Grammar
Countable / Uncountable nouns

3 Complete the chart with the words in the box. Write the plurals.

> apple   carrot   cereal   cheese   cookie
> egg   ham   orange juice   potato
> toast   tomato   water

Countable		Uncountable
Singular	**Plural**	**Singular only**
apple	apples	toast
1 _____	6 _____	11 _____
2 _____	7 _____	12 _____
3 _____	8 _____	13 _____
4 _____	9 _____	14 _____
5 _____	10 _____	15 _____

some / any

4 Choose the correct answer.

There's (some) / any milk in the fridge.
1 I had **some** / **a** orange juice for breakfast.
2 Can I have **some** / **a** water, please?
3 There's **an** / **some** apple in my bag.
4 There weren't **any** / **a** tomatoes in the store.
5 Did you eat **any** / **a** toast for breakfast?
6 I ate **a** / **some** banana before the game.

a lot of / much / many

5 Complete the dialogues with *a lot of*, *much*, and *many*.

A Is there much sugar in this soda?
B Yes, there is. There's a lot of sugar.

1
A Did you buy ¹_____ bananas?
B No, I didn't. There weren't any. I bought ²_____ oranges and potatoes.

2
A Is there ³_____ orange juice in the fridge?
B No, there isn't. We don't drink ⁴_____ juice, but my sister drinks ⁵_____ soda.

3
A Were there ⁶_____ vegetarian options on the menu?
B Yes, there were. There were ⁷_____ vegetarian pizzas.

4
A Did you make ⁸_____ cookies?
B Yes, I did, but I didn't make ⁹_____ chocolate cookies.

Student Book pp.54-55, 57   **Extra practice** online

How much ...? / How many ...?

6 Look at the pie chart about Gemma's diet. Complete the questions and answers with *How much ...?*, *How many ...?*, *a lot of*, *many*, and *much*.

<u>How much</u> pasta does Gemma eat?
She eats <u>a lot of</u> pasta.

1 _____ cookies does she eat?
She doesn't eat _____ cookies.

2 _____ water does she drink?
She drinks _____ water.

3 _____ carrots does she eat?
She doesn't eat _____ carrots.

4 _____ apples does she eat?
She eats _____ apples.

5 _____ tea does she drink?
She doesn't drink _____ tea.

a little / a few

7 Choose the correct answers.

We have (a few) / a little apples.

1 Mom puts **a little** / **a few** milk in her coffee.
2 We watched **a few** / **a little** DVDs.
3 Can I ask you **a little** / **a few** questions?
4 I only put **a little** / **a few** salt on my food.
5 Carlo knows **a few** / **a little** English songs.

Round-up

8 Read the interview about the South African swimmer, Chad le Clos. Choose the correct answers.

_B_ **Olympic medals did Chad le Clos win in the London Olympics?**

At the London Olympics in 2012, he won a silver and a gold medal, and beat the American swimming champion Michael Phelps! And at the Youth Olympics in 2010, he won ¹__ medals: five gold ones!

²__ **exercise does he do?**

Chad does ³__ exercise! Before the Olympics, he trained nearly every day, and completed about 24 hours of swimming a week. He also did exercise in the gym ⁴__ times every week.

⁵__ **food does he eat every day?**

Chad loves his father's cooking, so he eats ⁶__ his dad's pasta.

Does he have ⁷__ heroes?

Yes, he does. He is a big fan of Michael Phelps and has ⁸__ respect for the American swimmer.

Does he play ⁹__ other sports?

When Chad was little, he wanted to be a soccer player. These days, he goes surfing when he has ¹⁰__ free time. But there isn't ¹¹__ free time for Chad le Clos. He's a swimming star of the future!

	A	B
	A How much	B (How many)
1	A a lot of	B much
2	A How many	B How much
3	A a lot of	B any
4	A a few	B a little
5	A How many	B How much
6	A a lot of	B many
7	A some	B any
8	A a lot of	B much
9	A much	B any
10	A any	B some
11	A much	B many

Ordering food and drink

1 **Reorder the dialogues. Use the dialogues on page 56 of the Student Book to check your answers.**

1

__ A Is that for here, or to go?

__ B Yes, please. I'll have two chocolate cookies and a bottle of soda.

__ A OK, here you go. Anything else?

__ B Here you go.

_1_ A Can I help you?

__ B It's to go.

__ A OK. That's $6.59.

__ B No, thanks. That's all.

__ A Thanks. And here's your change.

__ B Thanks.

2

__ A What would you like to eat?

__ B Yes, please.

__ A Is that for here, or to go?

__ B I'd like a cheese and tomato sandwich, please.

__ A OK. Would you like your tea with milk?

__ B It's for here, thanks.

__ A Fine.

__ B Can I have some tea, too?

__ A Great. Thanks.

__ B Here you go.

__ A OK. That's $7.65 then.

2 **Complete the dialogue with the phrases in the box.**

> Anything else? ~~Can I help you?~~
> Is that for here? Small or large soda?
> Would you like a drink, too?

A _Can I help you?_

B Yes, please. I'll have a hamburger with cheese.

A ¹ _____

B No, it isn't. It's to go.

A ² _____

B Yes, please. I'd like a soda.

A ³ _____

B Large, please.

A ⁴ _____

B No, thanks. That's all.

A That's $7.12.

3 **Look at the pictures. Complete the dialogue.**

1

A What would you like to eat ?

B I'll have ¹ _____.

2

A Can I have some ² _____?

B Sparkling or still?

A ³ _____, please.

3

A Is that ⁴ _____
  or ⁵ _____?

B It's ⁶ _____.

4

A Anything ⁷ _____?

B Yes, please.
  ⁸ _____.

5

A That's ⁹ _____, please.

B ¹⁰ _____.

A Thank you.

4 **You are ordering a meal in a café. Choose from the food and drinks on the menu and complete your part of the dialogue.**

Café Menu

Sandwiches

Ham & cheese	$4.50
Chicken	$4.50
Egg	$4.00

Drinks

Soda	$3.90
Fruit juice (apple / orange)	$3.90

Server Can I help you?

You _____

Server Is that for here, or to go?

You _____

Server What would you like to drink?

You _____

Server Anything else?

You _____

Server OK. That's _____, please.

You _____

Server Thank you. And here's your change.

You Thanks.

That tastes good!

Mealtimes can often be a problem for children because they don't like the food in front of them. Their parents think the food tastes delicious, but the children think it's horrible. Why does this happen?

There's a simple explanation. People taste food with tiny things in their mouths called taste buds. Adults have about ten thousand of them. But children have a lot more taste buds. So when children eat something, the flavor can be incredibly strong for them, but pretty normal for their parents!

The way people enjoy food changes during their lives. Most children like candy, cookies, and chocolate. They don't usually like food or drink with strong flavors like coffee or tea. But as people get older, they

can enjoy these strong flavors because a lot of the taste buds in their mouths don't work any more. That's why teenagers start to enjoy more types of food.

There's another very important reason for people's changing enjoyment of food: their noses. They experience the flavor of food not only in their mouths, but in their noses, too. Some aromas are nice for adults, but children find them very strong. This can affect children's enjoyment of food.

Perhaps the most important influence on children's enjoyment of food is its appearance. If it comes in a nice packet, it's usually popular with children, but if it doesn't look good, not many kids want to eat it!

Did You Know?
- Insects have taste buds on their feet!
- Girls have more taste buds than boys!

Reading

1 Read the article. Then answer the questions.

Where are your taste buds?
They're in your mouth.

1 Why are some types of food delicious for adults, but horrible for children?
_____

2 What types of food do most children prefer?
_____

3 How do children usually react to things like coffee and tea? _____

4 What happens when some of your taste buds don't work any more? _____

5 At what age do we start to enjoy more types of food? _____

6 Which parts of our body help us to enjoy food?
_____

7 Flavor and aroma are important in food. What else is important for children's enjoyment of food? _____

8 Where do insects experience taste on their bodies? _____

Writing

2 Write a description of meals in your family. Include the following information:

- Who cooks the meals in your family?
- Describe the meals that the other people in your family make.
- How often do you cook?
- Describe the meals you make.

6 Grammar rules

Present progressive for future

1. We use the present progressive to talk about something that is happening now.
   Tom**'s doing** his homework at the moment.

2. We also use the present progressive to talk about future plans.
   We**'re flying** to Miami tomorrow.

3. When we use the present progressive for future, we need to say when.
   I'm meeting my friend **on Friday afternoon**.

Affirmative		
I	'm (am)	playing
you	're (are)	playing
he	's (is)	playing
she	's (is)	playing
it	's (is)	playing
we	're (are)	playing
you	're (are)	playing
they	're (are)	playing

4. We make the present progressive with the present simple of *be* + base form of the verb + *-ing*.
   I'm driv**ing**.
   They**'re** eat**ing**.

5. For most verbs, we add *-ing* to the base form.

6. However, there are some spelling variations:
   - verbs ending in *-e*. Drop the *-e* and add *-ing*.
     hav**e** → hav**ing**
   - short verbs ending in a vowel plus a consonant. Double the final consonant and add *-ing*.
     sit → si**tt**ing

Negative		
I	'm not (am not)	waiting
you	aren't (are not)	waiting
he	isn't (is not)	waiting
she	isn't (is not)	waiting
it	isn't (is not)	waiting
we	aren't (are not)	waiting
you	aren't (are not)	waiting
they	aren't (are not)	waiting

7. We make the negative form of the present progressive with *be* + *not* + base form of the verb + *-ing*.
   I**'m not** listening.
   We **aren't** speaking.

Questions		
Am	I	going?
Are	you	going?
Is	he	going?
Is	she	going?
Is	it	going?
Are	we	going?
Are	you	going?
Are	they	going?

8. We make the question form of the present progressive with *be* + subject + base form of the verb + *-ing*.

Short answers	
Affirmative	**Negative**
Yes, you **are**.	No, you **aren't**.
Yes, I **am**.	No, I'm **not**.
Yes, he **is**.	No, he **isn't**.
Yes, she **is**.	No, she **isn't**.
Yes, it **is**.	No, it **isn't**.
Yes, you **are**.	No, you **aren't**.
Yes, we **are**.	No, we **aren't**.
Yes, they **are**.	No, they **aren't**.

9. We make short answers of the present progressive with *Yes*, + subject pronoun + *be* or *No*, + subject pronoun + *be*.
   Are you working? **Yes, I am.**
   Is the bus leaving? **No, it isn't.**

Student Book p.63

Future time expressions

1 We use the present progressive for future with these time expressions:

- *this morning / afternoon / evening*
  They're leaving **this afternoon**.
- *tonight*
  He's going **tonight**.
- *tomorrow morning / afternoon / evening / night*
  We're going to London **tomorrow night**.
- *next Friday / weekend / week / month / summer / year*
  They're moving to a new house **next week**.
- *At* + the time
  at twelve o'clock, **at** midnight, **at** 3 p.m.
  We're meeting Jennifer **at 4 p.m.**
- *At* + longer period of time
  at Christmas, **at** Easter
  We're seeing our cousins **at Christmas**.
- *On* + the day or the date
  on 3rd August, **on** my birthday, **on** Monday, **on** Christmas Day
  I'm having a big party **on my birthday**.
- *In* + the month, season, year
  in August, **in** the summer, **in** 2016
  He's moving to Australia **in 2016**.

How long ...? + take

1 We use *How long + take* to ask about length of time.
  How long does it **take** you to walk to school?
  It **takes** me fifteen minutes.

2 We can use *How long + take* with or without the subject pronoun *you*.
  How long does **it take** to drive to Maine?
  It takes four hours.
  How long does **it take you** to have breakfast?
  It takes me about twenty minutes.

3 We can answer the question *How long + take* with these expressions:

about (five) minutes	three quarters of an hour
(ten) minutes	an hour
a quarter of an hour	an hour and a half
half an hour	two and a half hours

Student Book pp.63, 65

Word list

Review the Vocabulary. Write your own study notes (or translation) for each word.

Transportation

airplane _____

bicycle / bike _____

boat _____

bus _____

car _____

helicopter _____

motorcycle _____

subway _____

taxi _____

train _____

truck _____

Check it out!

Forget it! _____

Get lost! _____

Good luck! _____

Learn it, use it!

Are you free on ...? _____

Yes, I am. / No, I'm not. _____

What do you want to do? _____

Let's go / do / play ... _____

How about doing / going ...? _____

Why don't we go / do ...? _____

How about going / doing ...? _____

Yes. / OK. / All right. _____

Good idea. / No. / No, I'm sorry, I can't. / No, I don't like ...

_____

_____

Where do you want to meet? _____

Let's meet at ... _____

Student Book pp.62, 60, 64

6 Exercises

Vocabulary
Transportation

1 Look at the pictures. Complete the crossword.

		¹A		²	
³		I			
⁴	⁵	R			
		P	⁶		
⁷		L			
		A	⁸		
		N			
⁹		E		¹⁰	

Down ↓

1   2

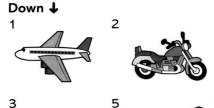

3   5   10

Across →

3   4   6

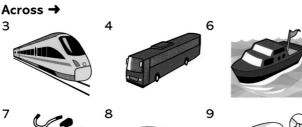

7   8   9

2 Choose the correct answers.

A **boat** / **subway** travels on water.

1 I had $2,000 in my bag, so I traveled home **in a taxi** / **on my bike**.
2 We flew over the city in a **helicopter** / **truck**.
3 The **truck** / **motorcycle** only has room for one passenger.
4 **An airplane** / **The subway** travels under the ground.
5 The **bus** / **car** had about fifty people in it.
6 The **subway** / **truck** brings fresh fruit and vegetables to the store every day.

Grammar
Future time expressions

3 Complete the sentences with the words in the box.

> at   in   next   on   this   tomorrow

I'm having a piano lesson _this_ afternoon.

1 Are you going to the Pink concert _____ week?
2 I'm not going to school _____ morning.
3 We're going to Hawaii on vacation _____ the summer.
4 My aunt is arriving _____ May 5ᵗʰ.
5 I'm meeting my friends _____ eleven o'clock.

Present progressive for future

4 Complete the message with the present progressive form of the words in the box.

> finish   go   go   have   meet   not come   study

Hi, Miguel,

Are you free on Saturday morning? Rob and I _are going_ skateboarding. Do you want to come with us? We ¹_____ at my house at 10 a.m. In the evening, Dad and I ²_____ to the movies. I want to see *Monsters University*. Do you like cartoons? Do you want to see the movie with us?
Simon
P.S. I ³_____ to basketball practice this evening. I ⁴_____ my science project and I ⁵_____ math! We ⁶_____ a math test at school tomorrow!!!

5 Write questions in the correct order

on / going / you / are / to / the / game / soccer / Saturday ?
Are you going to the soccer game on Saturday?

1 party / coming / Paul / to / is / the ?
_____

2 bus / what / leaving / time / is / the ?
_____

3 test / are / we / geography / when / our / having ?
_____

4 mom / is / tomorrow / you / your / driving ?
_____

6 Read the plans and messages. Write questions in the present progressive for future. Then write the answers.

> 10 a.m. go shopping with Mom
>
> 2 p.m.   meet Ross on Canal Street
>
> 6 p.m.   go to the movies with Norie

Who / Alicia / go / shopping with?
Who is Alicia going shopping with?
She's going shopping with her mom.

1 Where / Alicia / meet / Ross?

_____

_____

2 What time / she / go / to the movies with Norie?

_____

_____

Message ✕

> Sorry, Bruno. I can't come to your party on Saturday night.
> David

Send

3 When / Bruno / have / a party?

_____

_____

4 David / go to the party?

_____

_____

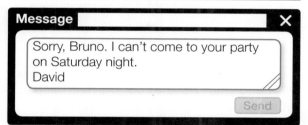

Hi, Camila,
See you at the bus stop at 11:30. The number 11 bus goes to Bellevue Street. We can have lunch at Pizza Paradise, and then we can go to the movies.
Lily ☺

5 Where / Camila and Lily / meet?

_____

_____

6 How / they / travel / to Bellevue Street?

_____

_____

7 Where / they / have / lunch?

_____

_____

8 What / they / do / after lunch?

_____

_____

How long ...? + take

7 Use the information to write questions and answers.

> drive from New York to Cape Cod = 5–6 hours
> How long does it take to drive from New York to Cape Cod?
> It takes 5–6 hours.

1 fly to Mars = between 150 and 300 days

_____

_____

2 travel from Seattle to Chicago by train = two days

_____

_____

3 walk one kilometer on foot = twelve minutes

_____

_____

4 fly from London to Sydney = 22 hours

_____

_____

5 travel from Battery Park to Times Square by taxi = fourteen minutes

_____

_____

Round-up

8 Complete the dialogue with the correct form of the verbs in the box.

> arrive come do drive fly go
> make stay take take visit

Luis Why are you so happy, Kayla?

Kayla My cousins from Scotland _are coming_ tomorrow. They ¹_____ from Edinburgh. It's a long way. I'm really excited.

Luis That's great news. How old are they?

Kayla Ian is 15, and Fiona is 14.

Luis What time ²_____?

Kayla At about 5 p.m., I think. Dad and I ³_____ to the airport to meet them when they land.

Luis How long ⁴_____?

Kayla For two weeks with us. Then they ⁵_____ a train and they ⁶_____ our grandparents for a week.

Luis How long ⁷_____ to go from here to your grandparents?

Kayla It takes an hour and a half. Mom ⁸_____ a lot of food because Ian eats a lot!

Luis What ⁹_____ with them when they are here?

Kayla We ¹⁰_____ to Disney World in Florida. I can't wait!

Inviting and making arrangements

1 Complete the dialogues with the words in the box. Use the dialogues on page 64 of the Student Book to check your answers.

Are	doing	free	How	Let's	meeting
mind	No	not	OK	time	want

1

David   Hi, Alvaro. Are you _free_ on Sunday morning?

Alvaro   Yes, I am.

David   Great. ¹_____ do something together.

Alvaro   Good idea. What do you ²_____ to do?

David   ³_____ about going to the new swimming pool?

Alvaro   ⁴_____. Where do you want to meet?

David   Let's meet at the subway.

Alvaro   Fine. At what ⁵_____?

David   Is ten o'clock OK?

Alvaro   Yes, that's fine. See you on Sunday!

2

Maria   I'm going to the movies on Thursday, Clara. ⁶_____ you free?

Clara   No, I'm sorry, I'm ⁷_____. I'm ⁸_____ my cousin on Thursday.

Maria   Oh, OK. How about ⁹_____ something on Saturday afternoon?

Clara   ¹⁰_____, I'm sorry, I'm playing soccer on Saturday afternoon.

Maria   Never ¹¹_____. Let's go another time.

Clara   Yes, OK. Thanks, Maria.

2 Write the dialogues in the correct order.

1

___ Yes, I can! Thanks, Lily! See you on Saturday!

___ Let's meet at my house. Mom's taking me to the concert. You can come with us.

___ Yes, I am! Thanks! Where do you want to meet?

_1_ I have tickets for the One Direction concert on Saturday. Are you free to come with me?

___ Great! What time are you leaving?

___ We're leaving at six thirty. Can you be here at six?

2

___ Sorry, but I can't. My aunt and uncle are coming for lunch on Sunday.

___ Oh, OK. What about Sunday?

___ No, sorry, I'm not. I'm watching a soccer game with my dad on Saturday.

___ Are you free on Saturday?

___ Never mind. Let's go another time.

3 Use the prompts to write invitations. Accept (✓) or refuse (✗) the invitations and give an excuse.

play tennis / Saturday / free? (✗ playing soccer)

A   I'm playing tennis on Saturday. Are you free?

B   No, I'm sorry, I'm playing soccer.

1 have a party / Friday evening / free? (✓)

A _____

B _____

2 free Wednesday afternoon? / go shopping (✗ babysitting my little brother)

A _____

B _____

3 watch a movie at my house / tomorrow evening / free? (✗ my mom's birthday)

A _____

B _____

4 free Sunday morning? / go swimming (✓)

A _____

B _____

4 Use the instructions to write two dialogues inviting your friend to do different things. Choose the activities from the pictures.

 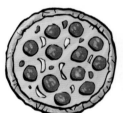

Invite your friend to do one of the activities in the pictures on Thursday afternoon.

A _____

Accept the invitation and ask where to meet.

B _____

Suggest meeting at the bus stop.

A _____

Accept and ask what time to meet.

B _____

Suggest half past four.

A _____

Accept.

B _____

Student Book p.64   **Extra practice** online

Ana's Blog

I'm so excited. Tomorrow, I'm flying to Guadeloupe, a French island in the Caribbean! It's my first time there. My cousin, Jose Luis, is working in a hotel there for the summer, so I have a free place to stay. Tonight, I'm catching a train to Miami, and I'm staying with a friend for the night. Tomorrow afternoon, I'm taking another train to the airport. My airplane is leaving at about 7 p.m. It's a 26-hour journey, so I'm taking a lot of good books and music so I don't get bored! I'm also taking my old French books from school. People speak French in Guadaloupe, and I'd like to practice it while I'm there.

Jose Luis is meeting me at the airport and driving me to his hotel. Luckily it isn't far from the airport – it only takes twenty minutes by car.

Jose Luis is working all summer, so he doesn't have much free time. But he has weekends free, so we're exploring the island by bike – biking is very popular on Guadeloupe. I have a lot of other plans, too. First, I'm going to the Guadaloupe National Park on Tuesday. Then, on Wednesday, I'm going shopping and on Thursday, I'm going surfing. On Friday, I'm visiting the island's archaeological museum. On Saturday, Jose Luis is taking me to one if the island's most beautiful beaches, and after that, we're going to a party to meet his friends. So I need to practice my terrible French!

Reading

1 Read the blog. Then answer the questions.

Who is Ana visiting in Guadaloupe?
She's visiting her cousin, Jose Luis.

1 Where is she staying tonight?

2 How long does Ana's journey take?

3 How are Ana and Jose Luis traveling to his hotel?

4 Is Ana spending all of her time with Jose Luis?

5 What form of transportation is she using to explore the island?

6 Who is she meeting on Saturday evening?

7 What does Ana think of her French?

Writing

2 Imagine you are spending next Saturday with your friend. Write a description of your plans. Remember to include language for ordering events in your description. Include the following information:

- Who are you spending the day with?
- Which places are you going to?
- Which forms of transportation are you using?
- How long do the journeys take?

Grammar rules

Comparative adjectives

1 We use comparative adjectives to talk about differences between two things or people.

Tom **is** tall**er than** his brother.

2 We use *than* after the adjective and before the second thing or person:

The Mississippi River is longer **than** the Hudson.

New York is bigger **than** San Francisco.

Regular adjectives

Short adjectives		
Adjectives	**Comparative**	
fast high small	add -er	faster (than) higher (than) smaller (than)
large nice	add -r	larger (than) nicer (than)
big sad	double the consonant and add -er	bigger (than) sadder (than)

1 With short adjectives, we add *-er*.

long + **-er** ➝ long**er**

deep + **-er** ➝ deep**er**

strong + **-er** ➝ strong**er**

2 With adjectives that end with *-e*, we add *-r*.

close + **-r** ➝ close**r**

late + **-r** ➝ late**r**

nice + **-r** ➝ nice**r**

3 With short adjectives ending in a vowel plus a consonant, double the final consonant and add *-er*.

thin + **ner** ➝ thin**ner**

big + **ger** ➝ big**ger**

hot + **ter** ➝ hot**ter**

Adjectives ending with consonant + -y		
Adjectives	**Comparative adjectives**	
happy funny	drop -y and add -ier	happier (than) funnier (than)

4 With adjectives ending in a consonant and *-y*, we drop *-y* and add *-ier*.

heavy ➝ heav**ier**

easy ➝ eas**ier**

Long adjectives		
Adjectives	**Comparative**	
important	more + adjective	more important (than)
boring		more boring (than)
interesting		more interesting (than)

5 With long adjectives, we put *more* + adjective + *than*.

Delhi is **more populated than** Bangalore.

Action movies are **more exciting than** love stories.

6 Some adjectives of two syllables follow the same rules as short adjectives.

clever ➝ clever**er**

narrow ➝ narrow**er**

quiet ➝ quiet**er**

simple ➝ simpl**er**

Cats are **cleverer** than dogs.

7 With some two-syllable adjectives, the short adjective and long adjective patterns are both correct (adding *-er* or *more*). You can check the correct comparative form of an adjective in a dictionary.

common ➝ common**er** (**than**)

      ➝ **more** common (**than**)

Irregular adjectives

Irregular adjectives	
Adjective	**Comparative**
good	**better** (than)
bad	**worse** (than)
far	**farther / further** (than)

• Some adjectives are irregular. You need to learn them.

Pablo is **better** than Yuki at soccer.

My school is **farther** than yours.

as ... as

as ... as		
Europe isn't	as big	as Africa.
Bikes aren't	as expensive	as cars.
Is Mount Cho Oyu	as high	as K2?

1 We put *as* before and after the adjective.

2 We use *as ... as* to say how two things or people are the same.
   You are **as** tall **as** my brother.
   My brother is **as** tall **as** you.

3 We use *not as ... as* to say how two things or people are not the same.
   English is**n't as** difficult **as** German.
   = German **is more** difficult **than** English.

   The Atlantic is**n't as** deep **as** the Pacific.
   = The Pacific is **deeper than** the Atlantic.

   The Blue Lake Hotel is**n't as** cheap **as** The Gardenia Hotel.
   = The Gardenia hotel is **cheaper than** the Blue Lake Hotel.

less ... than

1 We can use *less* before the adjective.
   This island is **less interesting than** the other island.

2 *Less ... than* means the same as *not as ... as*.
   The Gibson Desert in Australia **is less** famous **than** the Sahara desert in Africa.
   = The Gibson Desert in Australia **isn't as** famous **as** the Sahara desert in Africa.

3 We use *not as ... as* more often than we use *less ... than*.

Student Book p.77

Word list

Review the Vocabulary. Write your own study notes (or translation) for each word.

Geography
continent _____
country _____
desert _____
island _____
lake _____
mountain _____
ocean _____
river _____
sea _____
volcano _____

Check it out!
Go for it! _____
How's it going? _____
I'm terrible. _____
No way! _____

Learn it, use it!
How much are the tickets? _____
They're $20. / The tickets cost $20. _____
What time does it open / close / start / finish? _____
It's open / starts at ... _____
It closes / finishes at ... _____
It's open from ... to ... _____
Where is it? _____
It's on / near / in ... _____
How can I get there? _____
You can take the subway / take a bus / walk. _____

Student Book pp.74, 72, 76

7 Exercises

Vocabulary
Geography

1 Find nine more geography words in the puzzle.

V	O	L	T	R	I	V	E	L	S	I
N	A	C	K	A	R	E	L	A	N	T
O	H	A	M	S	O	P	S	D	D	E
A	B	C	O	U	W	R	Y	R	W	R
M	N	R	W	N	T	B	I	N	O	C
O	I	B	P	A	R	Y	R	T	I	D
U	A	Y	O	R	Y	D	N	E	N	M
N	T	R	C	E	N	A	T	M	D	P
P	R	W	N	A	C	R	B	Y	E	R
T	R	E	T	A	L	A	C	K	E	A
D	E	S	A	W	E	K	B	W	S	P

2 Complete the sentences with the words from exercise 1.

The Nile is a very long <u>river</u>.
1 Guadeloupe is an _____.
2 Mount Everest is a _____ in the Himalayas.
3 Mount Kilauea in Hawaii is an active _____.
4 Loch Ness is a famous Scottish _____.
5 The Mediterranean _____ lies between Europe, Asia, and Africa.
6 There's very little water in the Atacama _____.
7 In 1932, Amelia Earhart was the first woman to fly solo across the Atlantic _____.
8 Did you know that Australia is a country and a _____?

Grammar
Comparative adjectives
Short adjectives

3 Complete the chart with the comparative adjective.

Adjective	Comparative	
tall	<u>taller</u>	(than)
long	1 _____	(than)
windy	2 _____	(than)
hot	3 _____	(than)
easy	4 _____	(than)
slow	5 _____	(than)
nice	6 _____	(than)

4 Write comparative sentences. Use the adjectives from exercise 3.

There were strong winds yesterday. But there aren't any today.
<u>Yesterday was windier than today.</u>

1 My sister runs the 100 m in 13.5 seconds. I take 11.6 seconds.

_____

2 Today, it's 28°C. Yesterday, it was 22°C.

_____

3 I did my math homework without any problems, but my English homework was really difficult.

_____

4 I like the blue jacket, but I don't like the green one.

_____

5 The Nile River is 6,650 kilometers long. The Amazon River is 6,400 kilometers long.

_____

Long adjectives

5 Complete the text with the comparative form of the adjectives in the box. Use *than* where necessary.

> dangerous   difficult   ~~exciting~~   expensive
> interesting   popular

I love mountains. I have a lot of books about them, but climbing them is <u>more exciting than</u> reading about them! I find climbing ¹_____ other sports because there are always beautiful things to see. Climbing can be ²_____ other sports, but I know how to stay safe. Climbing isn't cheap. You need the correct shoes, etc. But a lot of other activities are ³_____! Perhaps for that reason climbing is becoming ⁴_____. When I am older, I want to climb Mount Everest. But I'm not sure about K2. K2 is smaller than Mount Everest, but it's ⁵_____ to climb!

Irregular adjectives

6 Complete the chart with the comparative adjective.

Irregular adjective	Comparative	
good	1 _____	(than)
bad	2 _____	(than)
far	3 _____	(than)

Student Book pp.74–75   **Extra practice** online

7 Complete the sentences with the comparative form of the adjectives in the box.

bad cheap dangerous famous ~~far~~ good

I walk one kilometer to school every day. But William walks two kilometers.
William walks farther / further than me every day.

1 It was mild yesterday, but it's freezing now.
The weather today is ________________ yesterday.

2 I feel safe in towns, but I don't feel safe in cities.
I think that cities are ________________ towns.

3 We all know about the Empire State Building in New York. But do we all know about the Shard in London?
Is the Empire State Building ________________ the Shard?

4 Leo doesn't like the restaurant's pizzas. He prefers his mom's!
Leo thinks that his mom's pizzas are ________________ the restaurant's.

5 It costs $589 to travel by train from Los Angeles to Minneapolis. But it costs $280 to fly there.
The airplane ticket is ________________ the train ticket.

as ... as

8 Read the sentences. Write sentences with the same meaning. Use *(not) as ... as* and the adjectives in parentheses.

The volcano Kilauea erupts more often than Hualālai. (active)
The volcano Hualālai isn't as active as Kileauea.

1 This book cost $10. The magazine costs $10. (expensive)
____

2 I wasn't interested in last night's movie. And this one isn't any better! (boring)
____

3 Africa is big: 30,244,049 km^2. But Asia is 44,391,162 km^2! (large)
____

4 Houston is a nice city. But I think there are more things to do in New Orleans. (interesting)
____

5 Your sister is very friendly. And I like your cousin, too. (nice)
____

less ... than

9 Write sentences about the people, things, and places below with *less ... than* and the adjectives in parentheses. You can use your own ideas.

books / movies (interesting)
Movies are less interesting than books.

1 Rio de Janeiro / Paris (beautiful)
____

2 soccer / basketball (popular)
____

3 Daddy Yankee / Don Omar (famous)
____

4 mountain biking / climbing (exciting)
____

5 happiness / money (important)
____

10 Rewrite your answers to exercise 9 using *not as ... as*.

Movies aren't as interesting as books.

Round-up

11 Choose the correct answers.

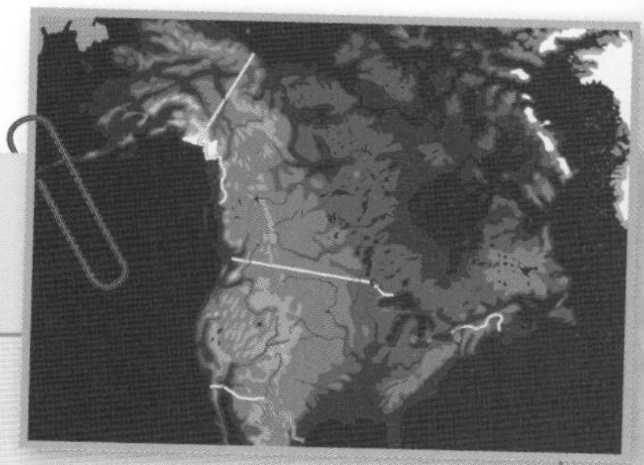

Canada and the U.S. are two large countries on the continent of North America.
The U.S. became a country in 1776, but Canada became a country in 1867, so Canada is **more young / younger** than the U.S.
And what about size? The U.S.'s total area [1]**isn't big / isn't as big** as Canada's. But the population of the U.S. is a lot [2]**biger / bigger**: 313.9 million live in the U.S., while only 34.5 million people live in Canada – the country is [3]**less populated / as populated** than the state of California, where 38.4 million people live!
Canada has more lakes than the U.S. But its mountains aren't [4]**as high / higher** as American mountains. Generally, the weather in the U.S. is [5]**better / gooder** than Canadian weather, but Canada's long, cold winters make it [6]**more popular / popularer** for its winter sports!
Reports show that in general, things like food, transportation, and clothes are [7]**more expensive / expensiver** in Canada than in the U.S. But they also show that Canadian cities are [8]**more nice / nicer** places to live in [9]**as / than** American cities. Where would you prefer to be?

Asking for tourist information

1 Complete the dialogue. Use the dialogue on page 76 of the Student Book as a model.

Assistant Good morning. *Can I help* _____ you?

Cesar Yes, please. I want to visit the New Orleans Museum of Art. ¹_____ are the tickets?

Assistant They're $10 for adults, and $6 for children.

Cesar What time ²_____?

Assistant ³_____ 10 a.m. to 6 p.m. on Tuesdays and Thursdays, and 11 a.m. to 5 p.m. on weekends. It's closed on Mondays, and Wednesdays are free.

Cesar ⁴_____?

Assistant It's on One Collins Diboll Circle, in City Park.

Cesar ⁵_____ there?

Assistant You can take the number 91 bus, or a taxi. You can get there by bike, too. That's cheaper than a taxi!

Cesar ⁶_____.

Assistant You're welcome. Have a nice day!

2 Write questions for the answers.

A *Can I help you?* _____

B Yes, please. I want to visit the Empire State Building.

1 A _____

B It's at 350 Fifth Avenue, between 33ʳᵈ and 34ᵗʰ Streets.

2 A _____

B It's open from 8 a.m. to 2 a.m. every day.

3 A _____

B You can take the subway, or the train.

4 A _____

B Tickets start from $25 for adults, and $19 for children.

3 Imagine that you work in a tourist information office. Look at the information and answer the tourist's questions.

Location: 2920 Zoo Drive, San Diego
Opening times: Open every day 9 a.m. – 6 p.m.
Tickets: Adults $44 / children $34
Transport: Number 7 bus from city center

You Hello. *Can I help you?* _____

Tourist Yes, please. I want to visit San Diego Zoo. Where is it, please?

You ¹_____

Tourist How can I get there?

You ²_____

Tourist How much are the tickets?

You ³_____

Tourist What time does it open?

You ⁴_____

Tourist That's great. Thanks very much.

4 Imagine that you are a tourist in a tourist information office in London, U.K. Use the information to write a dialogue. Use the dialogues in exercises 1 and 3 as models.

The London Eye

Location:
On the South Bank, London

Opening times:
Open every day, including Christmas Day
From 10 a.m. – 9:30 p.m.

Tickets:
Adults £19.20 /
Children: £12.30 /
Over 60s: £15.30

Transport:
Subway to Waterloo or Embankment stations
Train to Waterloo
Bus numbers 211, 77, or 381

Welcome to Beautiful Bahia

The state of Bahia is in the northeast of Brazil. It's the perfect place for a vacation! Here are some of the things you can see and do there.

Salvador – Capital of Happiness

Salvador is the capital city of the region. It's smaller than Sao Paulo or Rio, but some people say it's more Brazilian. The old part of the town has beautiful, colorful houses and monuments from the 17th century. The carnival in Salvador is spectacular. It takes place in February, and over 200 groups take part in the parades. The carnival party lasts for seven days and seven nights!

A Natural Paradise

The Chapada Diamantina National Park is in the center of Bahia. It's a beautiful region of mountains, rivers, waterfalls, and natural swimming pools. It's less populated than the coast, and it's perfect for active tourists, too. There are lots of things to do, like walking, mountain biking, swimming, and snorkeling.

To the Ocean

Whale watching is a popular activity in the Abrolhos archipelago off the south coast of Bahia. Thousands of tourists visit the region from July through November when the whales migrate there. It's also famous for its colorful, exotic fish, and spectacular coral formations.

Reading

1 Read the article about Bahia quickly and find the name of:

The capital city _____

A national park _____

An archipelago _____

2 Read the article again. Then answer the questions.

1 Where is Bahia?

_____

2 What can tourists see in the old part of Salvador?

_____

3 How long does the carnival party last?

_____

4 Where is the Chapada Diamantina National Park?

_____

5 What can tourists do in the park?

_____

6 What is a popular activity in the Abrolhos archipelago?

_____

7 Where is the Abrolhos archipelago?

_____

8 What is it famous for?

_____

Writing

3 Write an entry for a tourist brochure about a region in your country. Remember to use *also* and *too* in your text. Include the following information:

- location
- geography
- cities
- places to visit
- things to do

Welcome to ... It's the perfect place for a vacation ...

8 Grammar rules

Superlative adjectives

1 We use superlative adjectives to compare three or more things or people.

   Asia is **the largest** continent in the world.

2 We often follow superlative adjective + noun with *in* or *of*.

   – *in* + most phrases, *in* Ecuador, *in* my school, *in* my family

   Juana is the nicest girl **in** the class.

   Jaime is the fastest runner **in** the school.

   – *of* + other phrases, *of* my life, *of* the year

   It was the longest vacation **of** my life.

Regular adjectives
Short adjectives

Short adjectives		
Adjectives	**Superlative**	
	put **the** before all adjectives	
fast proud tall	and add **-est**	the fast**est** the proud**est** the tall**est**
large safe	and add **-st**	the large**st** the safe**st**
big sad	double the final consonant and add **-est**	the big**gest** the sad**dest**

1 With short adjectives, we add *-est*.

   long + -est → the long**est**

   slow + -est → the slow**est**

   strong + -est → the strong**est**

2 With adjectives that end with *-e*, we add *-st*.

   close + -st → the close**st**

   wide + -st → the wide**st**

   nice + -st → the nice**st**

3 With short adjectives ending in a vowel plus a consonant, double the final consonant and add *-est*.

   thin + **nest** → the thin**nest**

   big + **gest** → the big**gest**

   hot + **test** → the hot**test**

Adjectives ending with *-y*		
Adjectives	**Superlative**	
happy angry	put **the** before all adjectives, drop -y and add **-iest**	the happ**iest** the angr**iest**

4 With adjectives ending *-y*, we drop *-y* and add *-iest*.

   tidy → the tid**iest**

   heavy → the heav**iest**

   easy → the eas**iest**

Long adjectives

Long adjectives		
Adjectives	**Superlative**	
important	put **the most** before all adjectives	**the most** important
boring		**the most** boring
interesting		**the most** interesting

1 With long adjectives, we put *the most* before the adjective.

   Ana is **the most confident** girl in my class.

   That is **the most boring** book in the world.

2 Some adjectives of two syllables follow the same rules as short adjectives.

   clever   the clever**est**

   narrow   the narrow**est**

   quiet   the quiet**est**

   simple   the simpl**est**

   Spreuerhofstrasse in Germany is **the narrowest** street in the world.

3 With some two-syllable adjectives, the short adjective and long adjective patterns are both correct (adding *-est* or *most*). You can check the correct superlative form of an adjective in a dictionary.

Irregular adjectives

Irregular adjectives	
Adjective	**Superlative**
good	the best
bad	the worst
far	the farthest / the furthest

• Some adjectives are irregular. You need to learn them.
That was **the best** day of my life.

Comparative / Superlative

1 We can use the comparative to compare two people or things. We can compare them in three different ways:
  – in a positive way
    Today, I feel **happier than** yesterday.
  – in a negative way
    I feel **less happy than** yesterday.
    I **don't** feel **as happy as** yesterday.
  – to say things are the same
    I feel **as happy as** yesterday.

2 We can use the superlative to compare three or more people or things.

3 We can compare in two different ways:
  • in a positive way
    He is **the most excited** child in the room.
  • in a negative way
    He is **the least excited** child in the room.

the least

Long adjectives		
Adjectives	**Superlative**	
embarrassed	add **the least** before the adjective	the least embarrassed
nervous		the least nervous
confident		the least confident

1 We use *the least* to say that something is less than the others. *The least* is the superlative form of *less*.

2 We put *the least* before the adjective.
  I have **the least difficult** job in the office.

3 We often follow *the least* + noun with *in* or *of*.
  – *in* + most phrases, *in* Peru, *in* my school, *in* my family
    This is the least interesting place **in** Chile.
    He was the least nervous **in** the team.
  – *of* + other phrases, *of* my life, *of* the year
    Tom is the least interesting **of** my friends.

Student Book p.85

Word list

Review the Vocabulary. Write your own study notes (or translation) for each word.

Feelings and emotions
angry _____
annoyed _____
bored _____
confident _____
embarrassed _____
excited _____
fed up _____
frightened _____
happy _____
nervous _____
proud _____
sad _____

Check it out!
Here we come! _____
so far _____
That sucks! _____

Learn it, use it!
Can I speak with …? _____
Yes, of course. _____
Sorry, … isn't here right now. _____
Who's calling? _____
It's … _____
Is this …? _____
Yes, it is. / No, it isn't. _____
Do you want to leave a message? _____
Yes, please. Can you tell him / her …? / Can you ask him / her to return my call? _____
No, thanks. _____

Student Book pp.82, 80, 84

8 Exercises

Vocabulary
Feelings and emotions

1 Reorder the letters to form feelings and emotions.

d s a   _sad_

1 n o n y a d e   _____

2 t r e g n e f i h d   _____

3 s v u n r e o   _____

4 p h a y p   _____

5 d r u p o   _____

6 d f e p u   _____

7 a s b r e s e d m a r   _____

8 d e r b o   _____

2 Complete the sentences with the correct words from exercise 1.

I feel very _sad_ because my best friend is moving to another town.

1 I'm _____ because I have a test tomorrow.

2 Sam is very _____ with you. She thinks you broke her MP3 player.

3 Adrian is really _____ because he got some awesome presents for his birthday.

4 My parents are _____ of me because I'm doing really well at school.

5 I'm _____ because there aren't any interesting shows on TV!

6 Joana got really _____ when she heard a strange noise in the middle of the night.

Grammar
Superlative adjectives
Short adjectives

3 Complete the sentences with the superlative form of the adjectives in parentheses.

Nina is _the fastest_ runner on the team. (fast)

1 David is _____ boy I know. (happy)

2 How old is _____ person in the world? (old)

3 Mrs. Rodriguez is _____ teacher in my school. (nice)

4 This is _____ classroom in the school. (big)

5 The living room is _____ room in the house. (clean)

4 Look at the information in the chart. Write sentences with the adjectives below.

	Mom	Dad	Jorge	Angela
age	45	43	14	16
height	1 m 70	1 m 90	1 m 65	1 m 59
weight	73 kg	80 kg	54 kg	50 kg
hair color	blond	gray	black	brown

heavy   _Dad is the heaviest._

1 tall   _____

2 short   _____

3 light   _____

4 old   _____

5 young   _____

6 blond   _____

Long and irregular adjectives

5 Complete the dialogue with the correct form of the adjectives in parentheses.

Rosario What song are you listening to?

Claudia It's *I knew you were trouble* by Taylor Swift. It's one of _the most popular_ (popular) songs from her album. What do you think of her?

Rosario Oh, I love her, too. But I don't think that song is ¹_____ (good) one. I think *Love Story* is ²_____ (beautiful) song I know of Taylor's.

Claudia I saw her in concert last year, you know.

Rosario Wow! Awesome! You always do ³_____ (exciting) things. Did you get close to her?

Claudia No, our seats were ⁴_____ (far) from the stage – that was ⁵_____ (bad) thing. But it was ⁶_____ (amazing) night of my life!

W46

Student Book pp.82-83, 85   **Extra practice** online

8

6 Complete the sentences with the superlative form of the adjectives in the box.

> bad   confident   ~~good~~   interesting
> nervous   quiet   simple

I think that *Diamonds* is the <u>best</u> song on Rihanna's album, *Unapologetic*.
1 What was _____ thing about my vacation? It rained all week!
2 This museum has so much to look at. It's one of _____ places in the city.
3 The library is usually _____ room in the school.
4 Anabel is one of the most intelligent pupils in the school. So why is she always _____ before an exam?
5 The teacher chose Juan to make the presentation because he is _____ pupil in the class.
6 Sometimes _____ ideas are the best ones.

7 Write sentences that are true for you.

easy / school subject
I think the easiest school subject is art.
1 beautiful / place in my country
2 good / day of the year
3 funny / movie I know

Comparative / Superlative

8 Complete the text with the comparative or superlative form of the adjectives in parentheses.

When I was <u>younger</u> (young), I was a fan of Zac Efron. I thought he was ¹_____ (good) actor in the world. I also thought he had ²_____ (amazing) singing voice, and was definitely ³_____ (nice) to look at. My favorite actor now is Robert Pattinson. I think he is ⁴_____ (talented) than many other movie actors. And I think he gets ⁵_____ (good) looking every day! He's also a musician, and his songs are ⁶_____ (beautiful) than a lot of other music on the charts. I think he is ⁷_____ (great)!

the least

9 Write sentences with the same meaning. Use *the least* and the adjectives in the box.

> confident   dangerous   difficult
> expensive   ~~interesting~~

I think soccer is the most boring sport.
I think soccer is the least interesting sport.
1 These sneakers are the cheapest ones.
_____
2 For me, math is the easiest subject at school.
_____
3 Laura is the most nervous student before tests.
_____
4 People say that airplanes are the safest form of transportation.
_____

Round-up

10 Choose the correct answers.

Are you planning a trip to the U.S.? Here are some of its **most popular** / **popularest** places to visit.

At Disney World, in Orlando, Florida, you can meet your favorite Disney characters and learn about the history of Hollywood movies. Not surprisingly, it is one of the ¹**more** / **most** expensive vacation choices, but visitors say it is ²**better than** / **the best** other similar resorts.

If you prefer to be ³**closer** / **more close** to nature, then perhaps Yellowstone Park in Wyoming is the right choice for you. It's also one of the ⁴**beautifulest** / **most beautiful** places in the country. It attracts millions of visitors a year, but can sometimes feel like one of ⁵**quieter than** / **the quietest** and ⁶**least** / **less** populated places on Earth.

Washington, D.C. is our third suggestion, and some readers may feel ⁷**less** / **the least** excited by it than the first two. But the city has some of the ⁸**more** / **most** interesting museums in the country, and some of the ⁹**deliciousest** / **most delicious** food. It's also important to note that the city is perhaps the ¹⁰**least** / **most** expensive of our three ideas, because many of its attractions are free. So come and see what this city has to offer!

8 Communication

Making a phone call

1 Complete the dialogues with the words in the box.

> for you   ~~here~~   Is this Estela?
> leave a message   My number is
> return my call   speak with   Who's calling?

1
A Hello?
B Hi! It's Rafael
  here _____.
  1 _____
A No, it isn't. It's her cousin, Luisa. Estela isn't here right now. She's at the sports center. Do you want to
  2 _____?
B Yes, please. Can you ask her to
  3 _____ by nine o'clock at the latest? 4 _____ (212)-555-0444.
A That's (212)-555-0444. OK. Bye.
B Bye.

2
A Hello?
B Hello. Can I 5 _____ Antonia please?
A Yes, of course. 6 _____
B It's Mark, Antonia's boyfriend.
A Hi, Mark! Hang on a minute. Antonia! It's 7 _____. It's Mark.

2 Match the questions and answers.

1 Can I speak to Keisuke? _c_
2 Who's calling? ___
3 Does she have your number? ___
4 Is this Danilo? ___
5 Do you want to leave a message? ___

a No, she doesn't. It's (212)-555-0523.
b Yes, please. Can you tell Naiara I can't go to the concert tomorrow evening?
c ~~Sorry, he isn't here at the moment.~~
d It's Rosa, I'm Bastian's friend.
e No, it's his brother Ivan.

3 Read the information below. Then complete Eduardo's part of the dialogue.

You are Felipe's cousin, Eduardo. You answer the phone to Jaime. Felipe can't talk on the phone because he isn't at home. Tell Jaime that Felipe is at basketball practice. Ask if Jaime wants to leave a message, and ask if Felipe has his phone number. Repeat the number before you end the call.

Eduardo Hello? _____.
Jaime Hi! It's Jaime here. Is this Felipe?
Eduardo 1 _____
Jaime Where is he?
Eduardo 2 _____
Jaime Yes, please. Can you ask him to return my call by tomorrow morning?
Eduardo 3 _____
Jaime Oh, no, he doesn't. It's (212)-555-8833.
Eduardo 4 _____
Jaime Thanks. Bye.

4 Use the instructions to write dialogues.

1 You want to call Adriana, but you don't know her number. Phone Adriana's brother Caio and ask for her number.

_____
_____
_____
_____

2 Call your friend, Marcela. Marcela's sister Lisa answers. Marcela is in her bedroom. Tell Marcela you have two tickets for a concert tomorrow.

_____
_____
_____
_____

3 Phone your mom. Tell her you think you left your homework on the kitchen table. Ask her if it is still there.

_____
_____
_____
_____

Visit Mount Rushmore!

Visit Mount Rushmore, the most unusual monument in the U.S., and see the faces of four of our greatest presidents: George Washington (1732–1799), Thomas Jefferson (1743–1809), Abraham Lincoln (1809–1865), and Theodore Roosevelt (1858–1919). Each face is eighteen meters high, and they're the largest group of sculptures in the world!

The Mount Rushmore sculptures were the idea of a man called Doane Robinson in the early 1900s. The area around Mount Rushmore was very poor, and Robinson wanted to attract tourists to the region. Although at first he didn't know what kind of sculptures to build there, politicians in Washington agreed to create a memorial to four presidents from the first 150 years of U.S. history. But which four presidents were the best choice? The politicians had a lot of different opinions. However, the sculptor for the project, Gutzon Borglum, made the final decision.

Gutzon Borglum and his son created the Mount Rushmore sculptures between 1927 and 1941. Although they had about 400 local workers to help them, it was still one of the biggest and most difficult construction jobs in U.S. history. It was also one of the most dangerous. Amazingly, nobody died.

Today, the monument is one of the most popular tourist attractions in the U.S. and has more than two million visitors every year!

Reading

1 **Read the article. Then answer the questions.**

Which presidents can you see at the Mount Rushmore monument?
You can see George Washington,
Thomas Jefferson, Abraham Lincoln, and
Theodore Roosevelt.

1 What world record do the sculptures have?
_____

2 Who wanted to build sculptures in the area?
_____

3 Why did the area around Mount Rushmore need tourism?
_____

4 Who created the sculptures?
_____

5 How long did it take to create them?
_____

6 How many people helped them?
_____

7 How many tourists now visit the Mount Rushmore monument every year?
_____

Writing

2 **Read the factfile. Then write a review of the Grand Canyon Skywalk for a travel website. Remember to use *however* and *although*.**

Factfile

The Grand Canyon Skywalk

Where is it?
the Grand Canyon, Arizona

What is it?
a glass walkway over the deepest canyon in the world

What is special about it?
highest walkway in the world / can walk on it / look down at the canyon / one of the biggest tourist attractions in the south-west of America

How high is it?
1,200 meters above floor of the Grand Canyon

How wide is it?
3.1 meters wide

What is the walkway like?
looks pretty thin / very strong / exciting experience

Who built it?
the Hualapai Native American people (2006)

Why are some of the Hualapai unhappy about it?
built on an area of special ground for the Hualapai people

How can you get there?
nearest airport Grand Canyon West airport / at the moment very bad road to the Skywalk

OXFORD
UNIVERSITY PRESS

Great Clarendon Street, Oxford, OX2 6DP, United Kingdom

Oxford University Press is a department of the University of Oxford.
It furthers the University's objective of excellence in research, scholarship,
and education by publishing worldwide. Oxford is a registered trade
mark of Oxford University Press in the UK and in certain other countries

ISBN: 978 0 19 446337 9   Student Book & Workbook
ISBN: 978 0 19 446354 6   Student's Access Card
ISBN: 978 0 19 446345 4   Pack

Printed in China

This book is printed on paper from certified and well-managed sources

ACKNOWLEDGEMENTS

Cover photographs reproduced with permission from: Corbis (Ventura, California,
USA/David Pu'u), (Sydney Opera House/ Shaun Egan/JAI); Getty Images (teens
at a juice bar/Hola Images); OUP (glass marbles); Shutterstock (Young female
rock climber at sunset, Kalymnos Island, Greece/Photobac), (Climbers with
safety equipment on rock/Corepics VOF), (Abstract gray waving background/
Valenty).

Commissioned photography: Mark Bassett pp.10, 11, 18, 19, 30, 31, 38, 39, 52, 53,
60, 61, 72, 73, 80, 81.

Illustrations by: Mark Draisey pp.6 (ex 3), 15, 20, 50, 64, 97, W4, W13; Chuck
Gonzales pp.4, 5 (ex 7), 22, 32 (ex 1), 54, 55, 106; John Haslam pp.5 (ex 6), 8, 46,
62, 66, 74, 99, W29, W30, W34; Martin Impey p W36; Alan Rowe pp.6 (ex 4), 9,
14, 27, 34, 82, 107.

*The publisher would like to thank the following for their permission to reproduce
photographs*: Alamy pp.4 (Bruno/OJO Images Ltd, Gabriel/Paul Hakimata),
6 (Eduardo/Chris Rout), 7 (tennis player/Weberfoto), 37 (Everest/Irena Grizelj),
48 (Harry Potter theme park/Disney Magic), 58 (vending machine 1970s/
ClassicStock, healthy school meal/Foodfolio, unhealthy school meal/Jeff
Morgan 13), 59 (Okinawan meal/Amana Images Inc., hotdog/Joe Belanger),
66 (backpacker/Radius Images), 67 (Acapulco/Hemis), 70 (Masterchef
restaurant exterior/Bosiljka Zutich), 75 (brother and sister/Image Source),
76 (Central Park Zoo/D. Hurst, MOMA/Tips Images), 78 (beach/Douglas
Peebles Photography), 79 (Mt St Helens erupting/Lightroom Photos, barren
land/Richard Levine), 86 (birthday/Asia Images Group Pte Ltd), 87 (cycling/
Andrew Watson), 90 (burger/Paul Vinten), 101 (Airbus A380 cross section/
Steven May), 102 (Indian women eating/Louise Batalla Duran), W22 (boy/
Anyka), W31 (girl/BSIP SA), W37 (girl/David Young-Wolff, Guadaloupe aerial/
Jon Arnold Images Ltd, Guadaloupe street/Danita Delimont), W43 (Salvador
carnival/Pete M. Wilson), W47 (Disney World/Imagebroker), W48 (boy on
phone/Laura Dwight), W49 (Grand Canyon/National Geographic Image
Collection); Corbis pp.12 (Kiss/Jose Mendez), 16 (festival stage/Scott Moore/
Retna Ltd), 22 (Marie/Sven Hagolani, Gemma, Tina), 23 (Laurel and Hardy in
"Sons of the Desert". 1934 © Bettmann/CORBIS), 24 (JFK/Arnie Sachs/CNP, The
Supremes/Michael Ochs Archives), 25 (Greta Garbo/1950 © Sunset Boulevard),
26 (Bob Marley/Lynn Goldsmith), 28 (Montgomery race march background/
Steve Schapiro, black children in classroom/Bettmann), 35 (New Orleans/
Matthew Mcvay), 36 (Antarctica background/Ralph Lee Hopkins, Captain
Scott/Hulton-Deutsch Collection), 37 (Edmund Hillary/Bettmann), 47 (cinema/
Michael Hanson/Aurora Photos), 48 (JK Rowling/Chris Pizzello/Reuters), 56,
83 (blue whale/Denis Scott), 86 (girl in lift), 88 (Conor Maynard/Lee Harper, Ed
Sheeran/K.Dwek/London Ent, Bruno Mars/Darron Mark), 89 (Mount Snowdon/
Jim Richardson), 90 (Jeanne Calment/Pascal Parrot), 100 (Amelia Earhart/
Underwood & Underwood, Yuri Gagarin/Bettmann), 101 (WW1 German
plane/Brown & Dawson/National Geographic Society), W11 (Cassius Clay
boxing/Bettmann), W12 (girl/Sharie Kennedy, boy), W17, W19 (1888 blizzard/
Bettmann), W25 (*Wolverine* premiere/Ren Zhenglai), W29 (Chad le Clos/Clifford
White), W43 (whale watching/Michael S. Nolan), W46 (Taylor Swift/Mark
Blinch), W47 (Zac Efron/Derek Storm/Splash News, Robert Pattinson/Kevan
Brooks/AdMedia); Getty pp.12 (Katy Perry/Christopher Polk/Getty Images for
Clear Channel, Jay-Z/Debbie Hickey, Andre Rieu/Mark Westwood/Redferns,
Ziggy Marley/Frank Micelotta, Linkin Park/Kevin Mazur), 16 (festival child/
Tim Mosenfelder), 25 (Geoffrey Chaucer/c.1342/3-1400 English writer
Universal History Archive, Diego Rivera/Bettmann), 28 (Rosa Parks/Don
Cravens/Time & Life Pictures, white children in classroom/Lambert), 36 (tent
camp/Popperfoto), 48 (Daniel Radcliffe/Gamma), 58 (school meals 1940s/
Time Life Pictures), 96 (Suzuki students playing/Kazuhiro Nogi, Suzuki with
students/Chris Aldred/Keystone), 100 (Da Vinci's sketch/Hulton Archive, Virgin
Galactic Spaceship.2/Mark Greenberg/Virgin Galactic), 101 (Laika/Sovfoto/UIG
via Getty Images, Wright brothers' plane/Library of Congress), W5 (Paramore/
Jon Kopaloff), W43 (waterfall/Aldo Pavan); Kobal pp.24 (*The Simpsons Movie*/20th
Century Fox/The Kobal Collection/GROENING, MATT, *The Hunger Games*/
Lionsgate/The Kobal Collection), 41 (Walt Disney/The Kobal Collection),
44 (*The Hunger Games*/Lionsgate/The Kobal Collection, Liam Hemsworth in *The
Hunger Games*/Lionsgate/The Kobal Collection, *Legally Blonde*/MGM/The Kobal
Collection/Bennett, Tracy), W25 (*Wolverine* still/20th Century Fox/The Kobal
Collection); Oxford University Press pp.4 (flags, Laura, Hugo), 5 (skateboard,
guitar, MP3), 7 (Alanna), 12 (trumpet, flute, saxophone), 42 (car on fire), 43,
68, 69, 98 (Fall, Spring), 73 (karate/Photodisc), 100 (background), 101 (eagle),
102 (looking at map, Japanese businessmen, background), W7 (band), W41,
W42 (tiger background), W49 (Mt Rushmore); Rex Features p.40 (*Live Free
or Die Hard*/20thC.Fox/Everett, *The Conjuring*/Warner Bros. Pictures/courtesy
Everett Collection, *The Great Gatsby*/Warner Bros/Everett, *Mamma Mia*/
Moviestore Collection, *Finding Nemo*/W. Disney/Everett, *Stardust*/Paramount/
Everett, *Dumb and Dumber*/Moviestore Collection, *The Hunger Games*/Snap Stills),
70 (Masterchef Junior contestants/Jim Smeal/BEI), 90 (Tommy Mattinson/2008
Rex Features); Shutterstock pp.4 (Esther, Julia, David, Samuel, Alicia, Sophia),
5 (phone, watch, bike, laptop), 12 (piano, drums, guitar, violin, recorder),
16 (crowd background), 48 (Gloucester Cathedral cloisters background), 51,
58 (cutlery background), 65, 66 (Kathmandu, travel stamps, road background),
70 (utensils background), 73 (baseball/Brocreative), 73 (basketball/dotshock),
78 (mountains, blue background), 84, 86 (silhouettes), 90 (gold background),
96 (music background), 98 (beach, snow, background), 102 (shaking hands),
103 (all), 105, W5 (girl), W7 (instruments), W18, W23, W29 (girl), W42 (tiger
face, London Eye).

Picture research and illustration commissioning: Alison Wright